PLAY ROCK
GUITAR

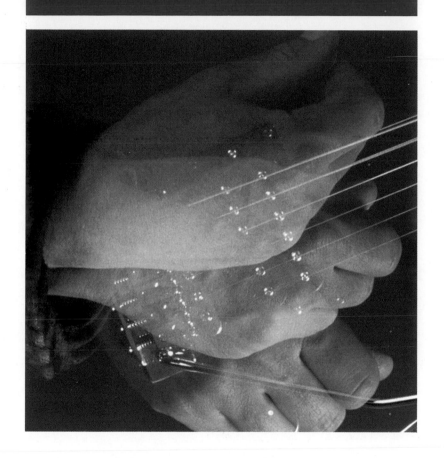

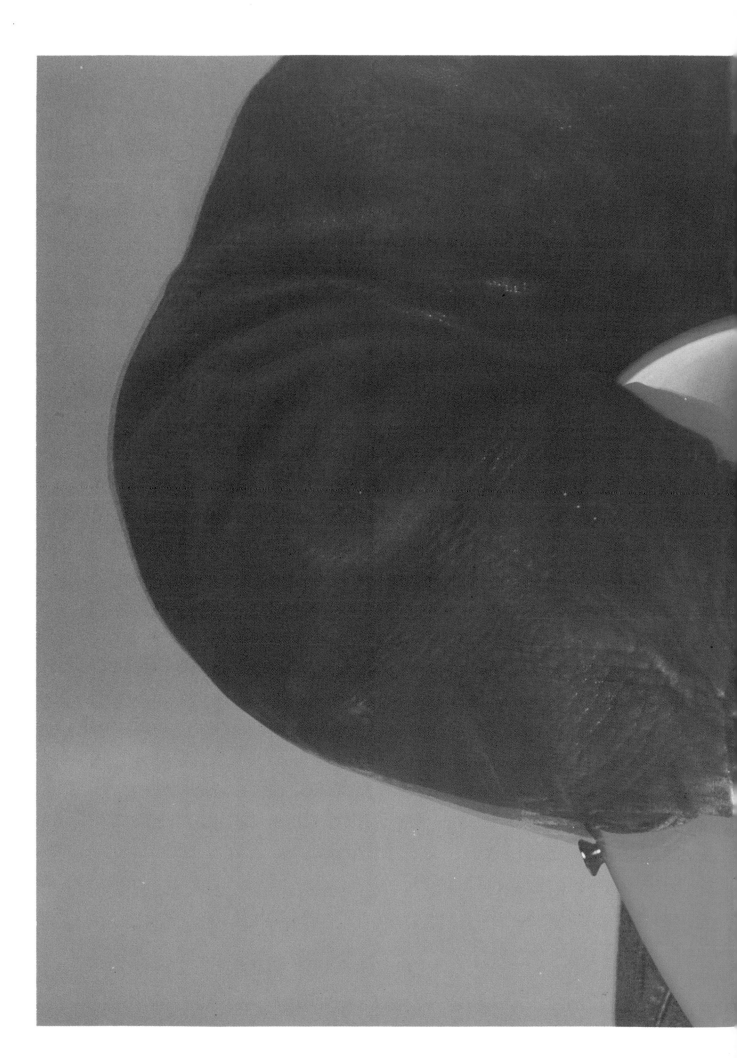

PLAY ROCK
GUITAR

LEARN TO PLAY STEP BY STEP • USING MAJOR HIT SONGS
GUITAR BUYERS GUIDE • A–Z OF ROCK GUITARISTS • HOW TO BREAK INTO THE MUSIC BUSINESS

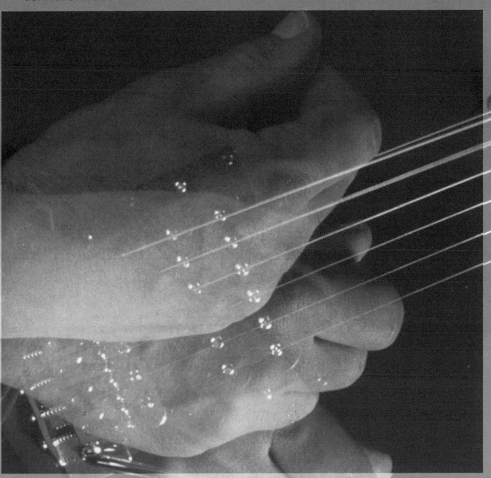

MIKE CLIFFORD
CONTRIBUTING AUTHORS: HEATHER ROBINSON • CHRIS TRENGOVE • PHIL McNEILL
FOREWORD BY STUART ADAMSON

a Salamander book

Published by Salamander Books Limited
LONDON • NEW YORK

A SALAMANDER BOOK

Published by
Salamander Books Ltd..
52 Bedford Row,
London WC1R 4LR,
United Kingdom.

© Salamander Books Ltd, 1987

ISBN 086101 299 2

Distributed in the UK by Hodder &
Stoughton Services, PO Box 6, Mill
Road, Dunton Green, Sevenoaks,
Kent TN13 2XX.

CREDITS

Project Manager: Ray Bonds

Editor: Phil McNeill

Art Editor: Mark Holt

Designer: Graham Smith

Diagram Artists: Neil Hyslop
and Terry Brand

Photographer: Mike Prior

Other photographs supplied by
London Features International Ltd.

Filmset by Flairplan Phototypesetting
Ltd.

Colour reproduction by Rodney
Howe Ltd.

Printed by Proost International Book
Production, Turnhout, Belgium

Produced for Salamander
Books by London
Features International Ltd.

ACKNOWLEDGMENTS

The publishers wish to thank
Yamaha-Kemble Music (UK) Ltd. for
the use of the guitars pictured in this
book. We would also like to thank all
the music publishers involved for their
cooperation in the use of music and
lyrics. Full acknowledgments page 128.

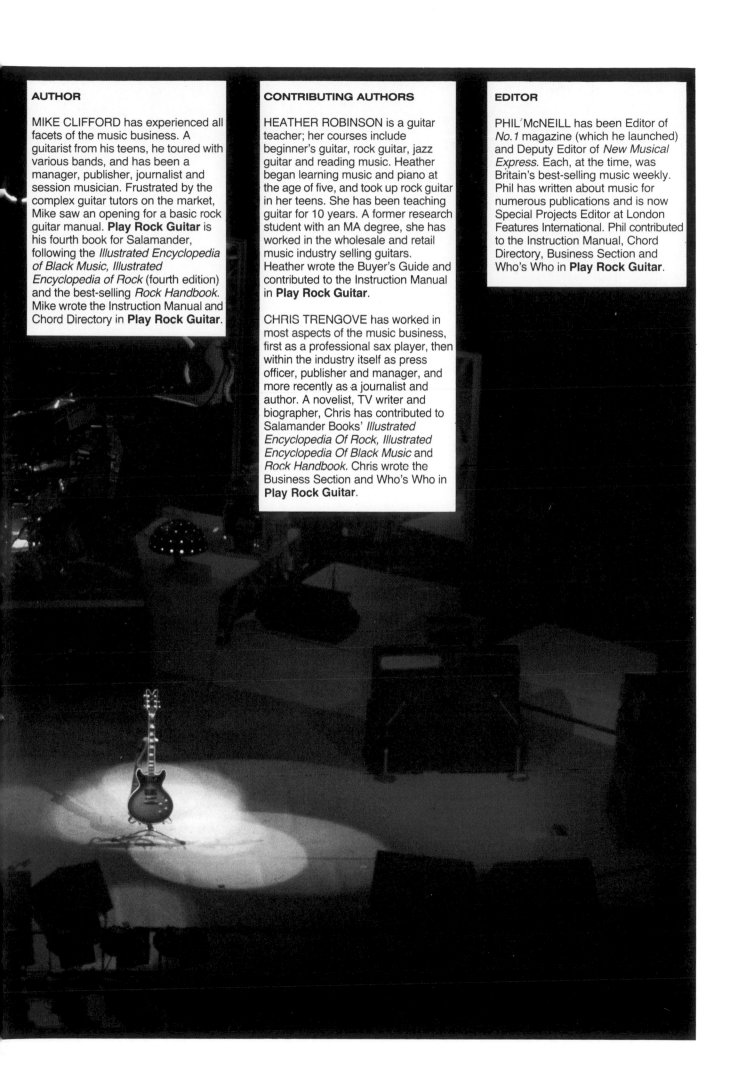

AUTHOR

MIKE CLIFFORD has experienced all facets of the music business. A guitarist from his teens, he toured with various bands, and has been a manager, publisher, journalist and session musician. Frustrated by the complex guitar tutors on the market, Mike saw an opening for a basic rock guitar manual. **Play Rock Guitar** is his fourth book for Salamander, following the *Illustrated Encyclopedia of Black Music, Illustrated Encyclopedia of Rock* (fourth edition) and the best-selling *Rock Handbook*. Mike wrote the Instruction Manual and Chord Directory in **Play Rock Guitar**.

CONTRIBUTING AUTHORS

HEATHER ROBINSON is a guitar teacher; her courses include beginner's guitar, rock guitar, jazz guitar and reading music. Heather began learning music and piano at the age of five, and took up rock guitar in her teens. She has been teaching guitar for 10 years. A former research student with an MA degree, she has worked in the wholesale and retail music industry selling guitars. Heather wrote the Buyer's Guide and contributed to the Instruction Manual in **Play Rock Guitar**.

CHRIS TRENGOVE has worked in most aspects of the music business, first as a professional sax player, then within the industry itself as press officer, publisher and manager, and more recently as a journalist and author. A novelist, TV writer and biographer, Chris has contributed to Salamander Books' *Illustrated Encyclopedia Of Rock, Illustrated Encyclopedia Of Black Music* and *Rock Handbook*. Chris wrote the Business Section and Who's Who in **Play Rock Guitar**.

EDITOR

PHIL McNEILL has been Editor of *No.1* magazine (which he launched) and Deputy Editor of *New Musical Express*. Each, at the time, was Britain's best-selling music weekly. Phil has written about music for numerous publications and is now Special Projects Editor at London Features International. Phil contributed to the Instruction Manual, Chord Directory, Business Section and Who's Who in **Play Rock Guitar**.

CONTENTS

Opposite: some of rock's foremost guitar players in action. From left, from the top: Eric Clapton, Prince, Ry Cooder,
Chuck Berry, The Edge, Jimi Hendrix, Gary Moore, Jimmy Page and Carlos Santana.

I FIRST took up guitar in the '60s. Like many others, I was inspired by The Beatles and The Rolling Stones.

At that time I'd been playing classical accordion for about ten years. I'd even won a number of inter-state contests, but I soon became more interested in rock.

The problem was that, like any studied music, you get a sheet of music and there's only one way to play it. The only room for interpretation is the emotional content within the notes written. What I really liked about rock guitar was the freedom.

I started on an old guitar which my father had had lying around the house since he was a kid. My brother Tommy gave me my first lessons along with a friend called Tom Miller who was in my first band, The Waifs. In fact I started in the band as an accordion player!

There were no books like this then, so I had to pick it up where I could. They taught me a few basic chords, and then I went to a guitar player who was the hotshot in a local band, and persuaded him to give me lessons.

He showed me a lot of the things in this book, like a basic understanding of seventh and minor chords, what they mean and how they are used, and a couple of simple blues scales.

Basically the lessons I took replaced what's in **Play Rock Guitar**. But whether you take your lessons from this book, or another guitar player, or both, here are a few points which I hope may be useful.

THE MOST important thing is to get plenty of practice. Personally I play for a couple of hours every day without fail. To anybody that's learning, I'd recommend that you set aside at least an hour a day when you practise and try to improve. But on top of that, it's helpful if you just play.

One of the best things you can do, if you've got an electric guitar, is to hold it while you're watching TV or talking to friends on the phone, and play it to yourself. Because as long as you don't plug it in, nobody can hear it. Don't worry about what you're playing—whether it's chords or a blues scale, finger exercises or a solo—the important thing is just to have the guitar in your hands, because the more you have it in your hands, the better the rapport you'll get with it. And when you do plug it in, you'll be much more comfortable with it.

ANOTHER POINT about practising: make it enjoyable. For every hour you spend cramping your hand trying to make new chord shapes, you should spend a half hour or so playing what you know and having fun.

As you go through the book, find what appeals to you the most, and use that to wind down from the hard stuff. For me, it would have to be the blues scales, which have always given me a lot of enjoyment.

The opposite side of the coin in my case was the barre chord—it took about three

Nils Lofgren is a brilliant guitarist both on record and in concert, with or without group. He played on Neil Young classics such as 'After The Goldrush', and has been a member of Bruce Springsteen's E Street Band since 1984.

months before my hand got strong enough for that. Playing a barre chord was a real landmark. So if you're having trouble with barre chords, don't worry, they are a struggle for every guitar player.

But remember, after half an hour or so of trying to clamp your hand down and not getting it right, don't just put the guitar down in frustration. Go back to playing the first blues scale, or just play **G Em C D** and sing 'Stand By Me' to yourself. Make sure you finish every day with a bit of fun.

OF COURSE, it's also important to listen to different guitar players and try to learn from them. I went through a phase where I spent most of my days listening to Jimi Hendrix, Eric Clapton and Jeff Beck.

I used to take their albums and slow them down on the turntable in order to learn their solos note for note—and I'd recommend it even now. Obviously if you're just starting out, you should choose something simple—one of the first solos I learned was 'The Last Time' by The Rolling Stones. There are plenty of great records with easy riffs and solos that you can learn.

It's also important to watch guitar players in action. I was lucky enough to spend a lot of time hanging out with a great rock and roll guitarist called Roy Buchanan, who used to play the redneck clubs all over Maryland. Normally I wouldn't have been welcome in those places with my long hair, but he told everyone to leave me alone as I was a friend of his.

I used to just sit and watch him play, and sometimes I'd sneak in a tape recorder. One technique I picked up from him was rolling the volume pedal down and back to get a wah wah cry baby effect, and that pedal steel guitar sound of fading the note in.

Along with Jimi Hendrix, Roy was my main influence. But whoever you're a fan of, don't just listen to them; watch them, and find something they do that's simple enough to learn.

ONCE I KNEW a few basic chords, one of the biggest steps for me was learning a couple of blues scales.

I used to give guitar lessons as a teenager, and the first thing I'd show someone was how to play the chords of **C**, **F** and **G**—just like this book—and then I'd show them how to use those three chords in a simple blues chord progression, which you can also find in **Play Rock Guitar**.

As the book recommends, you play that onto a cassette, then run it back. As soon as you start to learn your blues scales, you'll find that whatever combination of those notes you hit, it's going to sound kind of neat against that simple blues progression.

That to me is the greatest way to get started. It's so easy, and it will sound good, even before you get onto special techniques like bending strings and vibrato. You'll improve so fast that it will keep up your interest in the instrument.

I KEEP talking about electric guitars, and I have to say it's the instrument I'd recommend for a beginner, because the strings are easier to hold down than on an acoustic guitar. I know a lot of people who started on an acoustic guitar, and I've tried to teach them things, but their hands are weak—and before their hands get strong enough to hold down barre chords or even finger regular chords or play a blues scale, they get impatient and give up.

So I think an electric guitar is fine, plus of course a little amplifier. I see there's a section in the book that tells you what to look out for when buying electric guitars and amps.

The main thing is to find something comfortable to play, so you don't have to spend three months getting your hands strong enough even to make a chord.

If you *have* got an acoustic guitar, I recommend that you start with very light guage strings.

ONCE YOU'VE got started on some chords and scales, you can begin to try out other techniques, such as fingerpicking and bottleneck guitar. These styles aren't usually associated with rock guitar— fingerpicking is a folk or country music style, and bottleneck is a blues style—but as a rock player, I find them both invaluable.

When I started, it just happened that the only guitar pick my father had in his guitar case was a thumb pick, and I did all my initial learning with that. A thumb pick isn't very pliable, so it took a lot longer to learn than if I'd used an ordinary plectrum, but the advantage is that it sets your other fingers free.

To this day, I play almost exclusively with my fingers, rather than using a flat pick, because it gives me a greater range and the ability to reach different strings very quickly.

The important thing is, techniques like this give you more scope. Fingerpicking doesn't mean you have to play country or pretty music—you can play some of the nastiest, grittiest solos that way. Whatever style you play, you may come up with a particular guitar line that you can only play by fingerpicking, or you may get an idea for a slinky part that you just have to use bottleneck for.

Any guitar technique is just a physical tool. It's what's in your heart and your head that counts.

ONE THING a guitarist should always bear in mind is the song. That always comes first.

I'm very happy to have a reputation as a guitarist, but when I'm working with someone like Neil Young or Bruce Springsteen, my main priority is what's best for the song. Even on my own records, I feel my most valuable asset is as a songwriter, so I don't do that much soloing.

Remember, playing rhythm properly is every bit as important as being a good soloist.

When I play with Bruce, there's one acoustic song in particular, 'Johnny 99', where I play the entire song alone. It's just a simple rhythm part—the kind of thing that a lot of flashy guitarists might find boring—but if you asked them to play it they wouldn't have a groove to it. There'd be no 'pocket'.

When I'm with The E Street Band I get satisfaction out of being a part of the band, even if I only play a couple of little lines throughout a song—whether it's a slide part or a rhythm part, or some very simple fingerpicking on an acoustic guitar.

I take just as much pride in executing that properly as in firing off a five-minute solo.

AS I SAID at the beginning, I spent ten years studying classical accordion before I picked up the guitar—and although I eventually switched to guitar, that musical training was very useful to me.

If you want to play rock guitar, you don't *need* to know about music, but it does help. Any theory you pick up will make it easier once you get more advanced, and you'll be able to understand what you're playing. This is especially true today, because standards are so high.

You can take or leave the basic musical

Stuart Adamson sings and plays lead guitar alongside Bruce Watson in Big Country. Previously a member of The Skids, Stuart formed Big Country in 1982. Along with U2, they have helped reassert the guitar's role in rock.

theory in **Play Rock Guitar**—but I suggest you make the most of it.

IT'S BEEN said that the guitar is out of date in the world of synthesisers and sampling keyboards, but I'm real proud to be a guitar player.

I run into an enormous number of musicians now who I call programming fools—they're excellent programmers, but if you play them a simple rock and roll progression and say, "Improvise!", they can't do it.

The problem with keyboards is that you can only change the sound by the programming—you can't change the sound by the way you play. If you turn the amp up, well, it's just a louder version of the same sound.

With the guitar, every time you turn the dial you get a different sound. And you get new sounds depending on how hard you push it, how subtly you play it, where you pick the string—whether close to the bridge or high on the neck . . .

So I think it's a more expressive instrument, and it's as valuable now as it ever was.

The guitar has come a long way thanks to people like Keith Richards, Pete Townshend, Hendrix, Clapton, Beck and many others, and I'm proud to be able to play it.

I hope you will be too.

THE LIGHTS dim, the crowd roars, the compere's voice is long gone. You're on your own now.

Stepping out onto the stage, you cradle that old friend like it was the key to everything. A long white spotlight picks you out as you look up and draw out some long soaring notes that talk to the whole world . . .

THAT'S WHY we're here, right! You want to play rock guitar, me too!

Before the fantasy comes the fumbling. I have painful memories of the grooves in my fingertips during those first few months of stumbling from chord to chord with much tearing of hair and grinding of teeth. Give it time, they say. Fifteen years on I'm still learning.

I know, however, that all the great moments I've had, watching players who could bring tears to my eyes, started in exactly the same way. With the basics, with the pain.

No matter which style you develop or what standard you achieve (whatever that means), basic chords and scales are the foundation on which all players have built. So mark this time well, for what you give is what you get.

Make every note count. It's exciting driving at 150mph but you miss most of the scenery, so let what you play be the whole picture.

It's also worth remembering that expressive sounds don't always come from expensive guitars.

Once you start feeling comfortable on the fretboard (it does happen), don't put up barriers for yourself. Experiment with different styles, play with other players, increase your musical vocabulary, all the better to express yourself.

Although my own playing has become stylised over the years, this has come about through dabbling with all sorts of music until I felt confident enough to let myself show through.

FOR THIRTY years or so, the guitar has been the backbone of popular music and rightly so. There is no more emotive instrument for me, no more fitting soundtrack for my life.

So no matter whether you play for your own enjoyment or for your daily bread, and ideally a healthy mixture of the two, revel in the legacy of all the great players and add to it yourself.

You hold it here and now in your own hands.

Stay alive.

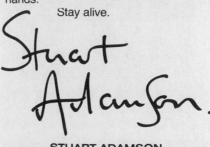

STUART ADAMSON

NILS LOFGREN

AUTHOR'S INTRODUCTION

When I first started playing guitar, the quickest way to learn was 'listen and copy' the contemporaries of the day: Chuck Berry, BB King, Steve Cropper, and later, Jimi Hendrix and Eric Clapton.

Guitar instruction books were few and far between. The most notable was Bert Weedon's *Play In A Day,* but the title was a sham. You might learn to hold the plectrum correctly, or sit yourself comfortably, but 'play in a day'? Never!

We won't pretend that you will be making your stage debut within 24 hours of purchasing the book, but a little perseverance will set you on the right track.

In compiling **Play Rock Guitar**, the objective was to teach some basic chords which could be used in a well known rock classic, and develop things from there.

I hadn't, however, reckoned on the staying power of the Colonel-in-Chief of our collection of writers, editor Phil McNeill, who argued for expanding the boundaries of the book to include a complete framework for the aspiring musician.

Well, we went along with that thinking, but devised a system of learning with several options attached.

The pages in our Instruction Manual are divided into two. The bottom half of each page is the basic tuition—the chord shapes, songs, etc. Above this lies the explanation for what you're learning below.

You do not, and I cannot emphasise this enough, need to know a gnat's knee about music in order to play guitar.

If you want to explore the technical matter behind the guitar, we have provided the food for thought. If you just want to get on and play that thang, so be it. Just follow the practical instruction course in the bottom half of each page, and don't worry too much about the theory above it.

The rest of the book is intended to inspire and educate. All young musicians come unstuck at one time or another because they're unsure of the rules of rock 'n' roll. Chris Trengove has provided them in the Business Section.

Heather Robinson's hardware section should help you ease your way into the complex world of electronic musical equipment and avoid paying out good cash for second-rate gear.

Chris Trengove's A–Z of guitar superstars is a gallery of leading axemen from the past 25 years or so—some even older, some yet to make their mark.

Learning to play guitar can appear a daunting task. The combination of **Play Rock Guitar** and good old-fashioned practice will make that task fun.

MIKE CLIFFORD

Right: rock guitar takes many guises. From the top, from left: Bruce Springsteen, Chrissie Hynde of The Pretenders, Pete Townshend, Chris Holmes of WASP, Billy Idol, Vicki Peterson of The Bangles.

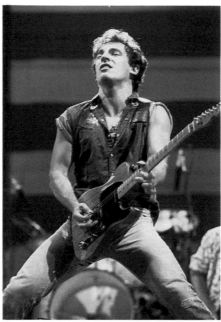

INSTRUCTION MANUAL

This is our step-by-step guide to guitar playing. Take it gradually, and by the time you reach page 66 you'll be a useful performer.

Each page of the Instruction Manual is split in half. The bottom section will give you practical playing experience, while the top section will fill you in on the background to what you are learning to play.

We think we've managed to put the basics of music across in the clearest way possible. But if you do find some of the top sections hard going, don't worry about it. Just make sure that you follow the practical course given in the lower half of each page.

At every stage of the Instruction Manual, try to play all the chords or lead scales on a page to the best of your ability before you continue. Keep practising until you get it right—and keep coming back and doing it again.

To make the task more enjoyable, you'll find some great songs to play in this Instruction Manual—'That'll Be The Day' by Buddy Holly, 'The Boys Are Back In Town' by Thin Lizzy, and 'Phone Booth' by Robert Cray. Each appears in more than one form, so that you can learn to use different skills within a familiar framework.

Take your time, and before you know it you'll really be able to Play Rock Guitar.

CONTENTS

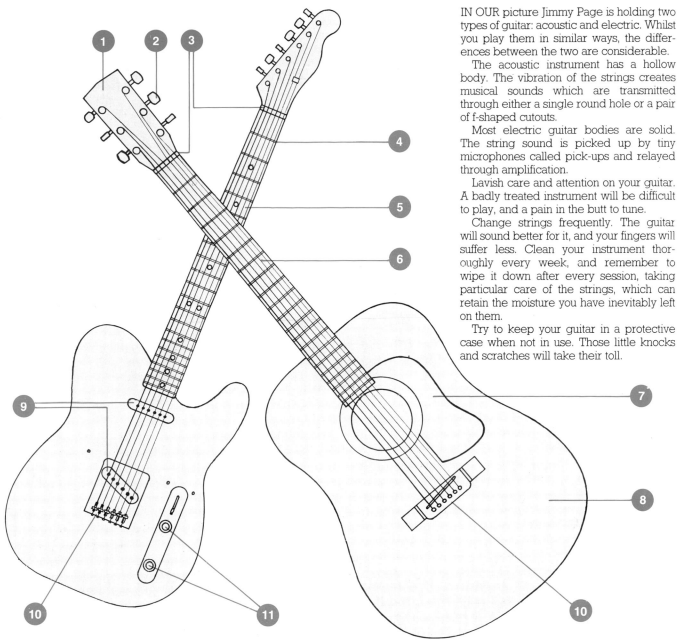

IN OUR picture Jimmy Page is holding two types of guitar: acoustic and electric. Whilst you play them in similar ways, the differences between the two are considerable.

The acoustic instrument has a hollow body. The vibration of the strings creates musical sounds which are transmitted through either a single round hole or a pair of f-shaped cutouts.

Most electric guitar bodies are solid. The string sound is picked up by tiny microphones called pick-ups and relayed through amplification.

Lavish care and attention on your guitar. A badly treated instrument will be difficult to play, and a pain in the butt to tune.

Change strings frequently. The guitar will sound better for it, and your fingers will suffer less. Clean your instrument thoroughly every week, and remember to wipe it down after every session, taking particular care of the strings, which can retain the moisture you have inevitably left on them.

Try to keep your guitar in a protective case when not in use. Those little knocks and scratches will take their toll.

1 HEADSTOCK The focal point of the tuning system, headstocks come in two distinctive designs. The square headstock has three tuners on either side, whilst Fender style instruments have all six tuners on the left.

2 TUNER There are six tuners—one for each string. They are used to tune strings to their proper pitch. Each tuner consists of a nut and cog to tighten or slacken the string. Also known as machine heads.

3 NUT The nut keeps the strings in position as they leave the head, by way of six small grooves. If you own an expensive guitar the nut will probably be made of ivory. If you're a conservationist—or just an economist—it'll be plastic.

4 FRETS Frets are wire inserts which mark the points on the neck where you press each string to make different notes. They are normally made of nickel alloy, hammered home.

5 FRETBOARD Generally made of rosewood, the fretboard is glued to the neck. It's usually decorated with tortoise shell or plastic inlays which help you to see where you are on the fretboard.

6 STRINGS The strings are the lifeblood of the instrument, and a poor or worn set can make even the most talented player sound bad. Generally constructed from alloy, strings vary in thickness from the bottom (thickest) to the top (thinnest). The three bass strings are wound to give them depth, whilst their skinny counterparts are simply tensioned alloy wire. Strings are measured by gauge—the lower the number, the thinner the string. It's important to select a set suitable for your guitar, whether electric or acoustic. The two aren't generally interchangeable.

7 SCRATCH PLATE Located next to the soundhole (acoustic) or pick-ups (electric), the scratch plate protects the main body of the instrument from plectrum scratches and finger marks.

8 SOUNDBOARD The acoustic guitar soundboard is the top piece of wood on the main body. The soundhole is cut into it.

9 PICK-UPS Pick-ups transmit the string sound from the guitar to the amplifier by way of an electric lead. In reality, pick-ups are no more than miniature microphones. You can in fact talk into a guitar pick-up and your voice will be broadcast through the amp.

10 BRIDGE Acoustic and electric guitar bridges come in all shapes and sizes, but their purpose is the same. They adjust the pitch, harmonics and string height. The classic set-up is the retaining tailpiece, and individual bridge, which is adjustable on electric models. Modern acoustic and many electric guitars have a one-piece bridge set-up, which eliminates the separate tailpiece. The bridge on an acoustic guitar is slightly offset to achieve perfect harmonics, whilst the electric counterpart has a series of independent mechanisms, one for each string. These are adjusted by a small screwdriver, until the pitch is correct.

11 VOLUME AND TONE CONTROLS Once your electric guitar is plugged in, and you have turned your amplifier on, you will be able to adjust volume and tone by the collection of knobs generally positioned to the right side of the bridge. The principle of tone and volume is exactly the same as your hi-fi. Moderation is sensible, but sometimes it's hard to resist 'cranking it up'.

13

HOLDING THE GUITAR

BEFORE YOU start playing, it's important to make sure you feel comfortable.

When standing you should not be labouring to support the main body of the guitar, and the strap should not be tugging at your neck.

With the strap resting on your shoulder, remove your hands from the guitar. There should be an equal balance of weight, with no great pressure on any part of your body.

The guitar is a heavy instrument, but if you distribute the weight sensibly it will cause little discomfort. If Angus Young or Susanna Hoffs can career around the stage whilst playing, so can you.

WHETHER YOU sit or stand probably depends on the type of guitar and style of music you play.

If you've got an electric guitar, shorten the strap until the guitar hangs as comfortably as if you were standing.

If you're using an acoustic model, there are several ways of holding it.

Some acoustic players cross their legs – right over left – and rest the guitar just above their right knee.

Others plant both feet on the floor and rest the body across their thighs. Others use a foot stool to raise one leg and rest the guitar there.

WHICHEVER METHOD you choose, if you can remove your hands from the guitar without dropping it on the floor, you're in business.

The important thing to remember is that the arms should never take the weight of the guitar. You need them to play it, not carry it.

When standing, make sure the weight of your guitar is spread evenly.

TUNING THE GUITAR

METHOD 1: Tuning to a piano. If you have a keyboard instrument, or some other instrument with fixed notes, you can tune up to it.

On your piano, play an **E** note – it's the 12th white note below middle **C**. That's the note you want on your sixth (bottom **E**) string.

Leave the sixth string 'open' by taking your left hand off the fretboard. Now gently strike the string with your right thumb, and keep thumbing it whilst gradually turning the sixth string tuning peg with your left hand.

When the guitar note matches the piano note, it's in tune.

You can now repeat the action for each string, matching it to the appropriate keyboard note – **E**, **A**, **D**, **G**, **B**, **E** – moving to your right along the keyboard each time.

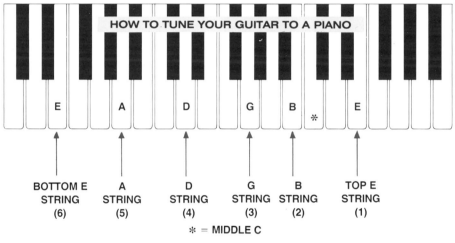

HOW TO TUNE YOUR GUITAR TO A PIANO

| BOTTOM E STRING (6) | A STRING (5) | D STRING (4) | G STRING (3) | B STRING (2) | TOP E STRING (1) |

✳ = MIDDLE C

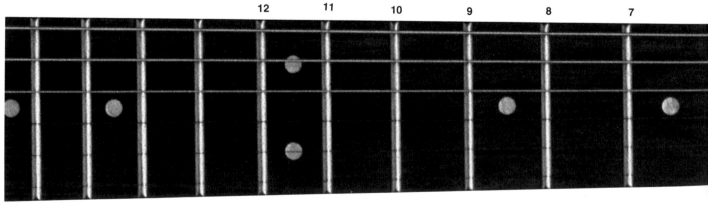

METHOD 2: Tuning the guitar to itself – perhaps the most common method, and the one you'll need when no other instrument is at hand.

Tune the sixth (bottom **E**) string as accurately as you can. Chances are that it's in tune anyway – being the thickest string, it's less likely to detune itself than the others.

Listen to the sound of your bottom **E**. It should be a deep, full note. As we move through the strings the notes will get progressively higher, until we reach top **E** which will give a light, ringing note.

Now to tune the fifth (**A**) string. Place the first finger of your left hand just behind the fifth fret of the bottom **E** string. That's an **A** note.

Keep your finger on the fret. Now thumb the fifth and sixth strings in turn, gently turning the fifth string tuning peg until the two notes are the same.

That's got your fifth string in tune.

Put your finger just behind the fifth fret, fifth (**A**) string. That's a **D** note. Tune your fourth (**D**) string to it.

Put your finger just behind the fifth fret, fourth (**D**) string. That's a **G** note. Tune your third (**G**) string to it.

Put your finger just behind the fourth fret, third (**G**) string. That's a **B** note. Tune your second (**B**) string to it.

Finally put your finger just behind the fifth

fret, second (**B**) string. That's an **E** note. Tune your top (**E**) string to that.

To put it briefly, tuning from the bottom string up, the frets to use are 5, 5, 5, 4 and 5.

If you've done it right, your top **E** and bottom **E** strings should give the same note. The only difference is the pitch – one high pitched, one low.

METHOD 3: Buy yourself a set of plastic or metal pitch pipes – they cost next to nothing and they're designed for guitarists.

The six notes on the pipe correspond with the notes on the six guitar strings. Just blow and tune, leaving all the strings 'open'.

When sitting, a strap can still help an electric guitar to hang steady.

The most common way of holding an acoustic guitar is to steady it across one thigh.

Then again, when it comes to playing live, anything goes for a showman like Chuck Berry!

Unlike a piano, which can stay more or less in tune for years, a guitar can go out of tune at any minute. The heat, the cold, the way you hit the strings . . . there are a thousand ways your instrument can become literally tuneless. So it's important that you learn to tune your guitar quickly and efficiently.

WE CANNOT pretend that our fingering system is particularly innovative, but it's simple and as long as you can count to four you'll probably get the hang of it.

Here's how the fingers of your left hand will be numbered throughout the book: (1) is the first finger, (2) is the second, (3) is the third, and (4) is the fourth or little finger.

Although the four fingers are used prodigiously, the left thumb rarely comes into play. It's mainly there to keep the guitar neck steady and help you press down firmly with your fingers.

You are advised to keep fingernails trim on both hands. Long nails make chord formation almost impossible, as the fleshy part of the fingertip struggles in vain to meet the fretboard.

TOP E NOTE

G NOTE

B NOTE

D NOTE

A NOTE

5   4   3   2   1

A
D
G
B
E

BOTTOM E STRING (6)
A STRING (5)
D STRING (4)
G STRING (3)
B STRING (2)
TOP E STRING (1)

HOLDING THE PLECTRUM

THE FINAL piece in the guitar set-up is the plectrum, or guitar pick. Later we'll get into different ways of using a plectrum, and playing with the fingers of your right hand.

To get you off on the right track here, pick up the plectrum between the first and second fingers of the right hand, and form the hand into a 'semi-fist'.

You'll find it best to use a fairly large, flexible plectrum in these early learning days. It will be easier to manipulate, and whilst volume tends to suffer, technique doesn't.

Your local guitar store will carry mountains of these plastic triangles.

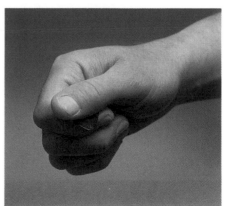

CHORDS

YOU ARE now ready to learn your first chord. A chord is a combination of notes which sound good together. In musical terms, they harmonise.

The following pages will quickly get you on the right road for chord formation, and you need know absolutely nothing about musical theory to begin practising.

As we go along we will cover the basic elements of music. But right now we just want your guitar, your hands, a little common sense and a lot of determination.

Dozens of notable guitarists have made their way with little or no musical theory. Legendary blues master Albert King plays the guitar upside down, with the strings the wrong way round. Enough said?

For now, just concentrate on getting your fingers in the right place. The rest will follow.

Being left-handed didn't stop Albert King cutting blues classics like 'Crosscut Saw' and 'Born Under A Bad Sign'. He just turned his guitar back-to-front! His thinnest (top E) string is literally at the top.

GET TOUGH

THESE FIRST few weeks are going to be rough on your fingers, as they struggle to assume a series of unnatural positions. There's not much you can do except persevere. You'll be amazed how even the strangest chord shape will eventually become second nature.

The fingertips of your left hand will suffer most, as they press down on the strings. Regular practice will soon toughen them up. You'll sense the turning point when your finger prints start to disappear.

The first time you try it, you'll find it hard to get your fingers in place, let alone press down. You might find it helps to physically grab each finger with your right hand and force it into position.

Don't worry, Eric Clapton probably had to do that when he played his first C chord.

CHORD OF C MAJOR

THE CHORD we've selected to start you on is **C** major, generally known as just **C**. This chord relates to many others that you will learn later.

The blue dots in the diagram indicate the position for each finger. Take your finger and place it *just behind* the fret indicated. If necessary, use your right hand to put your left-hand fingers in place.

THE **C** CHORD is formed like this:
First finger (1) just behind the first fret (the one nearest the nut) on the second (**B**) string.
Second finger (2) just behind the second fret on the fourth (**D**) string.
Third finger (3) behind the third fret on the sixth (bottom **E**) string.
Little finger (4) just behind the third fret on the fifth (**A**) string.

NOTE THAT the third finger is pushed further across the neck than the little finger. Because they are both pressing down behind the same fret, the third finger will have to sit midway between the second and third frets.

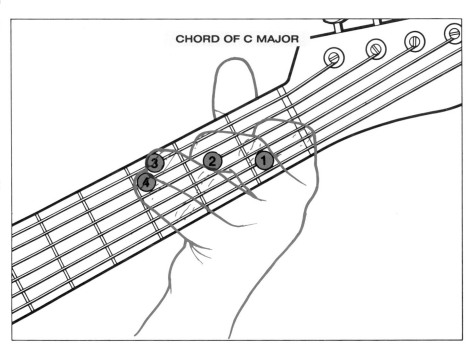

CHORD OF C MAJOR

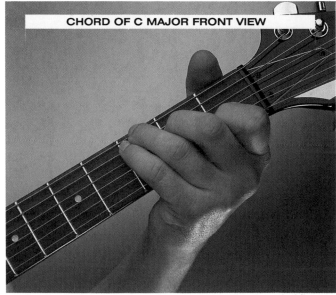

CHORD OF C MAJOR FRONT VIEW

The **C** major chord, first step in our three chord trick. Note the arched fingers, tips just behind frets.

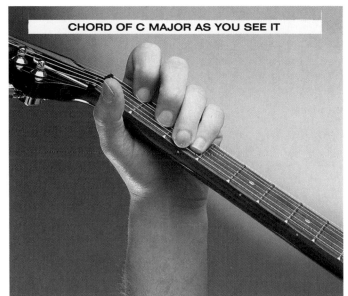

CHORD OF C MAJOR AS YOU SEE IT

The thumb sits behind the guitar neck, enabling the palm to support it comfortably.

AS YOU probably know, musical notes take their names from the letters of the alphabet, from **A** to **G**.

However, they aren't the only musical notes. There are also notes called sharps or flats, and they fall between the 'main' notes.

Why are they called sharps and flats? Simple: because the sharp *is* 'sharp', in that it's pitched one note above the main note, whilst the flat note is literally 'flattened' down one note.

Here's the confusing bit. Sharps and flats are in fact the same note. The note between **A** and **B**, for instance, can be called either **A** sharp (**A#**) or **B** flat (**B♭**).

There are two places where there is no sharp note between two 'main' notes – between **E** and **F**, and between **B** and **C**. You can see this clearly on a keyboard, where the sharp notes are black.

NOTES ON THE TOP E STRING

| F | F# | G | G# | A | A# | B | C | C# | D | D# | E |

As the notes go up the first (top **E**) string, the sharps fall on alternate frets—except between **B** and **C**, and between the open **E** and **F**. The 12 notes follow one another in the same order whatever the string.

NOTES ON A PIANO KEYBOARD

It's easier to pick out sharps and flats on a keyboard – they're the black notes. But the 12 notes still run in the same order as on a guitar: **E F F# G G# A A# B C C# D D# E**.

CHORD OF F MAJOR

THE CHORD of **F** major is one of the trickiest to learn at first, but once you've cracked it you'll progress faster. Like **C** it's usually known as just **F**. Here's how it's formed:

First finger (1) laying just behind the first fret across both the first (top **E**) string *and* the second (**B**) string.

Second finger just behind the second fret on the third (**G**) string.

Third finger (3) just behind the third fret on the fifth (**A**) string.

Little finger (4) just behind the third fret on the fourth (**D**) string.

NOTE THAT the bottom string is the only one that's 'open' (unfretted). It's not part of the chord – unlike the open strings in the **C** chord. Don't play the bottom **E** string.

The fifth (**A**) string can also be left out, giving a four-string chord. You can use your third finger (3) to fret the fourth (**D**) string, and give your little finger a rest.

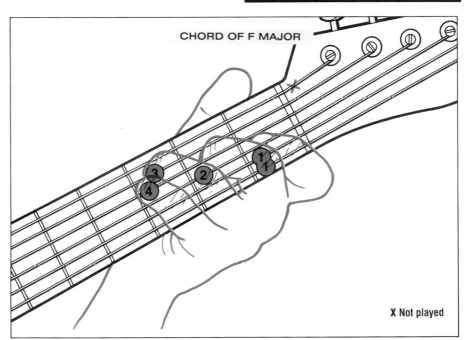

CHORD OF F MAJOR

X Not played

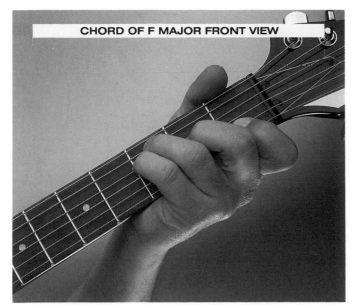

CHORD OF F MAJOR FRONT VIEW

This chord will be difficult at first, with the first finger holding down two strings at once. It might help to practise that finger on its own.

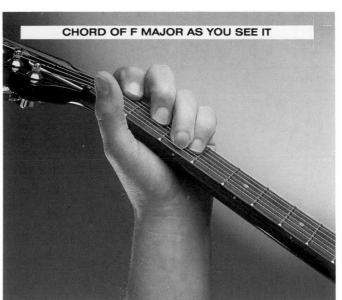

CHORD OF F MAJOR AS YOU SEE IT

You may also find it odd 'pulling back' the little finger. Keep at it, and it will become second nature.

MAJOR KEYS

BY NOW you may be wondering if your fingers will ever toughen up enough to master that **F** chord. Don't worry, they will.

You may also be wondering why we've chucked you in at the deep end like this – surely there are easier chords to play?

Well, yes, there are. But few are as important as **C**, **F** and **G**. Together they make up the 'three-chord trick'. Once you know these three chords, you can play a wealth of rock music.

THE CHORDS of **C**, **F** and **G** did not combine by some magical force. There is a precise science to it all.

When you play these three chords, you are playing in the key of **C** major.

It's important to know about keys, especially when playing with other musicians. Before you start a song, you need to know what key it's in, because that tells you which notes and chords you can use.

WE'VE SEEN how music consists of 12 notes: **A A# B C C# D D# E F F# G G#**. A# is also known as **B♭**, C# is also known as **D♭**, and so on. The note after G# is **A**, and the whole thing starts over again.

There is a major key based on each of the 12 musical notes – **A** major, **B♭** major, and so on.

For each major key there is an eight-note 'scale' – you probably learned it at school as doh, re, mi, fah, soh, la, ti, doh.

Try playing the scale of **C** major, starting on the first fret of your second (**B**) string. The notes in the scale are **C, D, E, F, G, A, B** and **C**.

These are the notes which 'work' in the key of **C** major – and any chord which uses a combination of these notes will also 'work' in the key of **C** major.

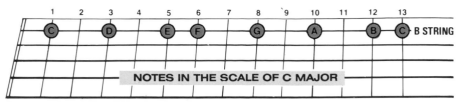

NOTES IN THE SCALE OF C MAJOR

These are the notes which 'work' in the key of **C** major. A song in **C** should stick to these notes.

CHORD OF G MAJOR

THE THIRD chord we've chosen is **G** – and you'll probably find it somewhat easier. Put it together with **C** and **F**, and you've got what's known as the three-chord trick, **CFG**. These three chords have combined to form countless songs.

The **G** chord has a different look to the **C** and **F** chords, because it's formed 'in reverse', with the first and second fingers going across the neck, and the third finger held back.

Here's how you do it:

First finger (1) just behind the second fret on the fifth (**A**) string.

Second finger (2) just behind the third fret on the sixth (bottom **E**) string.

Third finger (3) just behind the third fret on the first (top **E**) string.

NOTE HOW the first and second fingers arch over to come down on the strings from above, to avoid brushing against adjacent strings.

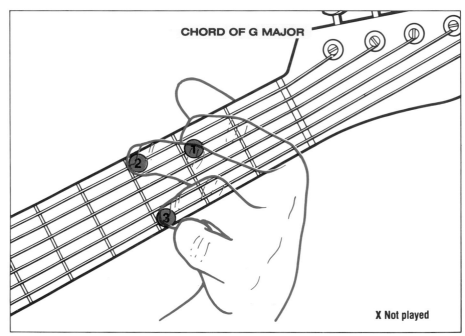

CHORD OF G MAJOR

X Not played

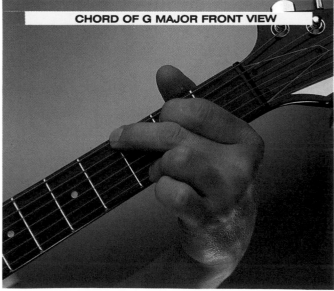

CHORD OF G MAJOR FRONT VIEW

A real finger twister, the **G** major chord has a 'reverse' position which is shared by few other chords.

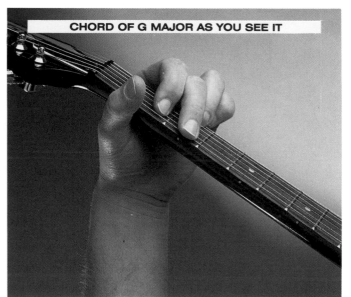

CHORD OF G MAJOR AS YOU SEE IT

Note how the fingers come down on the strings from above so that the 'open' strings ring loud and clear.

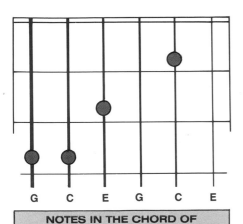

| G | C | E | G | C | E |

NOTES IN THE CHORD OF C MAJOR

The chord of **C** major works in the key of **C** major because it uses the notes **G**, **C** and **E**. These three notes are all in the scale of **C** major.

| X | C | F | A | C | F |

NOTES IN THE CHORD OF F MAJOR

The chord of **F** major works in the key of **C** major because it uses the notes **F**, **A** and **C**. These three notes are all in the scale of **C** major.

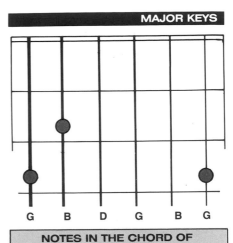

| G | B | D | G | B | G |

NOTES IN THE CHORD OF G MAJOR

The chord of **G** major works in the key of **C** major because it uses the notes **G**, **B** and **D**. These three notes are all in the scale of **C** major.

CHORD OF D MAJOR

THE CHORD OF **D** major has an interesting set-up. In previous chords you've been getting used to pushing the second finger across the neck beyond the first finger. Now that's reversed.

D major is a four-note chord in this basic form. In other words, you only play four strings. The strings you leave out are the bottom **E** and **A** strings.

THE SHAPE OF THE **D** major chord may look a little intricate, but it's quite simple really. Here's how it's formed:

First finger (1) just behind the second fret on the third (**G**) string.

Second finger (2) just behind the second fret on the top **E** string.

Third finger (3) just behind the third fret on the second (**B**) string.

The fourth (**D**) string is played open. The sixth (**E**) and fifth (**A**) strings are not played.

THERE IS an alternative way of fretting the **D** major chord – shown on the right, below.

CHORD OF D MAJOR

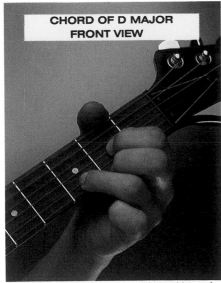

CHORD OF D MAJOR FRONT VIEW

The first and third finger must avoid touching and B string, in order for the chord to ring out loud and, more importantly, clear.

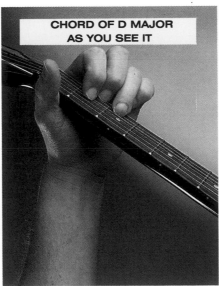

CHORD OF D MAJOR AS YOU SEE IT

Keep the little finger away from the action when forming the D chord, as it has a tendency to clutter the hand position.

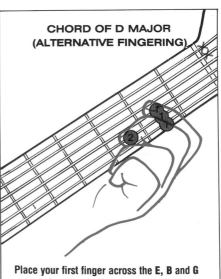

CHORD OF D MAJOR (ALTERNATIVE FINGERING)

Place your first finger across the E, B and G strings, just behind the second fret. The second finger falls in place just behind the third fret on the second (**B**) string.

19

PLECTRUM TECHNIQUE

ORIGINALLY MADE from bone and tortoise-shell, most plectrums are now moulded in plastic.

They vary considerably in size and flexibility. There's no hard and fast rule regarding which type to use for which style of playing.

Initially, a large, flexible plectrum is likely to be more suitable. The sound will be slightly muted, but there won't be too much resistance against the strings, so you should quickly gain the confidence to move to a smaller, stiffer type.

You'll probably find a small, stiff plectrum is better suited to lead playing. Some guitarists even play with a coin, to give a really hard attack on the strings and for scratching effects.

Certainly a smaller plectrum can be more useful for more controlled work. On some stringed instruments, the strings are so close together that only a small plectrum will do.

Whatever style you choose to play, most guitar tutors suggest holding the plectrum between your thumb and the first joint of your first finger.

Fine. But this again is very much a matter of personal choice.

Some very talented musicians play with the plectrum between thumb and second finger. It may look awkward, but if it feels right, alright.

The rule of, er, thumb is that as long as the plectrum is at the correct angle when striking the strings, you're OK.

HOLD THE plectrum as shown, but not too tightly. No white knuckles please.

Keep the plectrum steady—there should be a minumum of movement when it strikes the strings. But don't hold your wrist stiff or clench your fist, as it will make for less fluidity and speed.

The plectrum should be at ninety degrees to the strings as you play—so if the guitar is vertical, the plectrum should be horizontal.

Aim to get a sharp, clear sound. Stick with it, because it's easy to become satisfied as soon as you begin to make any sort of coherent sound from the guitar. As many guitarists have learnt to their cost, it's easy to ignore your right hand as you learn more chord shapes with your left.

Keep working on your plectrum technique, or you run the risk of becoming 'one-handed'.

To sum up: clear tone, flexible wrist, but a firm grip. And relax.

'THAT'LL BE THE DAY'

'THAT'LL BE The Day' is a simple yet timeless rock number built around the three major chords of **C**, **F** and **G**.

It's a little unusual in its structure, because it starts with the chorus, before reverting to the traditional verse/chorus pattern.

At first, we'll play the song entirely with downward strokes. Just take it slowly, and the rhythm will come naturally.

HOW TO USE THE GRID

Chords: Chords are represented by letters. Each chord change is highlighted by a change in colour.

A coloured box with no chord marked in it means that you should simply let the previous chord ring out without striking a new chord.

Rhythm: Each coloured box represents one beat. Tap your foot steadily, playing one strum for each beat. There are four beats to each bar.

Where a box is split in two, there is a chord change after half a beat. This may sound tricky, but if you follow the lyrics you'll find it quite straightforward.

KEY TO SYMBOLS AND COLOURS

⊓ One downward stroke
☐ **C** major
☐ **G** major
☐ **F** major
☐ **D** major

Elvis Costello: an '80s Buddy Holly?

TITLE		KEY	TEMPO
'THAT'LL BE THE DAY' (CHORUS)		C MAJOR	MEDIUM

1	2	3	4	1	2	3	4
F ⊓	F ⊓	F ⊓	F ⊓	F ⊓	F ⊓	F ⊓	F ⊓
That'll	be	the	day,	when	you	say	good-bye. Yes,

1	2	3	4	1	2	3	4
C ⊓	C ⊓	C ⊓	C ⊓	C ⊓	C ⊓	C ⊓	C ⊓
That'll	be	the	day,	when	you	make me	cry. You

1	2	3	4	1	2	3	4
F ⊓	F ⊓	F ⊓	F ⊓	F ⊓	F ⊓	F ⊓	F ⊓
Say you're	gon -na	leave me,	you	know it's	a	lie,	'cause

1	2	3	4	1	2	3	4
C ⊓					G ⊓	C ⊓	
That'll	be	the	da- a-	ay	when I	die.	Well you

TITLE		KEY	TEMPO
'THAT'LL BE THE DAY' (VERSE)		C MAJOR	MEDIUM

1	2	3	4	1	2	3	4
F ⊓	F ⊓	F ⊓	F ⊓	C ⊓	C ⊓	C ⊓	C ⊓
Give me	all	your lov-	ing and	your	tur- tle	dov- ing,	

1	2	3	4	1	2	3	4
F ⊓	F ⊓	F ⊓	F ⊓	C ⊓	C ⊓	C ⊓	C ⊓
All your	hugs and	kiss- es	and your		mon- ey	too.	Well,

1	2	3	4	1	2	3	4
F ⊓	F ⊓	F ⊓	F ⊓	C ⊓	C ⊓	C ⊓	C ⊓
You know	you love	me ba-	by,	un- til	you	tell me	may- be

1	2	3	4	1	2	3	4
D ⊓	D ⊓	D ⊓	D ⊓	G ⊓	G ⊓	G ⊓	G ⊓
That	some	day	well	I'll	be	through.	Well,

The relaxed wrist position, just prior to striking the strings.

The plectrum is swept across the strings at 90 degrees.

Striking the strings: keep the hand firm, but flexible.

LYRICS

CHORUS
That'll be the day, when you say goodbye. Yeah,
That'll be the day, when you make me cry. You
Say you're gonna leave, you know it's a lie. 'Cause
That'll be the da-a-ay when I die.

VERSE 1
(Well you)
Give me all your loving and your turtle doving,
All your hugs and kisses and your money too, well,
You know you love me baby, until you tell me maybe,
That someday well I'll be through. Well,

CHORUS
That'll be the day, when you say goodbye. Yeah,
That'll be the day, when you make me cry. You
Say you're gonna leave, you know it's a lie, 'cause
That'll be the da-a-ay when I die.

VERSE 2
(When)
Cupid shot his dart, he shot it at your heart, so
If we ever part and I leave you, well,
You say you told me and you, you told me boldly,
That someday, well, I'll be through. Well,

'THAT'LL BE The Day' was one of the key songs in rock and roll history. Released in summer 1957, it launched Buddy Holly on a meteoric career that was cut short by his death in an air crash in February 1959.

Inspired by the urgent rhythms of Bo Diddley and Elvis Presley, Holly added a fresh, melodic simplicity that was quite unique. The songs poured out: 'Peggy Sue', 'Rave On', 'Oh Boy', 'Not Fade Away',

'Everyday', 'Words Of Love', 'Brown Eyed Handsome Man', 'Heartbeat', 'Raining In My Heart', 'It Doesn't Matter Anymore' . . . every one a classic.

Artists influenced by Holly include The Hollies (who took his name), Elvis Costello and Marshall Crenshaw (who both copied his looks and much of his musical style), Don McLean (whose 'American Pie' was about him), The Beatles (who recorded 'Words Of

Love'), The Rolling Stones ('Not Fade Away').

Released under the group name of The Crickets, 'That'll Be The Day' was written by Holly with his drummer Jerry Allison and producer Norman Petty, who guided Holly's brief, brilliant career. It reached No.3 in the States and No.1 in the UK.

The song has since been recorded by at last 45 different artists, and gave its name to one of the best '70s rock movies.

The legendary Buddy Holly – left, with drummer and co-writer Jerry Allison, and right, in action on his Fender Stratocaster.

TONES AND SEMITONES

ON PAGE 18 we looked at the key of **C** major.

The scale of **C** major consists of the notes **C, D, E, F, G, A, B**. These are the notes which work in the key of **C** major.

The chords of **G** major and **F** major use notes from this scale, which is why they work in the key of **C** major.

NOW LET'S look at another key: **G** major. It too has a scale. The notes in the scale of **G** major are **G, A, B, C, D, E** and **F#**.

Compare this scale to the scale of **C** major. Although they start on different notes, and the **G** scale includes a sharp note, there is one very important factor the two scales have in common.

The spaces between notes on each scale are the same.

Each of these scales climbs the fret-board in gaps of **2, 2, 1, 2, 2, 2, 1** frets.

This is true for any major scale.

THERE IS a technical term for the gap from one fret, or note, to the next. It's called a semitone. And a space of two semitones is called a tone.

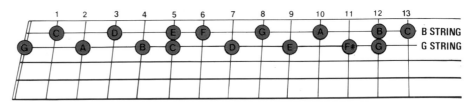

NOTES IN THE SCALE OF C MAJOR (ON THE B STRING) AND NOTES IN THE SCALE OF G MAJOR (ON THE G STRING)

So from **C** to **C#** is one semitone, and from **C** to **D** is one tone.

Using these terms, your major scale – 2, 2, 1, 2, 2, 2, 1 – goes up by jumps of *tone, tone, semitone, tone, tone, tone, semitone.*

You can use this formula to work out the notes in any major scale.

'THAT'LL BE THE DAY'

NOW THAT you've worked out on a simplified version of 'That'll Be The Day', you might like to try it with a slightly more developed rhythm.

Instead of simple downward strokes, this time you should try a downstroke followed by an upstroke, so that you play each chord twice in each beat.

At first this may seem difficult, so just concentrate on getting the rhythm right and don't let the chord changes distract you.

Don't worry if it sounds a little stilted. Find your own pace, and the rhythm will follow naturally.

THERE'S ANOTHER interesting rhythmic twist. The last line of the verse consists of one bar of downstrokes only, followed by a bar of triplets.

A triplet is three notes played in the space of a single beat. All you do is add an extra stroke into each beat. Check this bit out first by tapping it out with your middle three fingers: rat-tat-tat, rat-tat-tat, rat-tat-tat, rat-tat-tat.

This gives a strong percussive effect which you can hear on a lot of 'oldies'. Songs from the '50s often used a 'triplet' rhythm – James Brown's 'I'll Go Crazy' was a prime example, and Madonna's '50s pastiche 'True Blue' deliberately revived it. It's also to be found on modern hits such as Tears For Fears' 'Everybody Wants To Rule The World'.

KEY TO SYMBOLS AND COLOURS

⊓ One downward stroke
V One upward stroke
☐ **C** major
☐ **G** major
▣ **F** major
▣ **D** major

TITLE	KEY	TEMPO
'THAT'LL BE THE DAY' (CHORUS)	C MAJOR	MEDIUM

1	2	3	4	1	2	3	4
F	F	F	F	F	F	F	F
⊓ V	⊓ V	⊓ V	⊓ V	⊓ V	⊓ V	⊓ V	⊓ V
That'll	be the	day,		when you	say	good-bye.	Yes,

1	2	3	4	1	2	3	4
C	C	C	C	C	C	C	C
⊓ V	⊓ V	⊓ V	⊓ V	⊓ V	⊓ V	⊓ V	⊓ V
That'll	be the	day,		when you	make me	cry.	You

1	2	3	4	1	2	3	4
F	F	F	F	F	F	F	F
⊓ V	⊓ V	⊓ V	⊓ V	⊓ V	⊓ V	⊓ V	⊓ V
Say you're	gon -na	leave me,		you know	it's a	lie,	cause

1	2	3	4	1	2	3	4
C					G	C	
⊓					⊓ V	⊓	
That'll	be the	da- a-	ay		when I	die.	Well you

TITLE	KEY	TEMPO
'THAT'LL BE THE DAY' (VERSE)	C MAJOR	MEDIUM

1	2	3	4	1	2	3	4
F	F	F	F	C	C	C	C
⊓ V	⊓ V	⊓ V	⊓ V	⊓ V	⊓ V	⊓ V	⊓ V
Give me	all your	lov- ing	and your		tur- tle	dov- ing,	

1	2	3	4	1	2	3	4
F	F	F	F	C	C	C	C
⊓ V	⊓ V	⊓ V	⊓ V	⊓ V	⊓ V	⊓ V	⊓ V
All your	hugs and	kiss- es	and your		mon- ey	too.	Well,

1	2	3	4	1	2	3	4
F	F	F	F	C	C	C	C
⊓ V	⊓ V	⊓ V	⊓ V	⊓ V	⊓ V	⊓ V	⊓ V
You 'know	you love	me ba-	by,		un- til	you tell	me may- be

1	2	3	4	1	2	3	4
D	D	D	D	G	G	G	G
⊓	⊓	⊓	⊓	⊓ V ⊓	V ⊓ V	⊓ V ⊓	V ⊓ V
That	some	day	well	I'll	be	through.	Well,

THE NOTES in a scale are known not just by their names – **C**, **D**, **E**, etc – but also by numbers.

The first note in the scale – the one on which the scale is based – is called the first or root note. So the root note of the scale of **C** major is **C**.

After that, they're known simply by their numbers. So **B** is the second note in the scale of **C** major. The second note in the scale of **G** major is **A**.

This is useful when talking about chord structure.

ALL MAJOR chords are constructed from the root, third and fifth notes of their major scale.

So the chord of **C** major consists of the notes **C**, **E** and **G** – the root, third and fifth notes of the **C** major scale.

And the chord of **G** major consists of the notes **G**, **B** and **D** – the root, third and fifth notes in the scale of **G** major.

The technical name for this group of three notes is a triad.

So you now know how to work out the notes in any major scale, and from that you can work out the notes of any major chord.

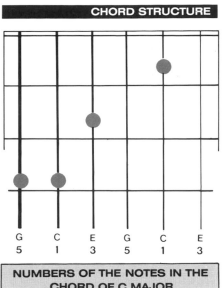

G	C	E	G	C	E
5	1	3	5	1	3

NUMBERS OF THE NOTES IN THE CHORD OF C MAJOR

NUMBERS OF THE NOTES IN THE SCALE OF C MAJOR						
C	D	E	F	G	A	B
Root	2nd	3rd	4th	5th	6th	7th

NUMBERS OF THE NOTES IN THE SCALE OF G MAJOR						
G	A	B	C	D	E	F#
Root	2nd	3rd	4th	5th	6th	7th

E MAJOR is a favourite chord of heavy metal and R&B guitarists. Its simple, full sound has inspired a thousand thumping guitar riffs.

Bearing in mind the musical alphabet, where **E** is the note before **F**, it follows that the **E** chord is one note or fret below the **F** chord. The shape is similar, but the way you form the chord with your fingers is not.

There are just three strings to be held down – the **G**, **D** and **A** strings. Here's how the **E** major chord is formed:

First finger (1) just behind the first fret on the third (**G**) string.

Second finger (2) just behind the second fret on the fifth (**A**) string.

Third finger (3) just behind the second fret on the fourth (**D**) string.

E major is a dramatic chord, as the open top **E** and bottom **E** strings provide the governing notes of the chord, and they sound out first, last and longest.

Combined with **A** major and **D** major, it forms the same three-chord trick in the key of **A** major as **C**, **F** and **G** in the key of **C** major.

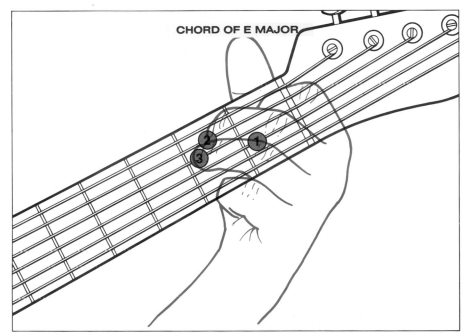

CHORD OF E MAJOR

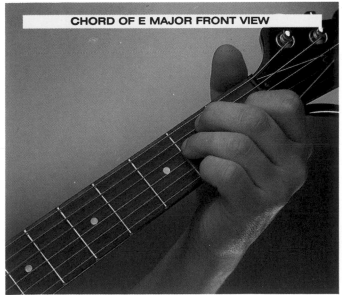

A relatively simple position, with three fingers in use, and three strings left open. The thumb should feel nice and relaxed.

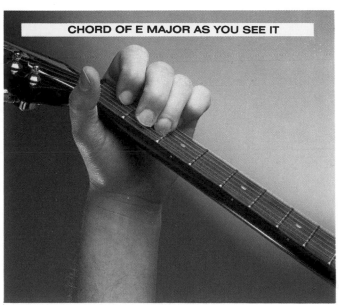

If the fingers do not maintain good contact with the strings, you may hear some fret 'buzz'. Relax, and arch that wrist for the best position.

THE KEY OF A MAJOR

OUR SECOND set of chords – **A**, **D** and **E** –form a three-chord trick in the key of **A** major.

The scale of **A** major follows the same pattern as the scale of **C** major: tone, tone, semitone, tone, tone, tone, semitone.

In other words, you can play the scale on your **A** string (the fifth), starting with the open string and sliding up the neck in gaps of 2, 2, 1, 2, 2, 2, 1 frets.

The chords of **A**,**D** and **E** all use notes in this scale. This means you can use them in a song in the key of **A** major.

KEY OF A MAJOR	
NOTES IN THE SCALE A B C# D E F# G#	
NOTES IN CHORD OF A MAJOR	A C# E
NOTES IN CHORD OF D MAJOR	D F# A
NOTES IN CHORD OF E MAJOR	E G# B

PLAYING SCALES

UP TO now we've been content to confine ourselves to chord work. Chords are the basis of nearly all guitar styles, and it makes sense to lay that firm foundation.

But as a rock guitarist, you will eventually need to play single notes. And with that in mind, it won't do any harm to begin practicising scales now.

Please don't be put off by the thought of playing scales. The phrase may have associations with dull classical music lessons, but in fact almost every major guitarist is an adept scales player. Scales are the lead guitarist's map of the fretboard.

You'll be lost without them . . .

FOR OUR first scale, we're going to show you the scale of **G** major – twice. First in a simplified format, and then in its more usual form.

Try the easy one first, using downward strokes of the plectrum.

You begin by playing your open third (**G**) string, then work your way up the strings, placing each finger where indicated. Note that the sixth note in the scale is the open **E** string.

When you get to top **G** (third fret, top **E** string), work your way back down again.

YOU SHOULD aim to move from bottom to top and back down again in one smooth, flowing motion, playing each note for an equal length of time. You may find it sounds better if you only play the top note once before starting back down again.

CHORD OF A MAJOR

WHEN WE were planning *Play Rock Guitar,* a colleague observed that "If you can conquer the **A** chord, you can conquer Everest."

It really hadn't occurred to us that **A** major was any more complicated to learn than any other chord. However it does have one confusing aspect, because it can be fingered in three different ways.

TRADITIONALISTS would point to the formation in picture 1:

First finger (1) holding down the third (**G**) string behind the second fret.

Second finger (2) just behind the second fret on the fourth (**D**) string.

Third finger (3) just behind the second fret on the second (**B**) string.

IN OTHER words, all three fingers are pressing down behind the second fret. This is the reason for alternative fingerings. It can get mighty cramped whichever way you play the **A** chord, and you have to find the variation that suits you best.

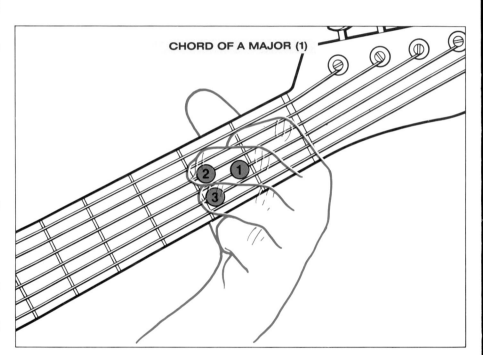

CHORD OF A MAJOR (1)

CHORD OF A MAJOR FRONT VIEW (1)

The 'D' style variation for the **A** chord gives your fingers the most room, as long as the first finger can fret the **G** string cleanly.

CHORD OF A MAJOR AS YOU SEE IT (1)

Although it looks a little awkward, there are advantages using this position particularly when moving to 'sympathetic' chords like **E**.

When you can do that, try out the 'real' scale of **G** major – the second shown here, which begins on the third fret, bottom **E** string.

This scale takes you right through two octaves, from bottom **G** to top **G**. The notes in between are **A**, **B**, **C**, **D**, **E** and **F#**. See if you can identify them as you play them. Once you know them, name each note in your head as you play it.

You'll notice there are no open strings in this scale. This gives you more control over each note: you can kill it or let it ring out, depending on how quickly you raise your finger off the string.

AFTER YOU'VE played this scale a few times using downward strokes of the plectrum, try another variation: down, up, down, up, down, up, etc.

Try not to take your fingers too far off the fretboard – it will slow you down.

The important thing when playing a scale is to get a smooth flow. That can only come through being relaxed – and that, in turn, can only come through practice.

So from now on, run through these scales every day before you begin your chord practice. It's all good preparation for your future career as a soloist!

SCALE OF G MAJOR

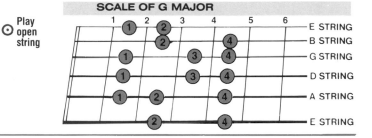

SCALE OF G MAJOR

PERSONALLY, I prefer the arrangement shown in picture 2 for playing **A** major:

First finger (1) behind the second fret on the fourth (**D**) string.

Second finger (2) behind the second fret on the third (**G**) string.

Third finger (3) behind the second fret on the second (**B**) string.

THAT IS the most comfortable position, as least as far as my fingers are concerned. But there's a further alternative, shown in picture 3, with the second, third and little fingers in the same sequence.

The advantage of this third alternative will become apparent when we get onto new chords which use the basic **A** major position, with added notes to be played by the first finger (1).

The essential thing with any chord is to get it ringing out loud and clear. Play each string separately. If there's a buzzing noise, that means the string isn't playing cleanly—one of your fingers is brushing up against it. As usual practice will eliminate this problem.

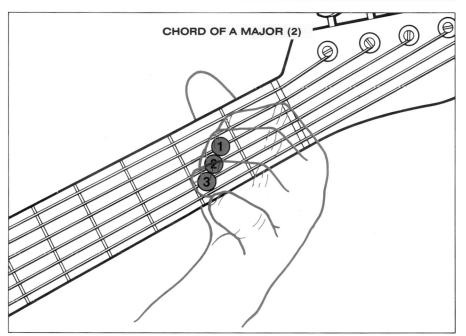

CHORD OF A MAJOR (2)

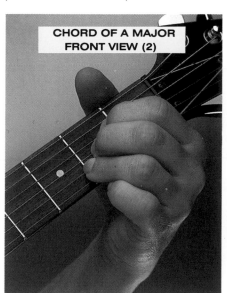

CHORD OF A MAJOR
FRONT VIEW (2)

The second variation of the **A** shape, with the first, second and third fingers nicely in a row on the second fret.

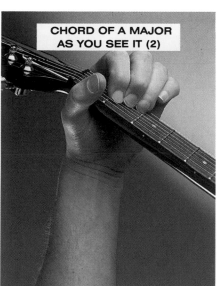

CHORD OF A MAJOR
AS YOU SEE IT (2)

Keep the little finger airborne when forming this **A** shape, as there is a tendency for it to drop onto the **E** string.

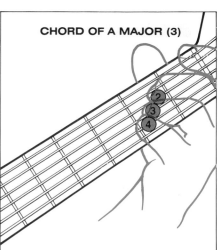

CHORD OF A MAJOR (3)

This position can be adapted for other chords, as you'll discover later. The second, third and fourth fingers line up just behind the second fret.

BARRE CHORDS

A BARRE CHORD is one where the first finger holds down all six strings.

It may sound easy, but it's not. Try holding down six strings with one finger yourself, and you'll soon see why to some players the barre position is as hard to tame as Rambo.

But although barre chords are difficult, they are also extremely useful. Indeed, there are several good reasons for playing a barre.

For a start, it's a way of bringing more strings into play. Take the chord of **F** major. Up to now we've played it as a five-string chord, leaving the open bottom **E** string unplayed.

Using a barre, with the first finger pushed right across the neck, we can play an **F** note on that bottom **E** string, and so bring it into the chord.

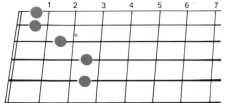

CHORD OF F MAJOR (NOT BARRED)

You needn't try this now—you'll get the chance to practise the chord on page 28. But the point to understand is why we use the barre: to bring all six strings into play.

THE SECOND important use of the barre is to help you play different chords using just one chord shape.

By keeping your fingers in the **F** shape,

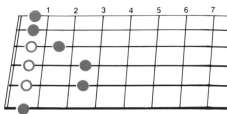

BARRE CHORD OF F MAJOR

and moving up two frets, you automatically have a barred **G** major chord.

If you move up two frets again, you have a barred **A** major chord. You don't have to change the hand position at all, other than to move it along the neck.

THE THIRD important use of the barre chord is to enable you to change chords

CHORD OF B MAJOR

AS YOU can see, the chord of **B** major is closely related to the chord of **A** major. In the same way that the note of **B** is two frets above the note of **A**, so the chord of **B** major is two frets above **A** major.

B major is an important chord. Along with **A**, it completes the three-chord trick in the key of **E** major: **E**, **A**, **B**.

But it's not an easy chord. In its simplest position, shown here, it is a four-note chord. In other words, the bottom two strings must not be played.

HERE'S HOW the basic **B** major is formed:

First finger (1) just behind the second fret on the first (top **E**) string.

Second finger (2) just behind the fourth fret on the fourth (**D**) string.

Third finger (3) just behind the fourth fret on the third (**G**) string.

Little finger (4) just behind the fourth fret on the second (**B**) string.

The bottom two strings (**A** and **E**) are not played.

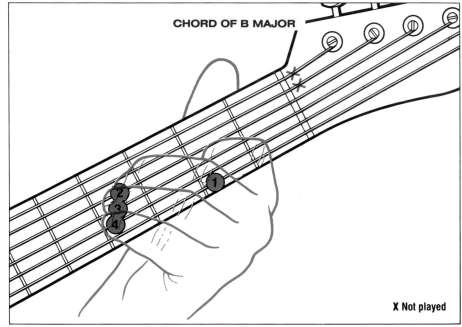

CHORD OF B MAJOR

X Not played

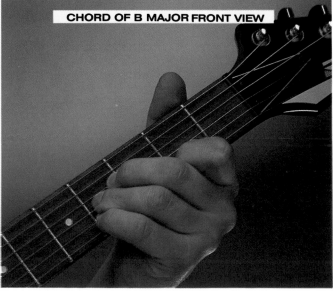

CHORD OF B MAJOR FRONT VIEW

Our most difficult chord to date, with a stretch of two frets. Establish the first and second fingers, then let the others drop into place.

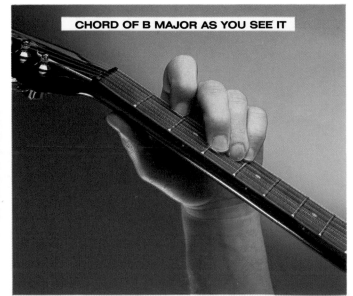

CHORD OF B MAJOR AS YOU SEE IT

If you feel pressure on your thumb, don't hold the chord too long. Try to pack the second, third and fourth fingers tight.

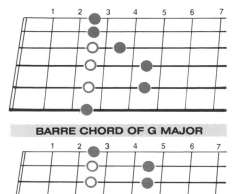

BARRE CHORD OF G MAJOR

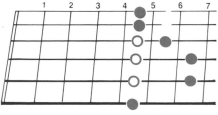

BARRE CHORD OF A MAJOR

BARRE CHORD OF C MAJOR

However, the two most used barre shapes are the ones in our **G** major and **C** major example. These two shapes are in fact derived from **E** major and **A** major.

Let's look at the **E** major shape. First, form a chord of **E** major using your second, third and fourth fingers (second finger, first fret **G** string; third finger, second fret **A** string; fourth finger, second fret **D** string).

This leaves the first finger 'free' to barre any fret. If it barres the third fret, that gives us our **G** chord.

Now let's look at the **A** major shape. Again, form an **A** major shape using the second, third and fourh fingers (all behind the second fret, **B**, **G** and **D** strings).

Again, the first finger is free to barre any fret. Move this chord shape along the neck to barre third fret, and you have the **C** major chord from our example.

more quickly.

Take for instance a **G** major barre chord, formed on the third fret. Without moving your first finger, you can shift smoothly to a **C** major barre chord.

There are other barre chords you could form on the same fret—minor chords, seventh chords—which we'll come to later.

BARRED B MAJOR CHORD

THE CHORD of **B** major is one that benefits immensely from the barre shape. Instead of the four-string chord opposite, we can bring all six strings into play.

Place your first finger right across all six strings on the second fret. The other four fingers line up in the same way as the unbarred chord:

First finger (1) barres all six strings just behind the second fret.

Second finger (2) just behind the fourth fret on the fourth (**D**) string.

Third finger (3) just behind the fourth fret on the third (**G**) string.

Little finger (4) just behind the fourth fret on the second (**B**) string.

AT FIRST you'll find barre chords almost impossible. Don't worry, it's the same for everyone.

Just keep practising—in time you'll find yourself using them as easily and naturally as any other chord.

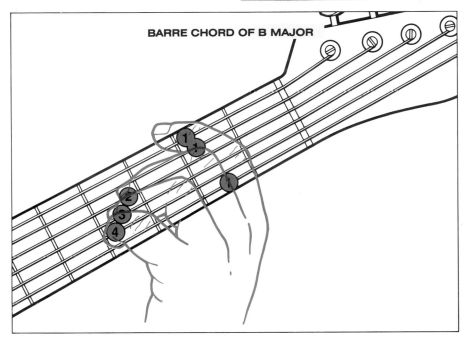

BARRE CHORD OF B MAJOR

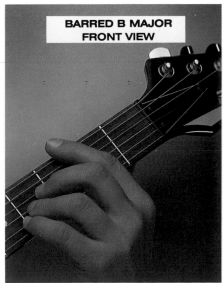

BARRED B MAJOR FRONT VIEW

This shape is even more difficult, but it's far more useful. If you can take the strain, you'll make a fine guitarist.

BARRED B MAJOR AS YOU SEE IT

Note that the barring finger isn't straight. As long as all the notes play clearly, that's OK.

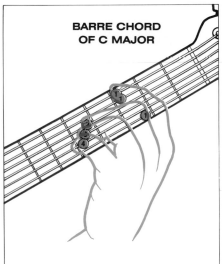

BARRE CHORD OF C MAJOR

IF WE move the barred **B** major shape up one fret we get **C** major. This is a useful variation on the 'open' **C** you already know.

BARRE CHORDS

THE BIG problem with barre chords is actually playing them. Holding down all six strings with one finger can be brutal. A simple exercise will soon get you into the 'feel' of the barre shape, and the more you do it, the more natural it will become.

Try this: without forming a chord shape, simply barre all six strings with your first finger and play through the strings. If you have six clear notes, with no buzzes, you're winning.

If this is too much of a strain, you can enlist the second finger to support the first.

If you can discipline yourself to repeat this arrangement for, say, five minutes a day, you'll get your reward.

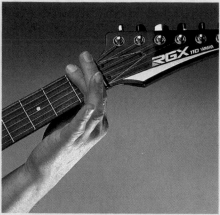
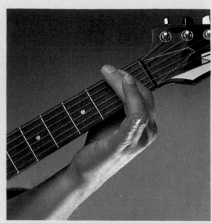

A helpful exercise for barre chords: the first finger barring first fret.

If the going gets tough for the first finger on its own, bring in the second finger to help.

BARRED F MAJOR CHORD

This is just about the most useful chord you'll every learn. Using this chord shape you can play every single major chord without changing your hand position—all you do is move the hand along the neck.

Here's how it's formed for its lowest version—the one nearest the headstock—**F** major:

First finger (1) barres all six strings just behind the first fret.

Second finger (2) just behind the second fret on the third (**G**) string.

Third finger (3) just behind the third fret on the fifth (**A**) string.

Little finger (4) just behind the third fret on the fourth (**D**) string.

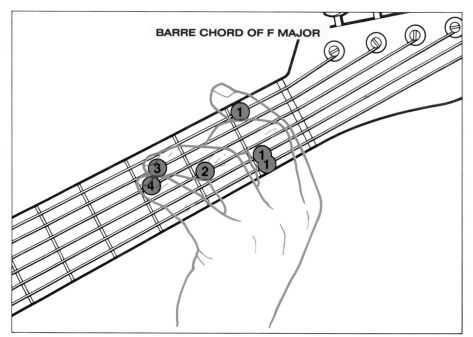

BARRE CHORD OF F MAJOR

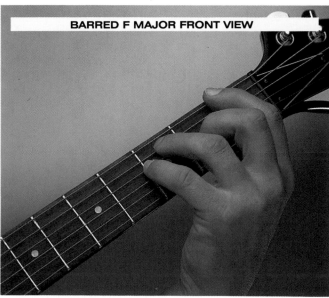

BARRED F MAJOR FRONT VIEW

The barre position adds an extra note to the **F** chord, giving you a full six-string shape. Make sure the first finger covers all frets.

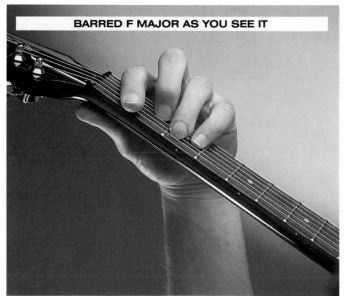

BARRED F MAJOR AS YOU SEE IT

It's difficult to keep the first finger straight, with the other fingers pulling it towards them. As long as the notes are clear, it doesn't matter.

USING BARRE chords, you can now work out different ways of playing all the major chords you've learnt so far.

To take one example: on page 25 you learned an open D major chord, comprising just four strings. Using a barre, you can now play two six-string chords of D major as well.

D major can be found as an 'A' style barre chord on the fifth fret, and as an 'E' type barre chord on the tenth fret.

ONE LAST point on barre chords. Some people complete a chord of this nature not by barring to cover the sixth string, but by hooking their thumb round the neck.

Generally this is frowned on by guitar teachers, but if it's good enough for Prince and Springsteen, who are we to tell you not to do it?

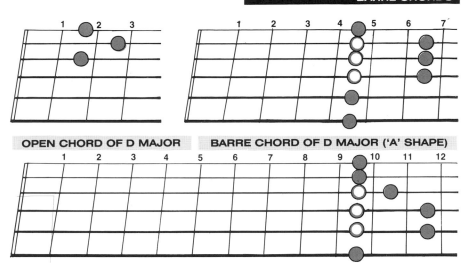

OPEN CHORD OF D MAJOR

BARRE CHORD OF D MAJOR ('A' SHAPE)

BARRE CHORD OF D MAJOR ('E' SHAPE)

BARRE CHORD OF G MAJOR

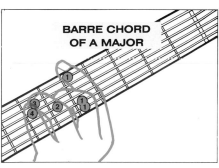

BARRED G MAJOR FRONT VIEW

BARRED G MAJOR AS YOU SEE IT

The barred G chord is exactly the same as F, two frets up. The first finger should feel a little easier away from the nut on the neck of the guitar.

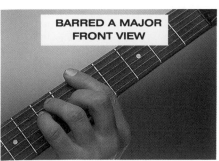

BARRE CHORD OF A MAJOR

BARRED A MAJOR FRONT VIEW

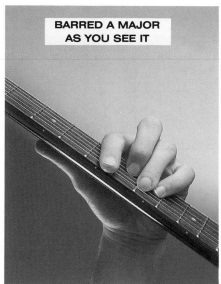

BARRED A MAJOR AS YOU SEE IT

This looks like a nice relaxed set-up because it is. Don't fear the barre chord: it could be your best friend.

THIS SHAPE is known as either the 'E' or 'F' shape. If you move it a couple of frets up the neck, you can form G major:

First finger (1) barring all strings just behind the third fret.

Second finger (2) just behind the fourth fret on the third (G) string.

Third finger (3) just behind the fifth fret on the fifth (A) string.

Little finger (4) just behind the fifth fret on the fourth (D) string.

TO FORM the barre chord of A major, we simply move two frets along. Because we barre this chord on the fifth fret, we sometimes refer to it as A played at the fifth fret.

First finger (1) barres all six strings just behind the fifth fret.

Second finger (2) just behind the sixth fret on the third (G) string.

Third finger (3) just behind the seventh fret on the fifth (A) string.

Little finger (4) just behind the seventh fret on the fourth (D) string.

Johnny Ramone of The Ramones plays the stock punk rock chord—a barred F.

MINOR KEYS

SO FAR, everything we've dealt with has been 'major'—major keys, such as the key of **A** major; major scales, such as the scale of **A** major; and major chords, such as the chord of **A** major.

As you know, there are 12 notes in music—**C, D, E, F, G, A, B**, plus the five sharp/flat notes **C#/Db, D#/Eb, F#/Gb, G#/Ab** and **A#/Bb**.

Each of these 12 notes has a major key based on its own major scale. And each note has its own major chord.

Now we come on to something new. For each 'major' there is a partner, known as a 'minor'.

Each of the 12 notes has a minor key based on its own minor scale. And each note has its own minor chord.

So you've got a total of 24 musical keys that you can work in—12 majors and 12

minors. And you've got 12 major chords and 12 minor chords which you can use—these are known as the primary chords.

THE TOP sections of the next six pages concentrate on minor keys, while the lower section shows you the most important minor chord shapes.

Once you understand how the major and minor scales and chords are constructed, and how they relate to one another, you could say that you basically understand music.

You can, if you wish, skip over this section and simply concentrate on learning to play the chords shown at the bottom of each page. But if you want to learn the complex language of music, we've done our best to give a simple explanation.

So let's get started . . .

MINOR SCALES

DO YOU remember how a major scale was made up? If you check back to page 18, you'll see how we played the scale of **C** major on our **B** string, with gaps of 2, 2, 1, 2, 2, 2, 1 frets—or tone, tone, semitone, tone, tone, tone, semitone.

The notes in the scale of **C** major were **C, D, E, F, G, A, B, C**.

To get the scale of **C** minor, we take the major scale and flatten the third, sixth and seventh notes by one semitone each.

So the notes in the scale of **C** minor are **C, D, Eb, F, G, Ab, Bb**.

The gaps between the notes in a minor scale are 2, 1, 2, 2, 1, 2, 2—or tone, semitone, tone, tone, semitone, tone, tone. (Technically, this is known as the Aeolian minor scale.)

CHORD OF E MINOR

OUR FIRST departure from the major chords is a simple and logical step, providing us with a necessary option in song structure.

The minor chords are often called the 'mood' chords, because they carry a sad, resonant sound, as opposed to the bright or forceful sound of a major chord. Yet you'll notice something familiar about them.

As you play the minor chord you'll recognise the root note and sound of its major counterpart—for example **A** minor will sound similar to **A** major, but will have a more mournful or soulful sound.

OUR STARTING point will be **E** minor (or **Em** for short). Just two fingers—the first and second—are required here:

First finger (1) just behind the second fret on the fifth (**A**) string.

Second finger (2) just behind the second fret on the fourth (**D**) string.

Strum this chord and hear the slightly sombre effect, in direct contrast to the dynamic **E** major chord.

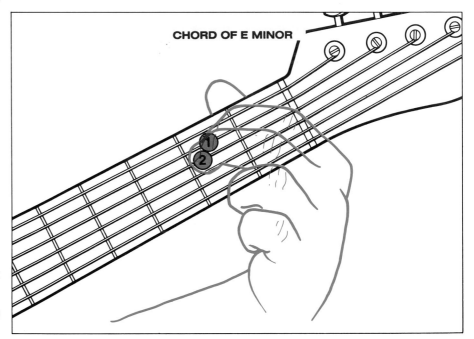

CHORD OF E MINOR

E minor is a simple two-finger chord. Note how the third finger stays well clear of the strings.

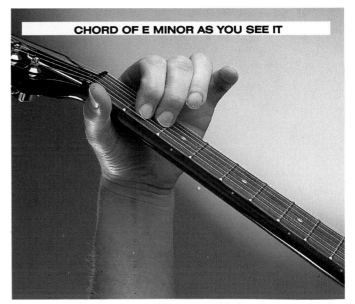

The thumb curls round the neck of the guitar, with the palm supporting the instrument's neck.

TAKE A LOOK at the scales of **C** major, **C** minor, **A** major and **A** minor. They are the notes you can use in the keys of **C** major, **C** minor, **A** major and **A** minor, whether playing single notes or chords.

You'll notice there's quite a difference between the notes in the scales of **C** major and **C** minor. But look at the scales of **C** major and **A** minor. One starts on **C**, the other on **A**— but the notes are exactly the same: C, D, E, F, G, A, B.

This is because **A** minor is the 'relative minor' of **C** major.

This means that any chord or note which can be used in the key of **C** major can also be used in the key of **A** minor.

It also means that the chords of **C** major and **A** minor are related—play them and you'll hear why. It's strange, but true, that you will often use **C** major and **A** minor together—but you'll almost never use **C** major with **C** minor. They just don't go.

The same goes for all major/minor chord pairs. Every major chord has its relative minor, with which it works well—for **C** major it's **A** minor, for **A** major it happens to be **F#** minor.

If you look at the table on the left, you'll see that **A** is the sixth note in the scale of **C** major, and **F#** is the sixth note in the scale of **A** major.

Armed with this knowledge, see if you can work out the relative minor for **G** major. The answer's on the next page.

HOW MAJOR AND MINOR SCALES RELATE							
SCALE OF C MAJOR	C	D	E	F	G	A	B	C
SCALE OF C MINOR	C	D	E♭	F	G	A♭	B♭	C
SCALE OF A MAJOR	A	B	C#	D	E	F#	G#	A
SCALE OF A MINOR	A	B	C	D	E	F	G	A

The scale of A minor has more in common with the scale of C major than with A major. In fact they share the same notes, because A minor is the relative minor of C major.

THE NEXT minor chord position involves the use of three fingers, to form **A** minor (**Am**).

Place your first finger (1) on the first fret of the second (**B**) string.

Second finger (2) just behind the second fret on the fourth (**D**) string.

Third finger (3) just behind the second fret on the third (**G**) string.

TRY PLAYING an **A** minor chord, then an **E** minor and a **C** major.

You'll notice that your second finger remains on the second fret of the fourth (**D**) string, playing the **E** note which links the three chords together.

Practise changing between the three chords, bring in **G** major as well—you'll soon hear some interesting chord patterns.

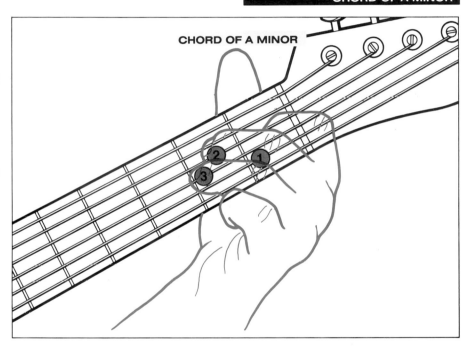

CHORD OF A MINOR

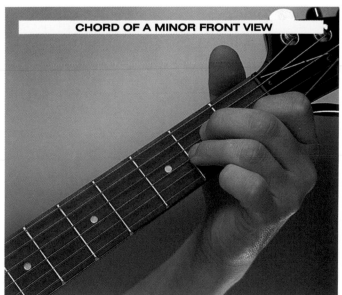

Like E minor, A minor is a resonant 'open' chord requiring accurate fingering for a full, clean sound.

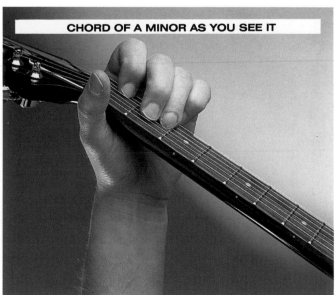

A minor and E minor sound really good together. Practise moving smoothly from one to the other.

RELATIVE MINORS

YOU CAN now add a relative minor chord to each of the three-chord tricks you already know, to make what we might call four-chord tricks.

So C, F, G, A minor (or Am for short) is the four-chord trick in the key of C major.

These four chords all work in the key of C major because they use notes which are in the scale of C major (the notes in the scale being C, D, E, F, G, A, B).

The chord of C major uses notes C, E, G.
The chord of F major uses F, A, C.
The chord of G major uses G, B, D.
The chord of A minor uses A, C, E.

IT'S ESSENTIAL to know the relative minor for each major chord, because the two go hand in hand.

The table below gives the relative minor for every major key or chord.

MINOR CHORD STRUCTURE

MINOR CHORDS are made up in exactly the same way as major chords: from the first, third and fifth notes of their scale.

The scale of A minor is A, B, C, D, E, F, G. Therefore the notes in the chord of A minor are A, C and E.

MAJOR KEYS AND THEIR RELATIVE MINORS											
MAJOR KEY	C	Db	D	Eb	E	F	F#	G	Ab	A	Bb	B
RELATIVE MINOR KEY	A	Bb	B	C	C#	D	D#	E	F	F#	G	G#

There is a logical way to work out which major key or chord relates to which minor key or chord. The relative minor is always three frets—three semitones—down from the major. From C, count down three semitones and you get A. Therefore A minor is the relative minor of C major.

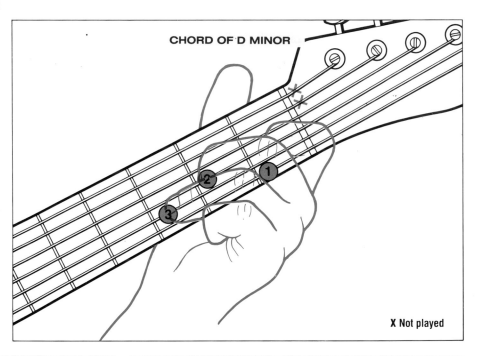

NOTES IN THE CHORD OF E MINOR

E B E G B E

CHORD OF D MINOR

THE Dm CHORD is perhaps the trickiest of the basic minor chords to form. Here it is:

First finger (1) just behind the first fret on the first (top E) string.

Second finger (2) just behind the second fret on the third (G) string.

Third finger (3) just behind the third fret on the second (B) string.

The fourth (D) string is played open. The bottom two strings are not played.

NOW YOU'VE got a three-chord trick of minor chords, consisting of Am, Dm and Em. These chords work together in the key of A minor.

Try different sequences of the three: together they combine to give a powerful, mournful effect.

And you can put them together with your original three-chord trick—C major, F major and G major—to form one giant six-chord trick to be used in the keys of C major or A minor. In other words, C or Am is your logical starting point—but it's you making the music, so suit yourself.

CHORD OF D MINOR

X Not played

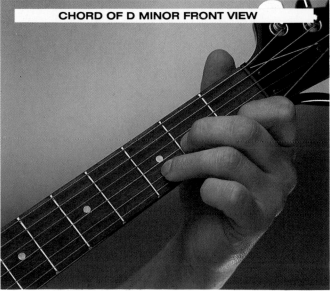

CHORD OF D MINOR FRONT VIEW

Your fingers should take on a 'spidery' look when forming Dm, with the first joints at the knuckle nicely bent.

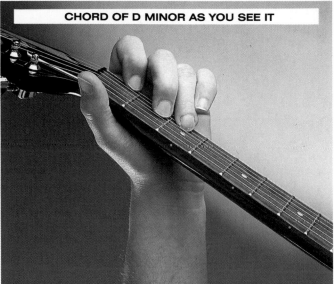

CHORD OF D MINOR AS YOU SEE IT

Your little finger may want to 'pop back' onto the strings, so remember to keep it tucked into the palm of your hand.

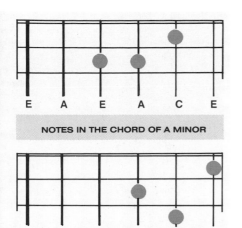

NOTES IN THE CHORD OF A MINOR

E A E A C E

NOTES IN THE CHORD OF D MINOR

X X D A D F

LET'S TAKE another look at some major chords and their relative minors. As we know, the major chords of **C**, **F** and **G** go together to form a three-chord trick in the key of **C** major.

Well, here's another useful fact: if you can use a major chord in a certain key, you can also use its relative minor chord.

So if we can use **C**, **F** and **G** in the key of **C** major, we can also use their relative minor chords—**Am**, **Dm** and **Em**.

These are the six primary chords that work in **C** major. They also work in the key of **A** minor.

ANOTHER WAY of putting it is to say that in every key there are six primary chords we can use. These six chords are based on six of the seven notes in the scale.

To take **C** major as our example, here's

the scale, along with the chords that work in the key of **C** major:

Root note: **C**.   Chord: **C** major.
2nd note: **D**.   Chord: **D** minor.
3rd note: **E**.   Chord: **E** minor.
4th note: **F**.   Chord: **F** major.
5th note: **G**.   Chord: **G** major.
6th note: **A**.   Chord: **A** minor.
7th note: **B**.   Chord: none.

In a minor scale, the only note which doesn't give us a chord to use is the second. Let's take the scale of **A** minor:

Root note: **A**.   Chord: **A** minor.
2nd note: **B**.   Chord: none.
3rd note: **C**.   Chord: **C** major.
4th note: **D**.   Chord: **D** minor.
5th note: **E**.   Chord: **E** minor.
6th note: **F**.   Chord: **F** major.
7th note: **G**.   Chord: **G** major.

This formula can be applied to any major

THE CHORDS of **B** minor and **C** minor take the **A** minor chord shape and move it along the fretboard.

The first—and most useful—of these two very similar chords is **B** minor. Unfortunately, in its easier unbarred form **B** minor is just a four-note chord. Here's how it's formed:

First finger (1) just behind the second fret on the first (top **E**) string.

Second finger (2) just behind the third fret on the second (**B**) string.

Third finger (3) just behind the fourth fret on the fourth (**D**) string.

Little finger (4) just behind the fourth fret on the third (**G**) string.

The bottom two strings are not played.

THE CHORD of **B** minor is useful because it's the relative minor of **D** major, and can be used in the same keys as its major relative.

So you can use it in the keys of **B** minor, **D** major, **G** major, **E** minor, **A** major and **F#** minor—and all bar **F#** minor are common keys.

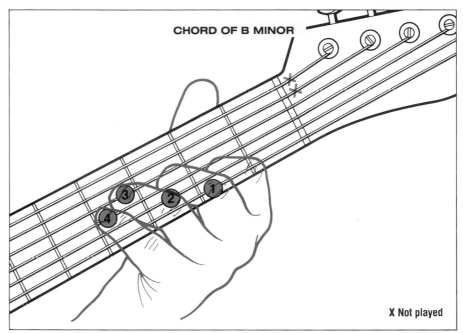

CHORD OF B MINOR

X Not played

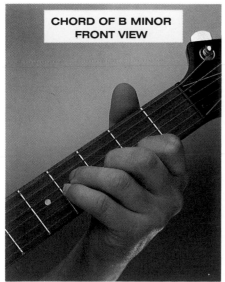

CHORD OF B MINOR FRONT VIEW

With the third and fourth fingers close together, there's a tendency to touch adjacent strings. Keep them well spaced if you can.

CHORD OF B MINOR AS YOU SEE IT

The thumb will fall back when forming **Bm**. Don't force it into an unnatural position. The left hand should always feel comfortable.

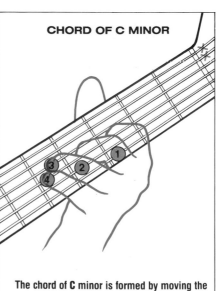

CHORD OF C MINOR

The chord of **C** minor is formed by moving the **B** minor fingering one fret up the neck. Again, the bottom two strings aren't played.

33

SHARPS OR FLATS?

AS WE know, a sharp/flat note can be called either sharp or flat—so how do we decide which it should be?

The simple explanation is that the note name changes according to what key you're using it in.

Here's how it works. You can't have two notes with similar names in the same key. So for instance you can't have **G** and **G♭**, or **G** and **G#**, **G♭** and **G#**. So if there's a **G** in the scale, the note **G♭/F#** will be called **F#**.

On top of that, you can't have both sharps and flats in the same key—a key may include up to six sharp notes (the key of **F#** major) or five flat notes (the key of **D♭** major). But never both.

For this reason, keys with sharps are

sometimes known as sharp keys, and keys with flats are sometimes known as flat keys.

One final point. In the table opposite, you may notice that in the keys of **F#** major and **D#** minor there's a note called **E#**. This is the note we usually call **F**, but because there's already an **F**-note (**F#**) in the key, it's called **E#**. This is the only time this occurs.

DON'T WORRY about what you call sharps or flats—if you refer to a note as **D#** when you should be calling it **E♭**, any musician will know what you mean.

But for any reader who wants to know how the system works, hopefully this has answered your questions.

or minor scale, to give you the primary chords that sound good in any key.

This doesn't mean these are the *only* chords you can use—there are lots of chords called sevenths, ninths, diminished and so on which we'll meet later.

It also doesn't mean you can't use other primary chords if you're writing a song—after all, rules are there to be broken. But these are the primary chords which use notes from each scale: the ones it's most natural to use.

THE TABLE opposite sets out all the major and minor scales, and all the chords that 'work' in every single key. You don't need to try to take it in all at once. Even the most experienced of musicians occasionally stumble over their scales. But as a reference table you'll find it invaluable.

CHORD OF F MINOR

LIKE ITS big brother **F** major, **F#** minor is formed around the first fret of the guitar. The first finger assumes a 'half-barre' position across the first three strings, because in effect you're just moving the **E** minor chord up one fret. Here's how it's formed:

First finger (1) barring just behind the first fret across the first, second and third (top **E**, **B** and **G**) strings.

Third finger (3) just behind the third fret on the fifth (**A**) string.

Little finger (**D**) just behind the third fret on the fourth (**A**) string.

The bottom **E** string is not played.

AS WITH the **F** major chord, this can be played as a four-string chord with the third finger fretting the fourth string and the bottom two strings unplayed.

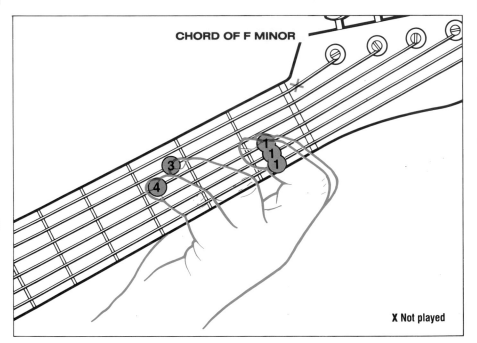

CHORD OF F MINOR

X Not played

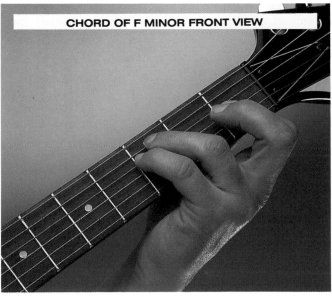

CHORD OF F MINOR FRONT VIEW

The first finger has a tough job holding down three strings here. Don't despair if the chord sounds fuzzy at first.

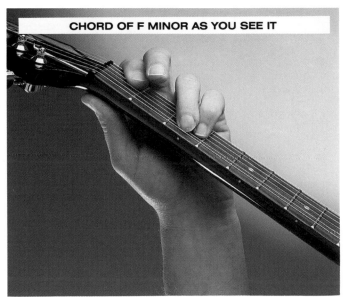

CHORD OF F MINOR AS YOU SEE IT

Try to help the first finger by using the second as support. The other two fingers will feel easier this way.

	NOTE IN SCALE	PRIMARY TRIAD CHORD	SCALE (READ DOWN FROM ROOT NOTE)											
			C	Db	D	Eb	E	F	F#	G	Ab	A	Bb	B
MAJOR KEY	Root	Root major chord	C	Db	D	Eb	E	F	F#	G	Ab	A	Bb	B
	Second	Minor chord	D	Eb	E	F	F#	G	G#	A	Bb	B	C	C#
	Third	Minor chord	E	F	F#	G	G#	A	A#	B	C	C#	D	D#
	Fourth	Major chord	F	Gb	G	Ab	A	Bb	B	C	Db	D	Eb	E
	Fifth	Major chord	G	Ab	A	Bb	B	C	C#	D	Eb	E	F	F#
	Sixth	Relative minor chord	A	Bb	B	C	C#	D	D#	E	F	F#	G	G#
	Seventh	– – – –	B	C	C#	D	D#	E	E#	F#	G	G#	A	A#

	NOTE IN SCALE	PRIMARY TRIAD CHORD	SCALE (READ DOWN FROM ROOT NOTE)											
MINOR KEY	Root	Root minor chord	A	Bb	B	C	C#	D	D#	E	F	F#	G	G#
	Second	– – – –	B	C	C#	D	D#	E	E#	F#	G	G#	A	A#
	Third	Relative major chord	C	Db	D	Eb	E	F	F#	G	Ab	A	Bb	B
	Fourth	Minor chord	D	Eb	E	F	F#	G	G#	A	Bb	B	C	C#
	Fifth	Minor chord	E	F	F#	G	G#	A	A#	B	C	C#	D	D#
	Sixth	Major chord	F	Gb	G	Ab	A	Bb	B	C	Db	D	Eb	E
	Seventh	Major chord	G	Ab	A	Bb	B	C	C#	D	Eb	E	F	F#

LIKE THE **F** major chord, the **F** minor chord shape slides easily along the neck to give other five-string minor chords. If you slide one fret, you have **F#** minor—a useful chord, because it works in the keys of **A** major, **D** major, **E** major, **B** minor and **C#** minor. It's the relative minor of **A** major, and sounds great played between **A** major and **E** major.

One fret further gives you **G** minor, and on the fifth fret you can play an alternative version of **A** minor to the one you already know.

Don't forget, though, that the open bottom **E** string is not played.

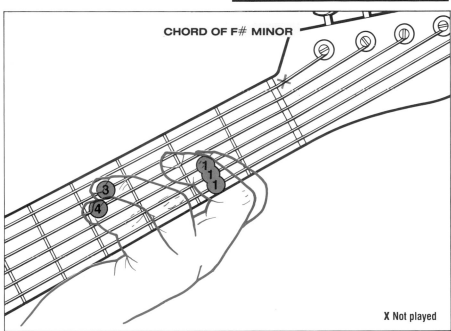

CHORD OF F# MINOR

X Not played

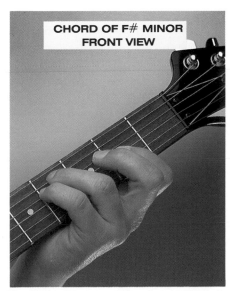

CHORD OF F# MINOR FRONT VIEW

The chords of F minor and F# minor are identical, but one fret apart. This chord sounds good with A, D or E major.

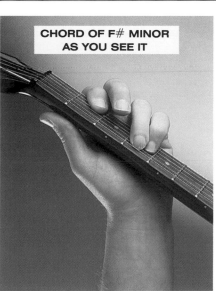

CHORD OF F# MINOR AS YOU SEE IT

Try sliding from F minor to F# minor, then on to G minor. You'll soon get to know your way around the fretboard.

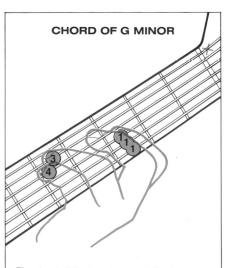

CHORD OF G MINOR

The chord of G minor is essentially the same as the chords of F minor and F# minor. You just play it on the third fret. The bottom E string is not played.

FINGER STYLE

A TRUCKLOAD of the most sophisticated equipment in the world can't disguise a weak right hand. Some guitarists work so hard on getting their chord shapes correct with their left hand, they forget about the right.

We've already looked at how to use a plectrum for rhythm work, and how to play the scale of **G** major with a plectrum. We'll be taking that further later, when we begin playing single-note solos, riffs and more scales.

But there's more to the right hand than just wielding a plectrum. Assuming you have the full set – four fingers and a thumb – it's purely a matter of practice before your right hand can perform tricks of its own.

The use of the fingers to pluck the strings is known as finger picking, or finger style.

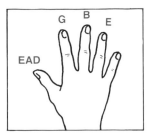
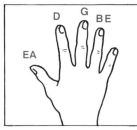
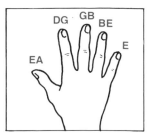

These diagrams show the different strings that may be played with each finger (and thumb) of your right hand.

Generally, it's associated more with folk than rock guitar, but it's more common in rock than is generally recognised: you can hear right-hand fingering skills in the work of guitarists as varied as Mark Knopfler, Steve Howe and Jeff Beck.

THE QUICKEST way to utilise the fingers as 'fleshy plectrums' is to consider them playing the strings in sequence, from bottom to top **E**. The thumb will strike downwards on the bottom **E** string, the fifth (**A**) string, and occasionally the fourth (**D**) string. The fingers will 'pick' upwards from the **D** string through to the top **E** string.

There is no set rule for which finger plays which string, but the three diagrams above show possible combinations.

BARRED MINOR CHORDS

AS WE explained on page 26, barre chords simplify the work of the left hand, enabling you to use familiar chord shapes anywhere on the guitar.

There are two important minor chord shapes – **Em** and **Am** – which can be barred to provide a simple set of chords using the same shape.

Barring **Em** on the first fret gives us **Fm**. The set-up is:

First finger (and second, if you like) across all strings, just behind the first fret.

Third finger just behind the third fret on the fifth (**A**) string.

Little finger just behind the third fret on the fourth (**D**) string.

Move the whole thing two frets further, and you've got **Gm**.

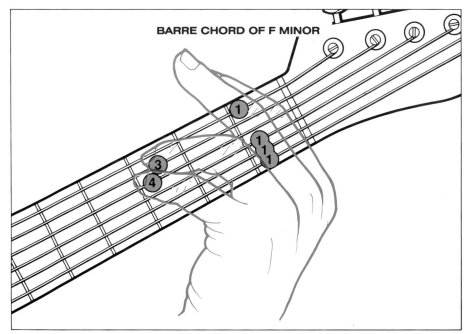

BARRE CHORD OF F MINOR

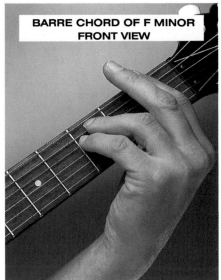

BARRE CHORD OF F MINOR FRONT VIEW

This is a fairly difficult barre chord to form, as it falls on the first fret where the strings are less forgiving.

BARRE CHORD OF F MINOR AS YOU SEE IT

When forming a barre chord such as **F** minor, remember to use your second finger to support the first, if that helps.

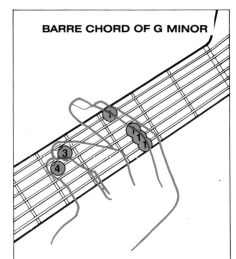

BARRE CHORD OF G MINOR

You can identify any of the **Em** style chords by their position in relation to the **E** strings. **Gm** falls on the third fret, which is the **G** note on the **E** strings.

LET'S TRY working out with the right hand on just one chord – an open **G** major.

First, form the chord with your left hand, then strike the bottom string a couple of times with your thumb. You will immediately notice the mellow tone it produces.

Now pluck the top string with your third finger, by pulling it upwards. Alternate these two notes until you feel relaxed and comfortable.

The note you're playing is of course the same on both strings, **G**.

Now here comes the tricky bit. Using the thumb only, strike the bottom **E** string and then the fifth (**A**) string. Forget about the other fingers for the moment; just concentrate on getting the thumb working on those bottom two strings.

The **A** string is being held down on the second fret, giving a **B** note.

Practise this until you're completely happy with your performance. Don't try and race ahead here. Whilst the sounds you are making may seem repetitive and dull, it's the right hand which is benefiting. You're only shortchanging yourself if you adopt a 'nuts to this bit' attitude.

IF WE are still on speaking terms, and you are happy to proceed, we will now make full use of the right hand in conjunction with the **G** chord.

The first finger will pluck the **G** string, the second finger the **B** string, and the third finger the top **E** string. Ignoring the thumb, pull these three strings together. A little fuzzy, eh?

Looking at the picture here, note the position of the fingers in relation to the strings. For maximum clarity of tone, pull

Finger picking stance, thumb poised over bottom E.

the strings from a point just below the tip.

The next move is to bring in the thumb. Try this: strike the bottom **E** string with the thumb, then pull the top three strings.

BARRING THE **A** minor shape on the second fret gives us **B** minor – the relative minor to **D** major, and an important link in a chord chain that includes **D**, **G** and **A**.

B minor is formed as follows:

First finger holds down all the strings on the second fret.

Second finger just behind the third fret on the second (**B**) string.

Third finger just behind the fourth fret on the fourth (**D**) string.

Little finger just behind the fourth fret on the third (**G**) string.

AS WITH all barre chords, this shape can be used at any point on the neck. Form this shape at the fifth fret, and you have **Dm**. You also have a convenient place to change either to **Em** (by sliding up to the seventh fret) or to **Am** (by holding the barre on the fifth fret, but adjusting the other fingers into the **Fm** shape).

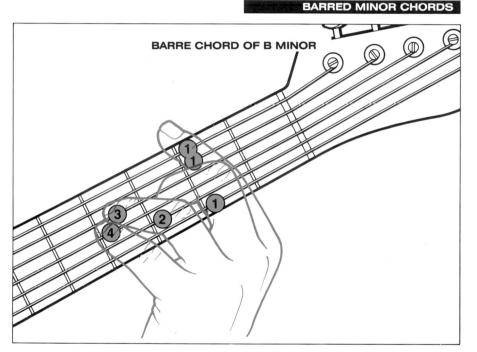

BARRE CHORD OF B MINOR

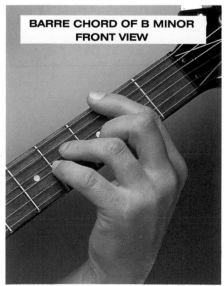

Bm is an important chord, as it is the relative minor to D major, and will therefore appear frequently in songs written in D, a common key.

The tightness of the second, third and fourth fingers takes some getting used to when forming these Am style chords in their barre positions.

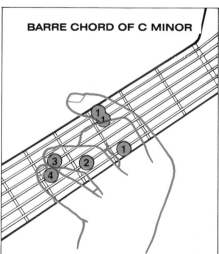

BARRE CHORD OF C MINOR

This is **Cm**, which surprisingly is not used as much as **C#m** (one fret along) because **C#m** is the relative minor of **E** major. You can use this shape to form any minor chord.

FINGER STYLE PRACTICE

Repeat these moves alternately until it feels comfortable.

YOU MIGHT describe the sound you are now making as *dum-ching, dum-ching.* Silly, I know, but it helps us get the message across.

To broaden the scope of the thumb, let's bring in the fifth (**A**) string. Alternate it with the bottom **E** string to give this effect:

Dum (bottom **E**) *ching* (top three strings). *Dum* (**A** string) *ching* (top three strings). *Dum* (bottom **E**) *ching* (top three strings). And so on.

Don't worry too much about your *ching* at this point. Just work on that thumb.

You should try to get it moving almost independently, so that while it plods along giving a regular bassline, the fingers play the tricky bits.

FINALLY, WE need to incorporate the **D** string. Working on the *dum-ching* principle, first strike the bottom **E** string with your thumb, then pluck the top three strings, as above. Now add the **A** string (thumb), followed by the *ching* effect. And then the new bit: strike the **D** string with the thumb, followed by the *ching.*

Incidentally, you can take each *dum-ching* as one beat. If you add a fourth *dum-ching* based on the **A** string, that will neatly complete one four-beat bar, and you can start at the **E** string again.

AND THAT, in its most basic form, is finger style. Once you've conquered the **G** chord in this style, you can apply the technique to other chords, and begin to work up chord changes.

Generally, it sounds best if the root note

of each chord is played by the thumb on the first beat of the bar. So if you are playing open chords, these are the strings to play first with the thumb:

E or **Em**: Sixth (bottom **E**) string;
A or **Am**: Fifth (**A**) string;
D or **Dm**: Fourth (**D**) string;
G: Sixth (bottom **E**) string;
C: Fifth (**A**) string;
F or **Fm**: Fourth (**D**) string.

Bearing that in mind, try these chord sequences:

C Am F G
Am Em
G D C G
Am G F E.

As always, take it slowly at first.

ON PAGE 40 we look at a few different fingerpicking patterns.

'THE BOYS ARE BACK IN TOWN'

NOW THAT we've looked at the minor chords, here's a song which employs an interesting selection of major and minor chords – 'The Boys Are Back In Town' by Thin Lizzy.

For our purposes here, we've modified the song a little. Later on you'll get the chance to play it in its full glory, complete with seventh and minor seventh chords – and in a different key. But for now, let's try it in the key of **C**, and with a simplified rhythm and chords.

You've already encountered most of the chords you'll need. Our version has seven: the original three-chord trick of **C**, **F** and **G**, along with their relative minors **Am**, **Dm** and **Em**, plus one new chord, **A♭**, which we'll show you along with the complete song on page 40.

THE RHYTHM is a regular four beats to the bar (**4/4** in musical terms), but you have a choice of two ways to play it, shown on the two grids here.

The easiest way (top grid) is simply to play one downstroke for each beat. That's not much like Thin Lizzy played it. but it will make sense, and it will certainly help at first while you're working out the chord sequence.

Once you're familiar with the chords, try adding the slightly more difficult rhythm element marked on the lower grid. It entails both down and up strokes, but not in a straightforward down-up-down-up pattern.

Tap your foot steadily, quite slowly, counting out 1-2-3-4. The rhythm pattern is down, down-up . . . down. Repeat it over and over, and should find the emphasis changing to DOWN, down-UP . . . down, DOWN, down-UP. . . down, DOWN, down-UP. . . down.

If you can't get the hang of this, don't worry. Just concentrate on playing downstrokes, but every now and then slip in an upstroke so that you gradually add a bit of swing to it.

When you feel you're ready, go on to page 40, where the whole song is laid out.

KEY TO SYMBOLS AND COLOURS

⊓ Downward stroke   V Upward stroke

☐ **C** major   ☐ **E** minor   ☐ **G** major
☐ **F** major   ☐ **A** minor

TITLE	KEY	TEMPO
'THE BOYS ARE BACK IN TOWN' (OPENING LINES)	C MAJOR	MEDIUM SLOW

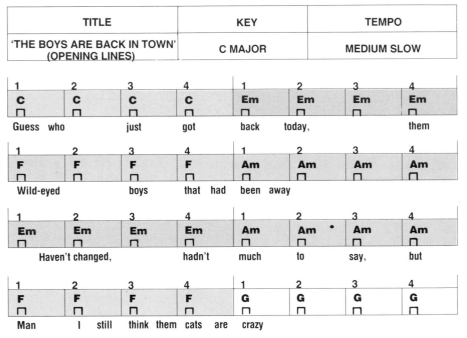

Above: This is how to play the song using all downward strokes: one stroke for each beat, regular as clockwork. If you want, you can play it all the way through like this.

Above: This is the rhythm we suggest you use. It can be applied to the whole of the grid on page 40. You don't play a chord on the third beat of the bar, but just let your previous chord ring out.

Four expert fingerpickers, from left: Mark Knopfler fingerpicks while smoking a cigarette; Albert Collins fingerpicks with a capo on his guitar neck; George Thorogood fingerpicks whilst playing bottleneck; Jeff Beck fingerpicks and palms his tremolo arm at the same time.

'THE BOYS Are Back In Town' was the high point in the saga of Thin Lizzy – a tale of a black Irish bass player, a drummer and about a dozen guitarists.

The bass player was Phil Lynott; the drummer, also from Dublin, was Brian Downey. From 1970 to 1983, they accompanied some of the finest hard rock guitar players in the world – Brian Robertson, Scott Gorham, Gary Moore, Snowy White, John Sykes, Eric Bell and even Midge Ure.

All these guitarists were great technicians. Each of them could have adorned any heavy metal band. But it was Lynott who elevated Lizzy above heavy metal, with his wit, charm and imaginative songwriting. His subjects ranged from rock and roll to blood and thunder, from cowboys to warriors. The common factor was romance, enhanced by the melodic double guitar sound.

Released in 1976, 'The Boys Are Back In Town' was taken from the 'Jailbreak' album, which sent Thin Lizzy high into the charts in both the US and UK. Other hits included 'Whiskey In the Jar', 'Dancin' In The Moonlight' and 'Don't Believe A Word', but Thin Lizzy will always be remembered for "them wild-eyed boys".

Sadly, Phil Lynott died in January 1986, but his songs remain as a testament to a great talent. 'The Boys Are Back' is typical of the freshness he managed to bring to fairly standard chord progressions, and the Thin Lizzy songbook is well worth picking up as an object lesson in how to write great guitar songs.

Right: Thin Lizzy leader Phil Lynott with three of his guitarists (from left: Brian Robertson and Scott Gorham, who played together on 'The Boys Are Back In Town', and Gary Moore).

FINGER STYLE PATTERNS

ONCE YOU'VE got your *dum-ching* working, you should try to use individual fingers to pluck individual strings, rather than all three at once.

Here are some possible finger picking patterns which you can apply to almost any chord. We've marked the thumb (**T**) as striking the bottom **E** string, but it could equally well play the fifth (**A**) string, depending on the chord.

Usually the thumb will play the root bass note—bottom **E** string for **E** major and **G** major, the fifth string for **A** major and **C** major, and so on.

You don't read these charts like chord diagrams, which is why the strings are open-ended. Just move from left to right, as if reading a book. Follow the blue ball.

So in the first chart, you play the sixth string with your thumb, then the top **E** string with your third finger, then the **B** string with your second finger, then the **G** string with your first finger.

In each pattern, when you reach the end you simply start at the beginning again.

When working on a new pattern, try it at first with just one chord, repeating it until you get it right. Then try changing chords, taking care to strike the correct bass note at the start of each bar.

SIX RIGHT HAND PATTERNS FOR FINGER STYLE PLAY

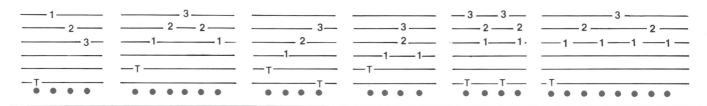

'THE BOYS ARE BACK IN TOWN'

HERE IT is, then – your biggest test to date: the long, complex chord sequence of 'The Boys Are Back In Town'.

It has a 12-bar intro (four bars repeated three times). Then there's a 16-bar verse and 12-bar chorus. And for good measure, there's an eight-bar 'bridge' to take you from the chorus back to the verse. This bridge is where the famous twin guitar riff occurs.

Looking at the running order opposite, you'll notice there's also a second bridge (Bridge 2), which isn't shown on the grid here. We'll include that later, when we develop the song – you can get along without it for now.

AS EVER, take this nice and slowly at first. Try to master each section on its own before stringing them all together.

Don't worry too much about the rhythm – as long as you've got something that sounds good to you, you can work your way through the song, practising the different chord changes.

The most unusual chord is **A♭** major, which you won't often find it in a song in **C** major. Phil Lynott uses it to break up the pattern and make a contrast. The 'natural' chord to put there would be **Am** (try it yourself).

Apart from that 'unnatural' **A♭**, this song is a classic illustration of the six chords which 'work' in a key – those chords, in the case of **C** major, being **C**, **Dm**, **Em**, **F**, **G** and **Am**.

AS WE said, the **A♭** chord is introduced to add contrast between the first and second parts of the verse. You can emphasize that contrast. For the first ten bars of the verse, use open chords near the nut of your guitar. But after you hit that **A♭** on the fourth fret, try playing an **F**-shape **G** (third fret), an **Fm**-shape **Am** (fifth fret), a **Bm**-shape **Dm** (fifth fret), and finally an **F**-shape **G** again. These can all be played either as barre chords or as four-string chords.

TITLE	KEY	TEMPO
'THE BOYS ARE BACK IN TOWN'	C MAJOR	QUITE FAST

1	2	3	4	1	2	3	4
C ⊓	C ⊓ ∨		C ⊓	C ⊓	C ⊓ ∨		C ⊓

1	2	3	4	1	2	3	4
Dm ⊓	Dm ⊓ ∨		Dm ⊓	F ⊓	F ⊓ ∨		F ⊓

VERSE

1	2	3	4	1	2	3	4
C ⊓	C ⊓ ∨		C ⊓	Em ⊓	Em ⊓ ∨		Em ⊓

Guess who just / got / back to- day, / them

1	2	3	4	1	2	3	4
F ⊓	F ⊓ ∨		F ⊓	Am ⊓	Am ⊓ ∨		Am ⊓

Wild- eyed / boys / that had been a- way.

1	2	3	4	1	2	3	4
Em ⊓	Em ⊓ ∨		Em ⊓	Am ⊓	Am ⊓ ∨		Am ⊓

Haven't changed, / hadn't / much to say,

1	2	3	4	1	2	3	4
F ⊓	F ⊓ ∨		F ⊓	G ⊓	G ⊓ ∨		G ⊓

But man, I still / think them / cats are cra- zy.

1	2	3	4	1	2	3	4
C ⊓	C ⊓ ∨		C ⊓	Em ⊓	Em ⊓ ∨		Em ⊓

They were asking / if you were around,

1	2	3	4	1	2	3	4
F ⊓	F ⊓ ∨		F ⊓	A♭ ⊓	A♭ ⊓ ∨		A♭ ⊓

How you was, / where you could be found.

KEY TO SYMBOLS AND COLOURS

⊓ Downward stroke   ∨ Upward stroke

▫ C major   ▪ E minor   ▫ G major
▫ F major   ▪ A minor   ▪ D minor
▫ A♭ major

CHORD OF A♭ MAJOR

As this chord falls between **F** and **G** in the song, we suggest that you play it as an **F**-shape chord on the fourth fret.

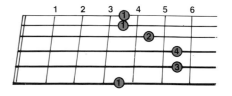

IF YOU'RE still practising the scale of **G** major, which we showed you on page 25, you should be fairly fluent by now. You could also probably do with a change – and now that we've looked at the minor chords, this is a good time to try a minor scale: **C** minor.

As before, there's an easy version and a 'proper' version. The simpler one takes you through a one-octave scale, from **C** to **C**.

The longer version is two octaves.

Try the shorter one first, starting on the fifth fret of your third (**G**) string. For the last note, slide your little finger from the sixth fret, top **E** string, to the eighth.

The notes in the scale of **C** minor are **C**, **D**, **E♭**, **F**, **G**, **A♭** and **B♭**. Try to identify each note as you play it.

You'll notice that there are no open strings in this scale. This means that you can move the whole exercise up and down the fretboard.

Move it all up two frets, and you've got the scale of **D** minor.

Bearing this in mind, you can return to the scale of **G** major – the second version, with no open strings – and try that scale in different parts of the fretboard.

Move it two frets up, and you'll be playing the scale of **A** major.

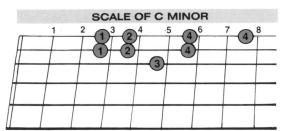

SCALE OF C MINOR

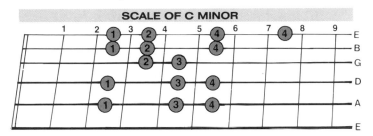

SCALE OF C MINOR

LYRICS AND RUNNING ORDER

INTRO (Three times)

VERSE 1
Guess who just got back today,
Them wild-eyed boys that had been away.
Haven't changed, hadn't much to say,
But man, I still think them cats are crazy.
They were asking if you were around,
How you was, where you could be found.
Told them you were living downtown,
Driving all the old men crazy.

CHORUS
The boys are back in town . . .
(Eight times)

BRIDGE 1 (Twice)
VERSE 2
You know that chick that used to dance a lot,
Every night she'd be on the floor shaking what she'd got,
Man, when I tell you she was cool, she was red hot,
I mean she was steaming.
And that time over at Johnny's place,
Well this chick got up and she slapped Johnny's face,
Man, we just fell about the place,
If that chick don't wanna know, forget her.

CHORUS
BRIDGE 1 (Twice)
BRIDGE 2
Spread the word around,
Guess who's back in town.
Just spread the word around.

VERSE 3
Friday night they'll be dressed to kill,
Down at Dino's bar and grill.
The drink will flow and blood will spill,
And if the boys wanna fight you better let 'em.
That jukebox in the corner blasting out my favourite song,
The nights are getting warmer, it won't be long,
Won't be long till summer comes,
Now that the boys are here again.

CHORUS/BRIDGE 1/FADE

1	2	3	4	1	2	3	4
G	G		G	Am	Am		Am
⊓	⊓ ∨		⊓	⊓	⊓ ∨		⊓
Told	them you were	living		down	town,		

1	2	3	4	1	2	3	4
Dm	Dm		Dm	G	G		G
⊓	⊓ ∨		⊓	⊓	⊓ ∨		⊓
	Driving	all the	old		men crazy.		The

CHORUS

1	2	3	4	1	2	3	4
C	C		C	C	C		C
⊓	⊓ ∨		⊓	⊓	⊓ ∨		⊓
Boys	are back		in town,	the boys	are back		in town.

1	2	3	4	1	2	3	4
Dm	Dm		Dm	F	F		F
⊓	⊓ ∨		⊓	⊓	⊓ ∨		⊓
							I said the

1	2	3	4	1	2	3	4
C	C		C	C	C		C
⊓	⊓ ∨		⊓	⊓	⊓ ∨		⊓
Boys	are back		in to-	o-	o-		own. The

1	2	3	4	1	2	3	4
Dm	Dm		Dm	F	F		F
⊓	⊓ ∨		⊓	⊓	⊓ ∨		⊓
Boys	are back		in town.				The

1	2	3	4	1	2	3	4
C	C		C	C	C		C
⊓	⊓ ∨		⊓	⊓	⊓ ∨		⊓
Boys	are back		in town,	the boys	are back		in town, the

1	2	3	4	1	2	3	4
Dm	Dm		Dm	F	F		F
⊓	⊓ ∨		⊓	⊓	⊓ ∨		⊓
Boys	are back		in town,	the boys	are back		in town.

BRIDGE 1

1	2	3	4	1	2	3	4
C	C		C	F	F		F
⊓	⊓ ∨		⊓	⊓	⊓ ∨		⊓

1	2	3	4	1	2	3	4
C	C		C	G	G		G
⊓	⊓ ∨		⊓	⊓	⊓ ∨		⊓

SEVENTH CHORDS

THE CHORDS we've covered to date are all known as primary chords.

C major is the primary chord in the key of C major. A minor is the primary chord in the key of A minor.

Each primary chord is made up from the first, third and fifth notes of the scale.

So the chord of C major consists of the first, third and fifth notes in the scale of C major—C, E and G. And the chord of A minor consists of the first, third and fifth notes in the scale of A minor—A, C and E.

Primary chords are the most important chords you'll ever learn. But there are vast numbers of other chords waiting to be played—most of them with weird names like augmented, diminished, sevenths, ninths and thirteenths.

You shouldn't feel intimidated by these strange names. Often you find the simplest chord imaginable hiding behind some long name—for instance, E minor seventh sounds complex, but it's the easiest chord ever invented.

Anyway, having introduced you to the primary chords, it's time to branch out—and by far the most common chords outside of primary chords are seventh chords.

THERE ARE three main kinds of seventh chord: major sevenths, minor sevenths and dominant sevenths.

Of these, the chord most used by guitarists is the dominant seventh. In fact, when guitar players talk about A seventh, or A7, they mean A dominant seventh.

As the name implies, seventh chords are all wrapped up with the seventh note of the scale. The way they're made up is very simple.

For each key, we start with the triad of notes that make up the primary chord—the first, third and fifth.

If you take a major triad and add the seventh note of the major scale, you have a major seventh chord.

If you take a minor triad and add the seventh note of the minor scale, you have a minor seventh chord.

Here's the tricky bit. If you take a major triad and add the seventh note in the *minor* scale, you have a dominant seventh chord.

And that, in a nutshell, is seventh chords.

THERE IS of course a little more to it than that. For one thing, guitar chords don't always include all the notes that make up a particular chord—take a look at C7, opposite. But any seventh chord *will* have the appropriate seventh note.

CHORD OF C SEVENTH

FOR A GUITARIST, the most common variation on the major chord is the dominant seventh chord. Generally known as just the seventh, it's written in musical shorthand with a figure 7, as in C7. Along with minor chords, sevenths serve to break the mood of the straight major chord sequence.

Let's start with our old three-chord trick, C, F and G. C7 is a tough, bluesy chord, and a favourite of guitar players brought up on a diet of Muddy Waters, Buddy Guy and BB King.

Here's how it's formed:

First finger (1) just behind the first fret on the second (B) string.

Second finger (2) just behind the second fret on the fourth (D) string.

Third finger (3) just behind the third fret or the fifth (A) string.

Little finger (4) pulls back to the third fret on the third (G) string.

The bottom E string is usually left unplayed, while the top E string is played 'open'.

C7 is the dominant seventh chord in the key of F major, and sounds good followed by F.

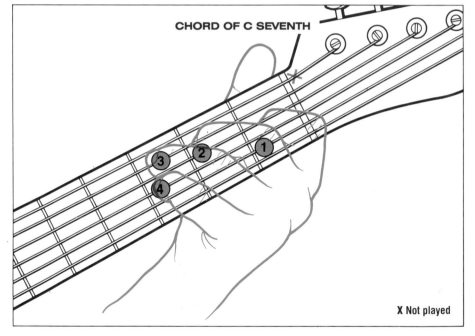

CHORD OF C SEVENTH

X Not played

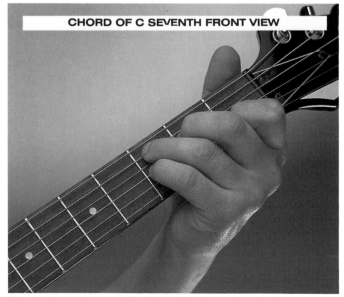

CHORD OF C SEVENTH FRONT VIEW

This C7 set-up looks more difficult than it is, although the little finger may want to wander the first few times.

CHORD OF C SEVENTH AS YOU SEE IT

The thumb falls between the first and second fingers behind the neck. Try to avoid pressure on the fleshy part of the thumb.

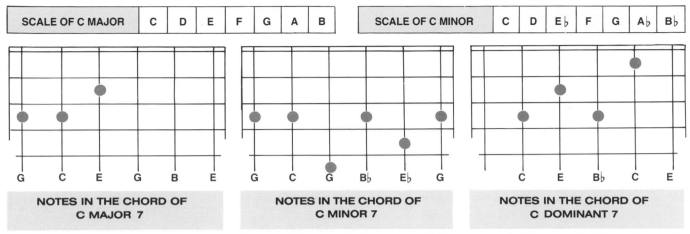

SCALE OF C MAJOR	C	D	E	F	G	A	B

SCALE OF C MINOR	C	D	E♭	F	G	A♭	B♭

G   C   E   G   B   E

G   C   G   B♭   E♭   G

C   E   B♭   C   E

**NOTES IN THE CHORD OF
C MAJOR 7**

**NOTES IN THE CHORD OF
C MINOR 7**

**NOTES IN THE CHORD OF
C DOMINANT 7**

The chord of **C** major 7 (**Cmaj7**) has the notes **C**, **E**, **G**, **B** (first, third, fifth and seventh notes in the scale of **C** major).

The chord of **C** minor 7 (**Cm7**) has the notes **C**, **E♭**, **G**, **B♭** (first, third, fifth and seventh notes in the scale of **C** minor).

The chord of **C** dominant 7 (**C7**) has the notes **C**, **E**, **B♭** (first and third notes in the major scale, plus the seventh note in the minor scale).

G7 IS a full six-note chord, with just three strings held down. Here's how it's formed:

First finger (1) just behind the first fret on the first (top **E**) string.

Second finger (2) just behind the second fret on the fifth (**A**) string.

Third finger (3) just behind the third fret on the sixth (bottom **E**) string.

Your pinkie can wander to its heart's content, but remember to arch your other fingers, or you run the risk of touching adjacent strings and muting the sound of the open notes.

G7 sounds good followed by **C** major, because it's the dominant seventh chord in the key of **C**.

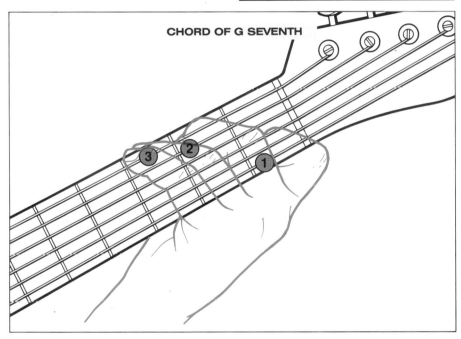

CHORD OF G SEVENTH

CHORD OF G SEVENTH FRONT VIEW

You will feel a twinge in your third finger as you stretch to make this **G7** chord. Pull the little finger back as far as you can.

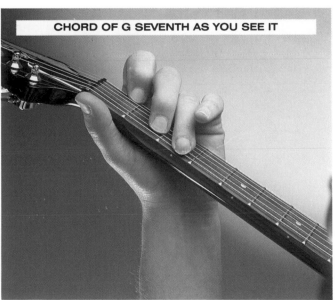

CHORD OF G SEVENTH AS YOU SEE IT

G7 is one of the most used seventh chords, as it is found in many blues songs in the key of **C**.

DOMINANT SEVENTH CHORDS

THERE IS of course a good reason why we call it the *dominant* seventh.

When you play with other musicians you may hear them refer to 'sub-dominant' and 'dominant'. These are simply musical terms for the fourth and fifth notes of a scale.

So if you're playing in C major, the sub-dominant is F and the dominant is G... CFG, our first three-chord trick.

As you know, the reason these three chords work in C major is because they all consist of notes found in the scale of C major. The same goes for their three relative minor chords, Am, Dm and Em.

The same also applies to most of the major seventh and minor seventh chords. The odd one out is G major 7, because it has the notes GBDF#, and F# is not in the scale of C major.

This is where the dominant seventh chord comes in. In G7 the F# is replaced by F, so that you can use it in the key of C.

THE DOMINANT seventh chord is almost always followed by the root chord of the major key it's related to.

Try playing G7 followed by C, or D7 followed by G—you'll soon recognise it as one of the most used and most satisfying chord changes in rock.

STRING NUMBER	6	5	4	3	2	1
NOTES IN THE CHORD OF C MAJOR 7	G	C	E	G	B	E
NOTES IN THE CHORD OF F MAJOR 7		C	F	A	C	E
NOTES IN THE CHORD OF A MINOR 7	E	A	E	G	C	E
NOTES IN THE CHORD OF D MINOR 7		A	D	A	C	F
NOTES IN THE CHORD OF E MINOR 7	E	B	D	G	B	E
NOTES IN THE CHORD OF G MAJOR 7			G	B	D	F#
NOTES IN THE CHORD OF G DOMINANT 7	G	B	D	G	B	F

All these seventh chords work in the key of C major, except for G major 7. So in the key of C, we use G dominant 7 (G7) instead.

MAJOR KEY	C	Db	D	Eb	E	F	F#	G	Ab	A	Bb	B
DOMINANT SEVENTH CHORD	G7	Ab7	A7	Bb7	B	C7	C#7	D7	Eb7	E7	F7	F#7

CHORD OF F SEVENTH

A FOUR-STRING chord, F7 uses a half-barre with the first finger (1) placed across the first four strings just behind the first fret. The second finger (2) then holds down the third (G) string just behind the second fret.

If you are still practising our barre chord exercise, you may find it more comfortable to use both your first and second fingers to barre the four strings, whilst using the third finger (3) to hold down the G string.

You may not use F7 very often—it's the dominant seventh chord in the key of B major—but this is a useful chord, because you can slide it up and down the fretboard.

If you move two frets along, to the third fret, you've got G7. Take it to the fifth fret, and you've got A7. These are alternatives to the versions of G7 and A7 shown here in their own right.

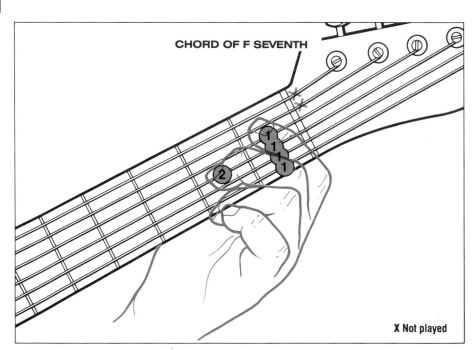

CHORD OF F SEVENTH

X Not played

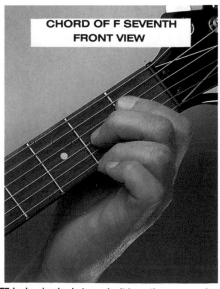

CHORD OF F SEVENTH FRONT VIEW

F7 looks simple, but you don't have the support of the second finger in this semi-barre position. It's got its own job to do.

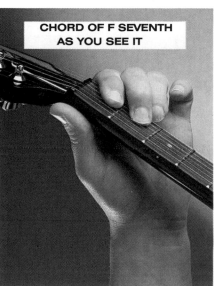

CHORD OF F SEVENTH AS YOU SEE IT

Try holding down the first four strings with the first finger a few times before adding the second finger to this F7 chord shape.

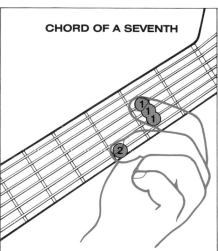

CHORD OF A SEVENTH

Like F7, A7 involves a half-barre. The first finger (1) barres the first four strings just behind the second fret. The second finger (2) holds down the first (top E) string on the third fret.

THE THREE DIFFERENT types of seventh chord—major sevenths, minor sevenths and dominant sevenths—all have very different qualities.

We'll talk about how to use minor seventh chords and major seventh chords in a few pages time.

The one thing they share with their dominant seventh counterparts is an air of being 'unfinished', as if they need to be followed by another chord.

This is particularly true of dominant seventh chords, where the chord that follows is almost always the root chord of the key.

Dominant sevenths are especially popular in blues and rhythm 'n' blues. They have a tough, hardhitting sound, with the 'unfinished' quality giving either an urgent edge (when a seventh chord is used as the leading chord in a song or part of a song), or a pleasing inevitability when used before the root chord.

THE MOST common use of dominant seventh chords is in a 12-bar blues. Almost every old blues song by Muddy Waters, BB King or Howlin' Wolf, and most '50s rock and roll songs by the likes of Buddy Holly and Chuck Berry used the 12-bar blues form. Many modern rock songs such as ZZ Top's 'Legs' fit the 12-bar format.

A 12-bar blues consists of three lines of four bars each. A typical 12-bar will go:

C F C C/
F F C C/
G F C G7.

Count four beats for each chord. You can use **G** instead of **G7**, but you'll notice at once that it doesn't have the same effect.

Robert Cray uses plenty of seventh chords in 'Phone Booth', which you can play on page 60.

CHORD OF E SEVENTH

E7 IS a simple two-fingered chord. The first finger (1) is placed just behind the first fret on the third (**G**) string, and the second finger (2) goes just behind the second fret on the fifth (**A**) string.

You'll notice the obvious similarity to the **E** major chord—we've simply removed the third finger from the fretboard.

E7 sounds good followed by **A** major, because it's the dominant seventh chord in the key of **A** major.

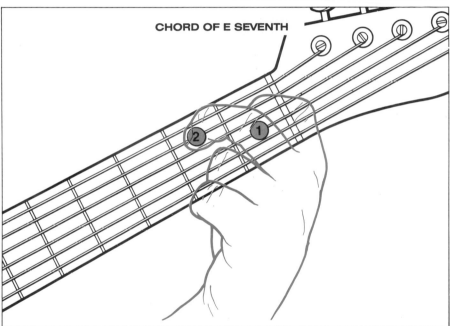

CHORD OF E SEVENTH

CHORD OF E SEVENTH FRONT VIEW

Do they come any simpler? The point here is to get a clear sound from the open strings, so maintain good position with the first and second fingers.

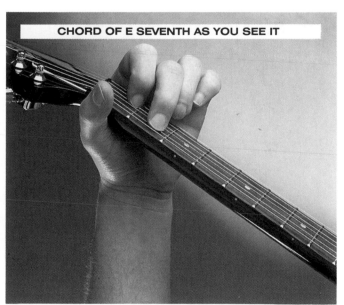

CHORD OF E SEVENTH AS YOU SEE IT

A real blues chord, which will only work if the open strings are kept clear. Keep that third finger tucked away from the top E string.

TREMOLO ARM

IT DON'T mean a thang if it ain't got that twang – or to put it another way, welcome to our brief rundown on tremolo.

The tremolo arm was probably most used in the early '60s, by twang merchants such as Duane Eddy and Hank Marvin of The Shadows.

With the notable exceptions of Jimi Hendrix and Jeff Beck, later guitarists tended to ignore it, but it has enjoyed a renaissance in the '80s, particularly among heavy rock players. Current exponents include Gary Moore, Steve Vai and Stevie Ray Vaughan.

Right: two members of the tremolo club, at opposite ends of the musical spectrum – Hank of the Shads and Richie Sambora of Bon Jovi

CHORD OF D SEVENTH

D7 IS relatively simple, and has a nice earthy sound. Here's how it goes:

First finger (1) just behind the first fret on the second (**B**) string.

Second finger (2) just behind the second fret on the third (**G**) string.

Third finger (3) just behind the second fret on the first (top **E**) string.

The fourth (**D**) string is played open.

The fifth (**A**) and sixth (bottom **E**) strings are not played.

D7 is the dominant seventh chord in the key of **G** major, and sounds most natural when followed by a chord of **G** major.

B7 IS probably the most awkward chord to date: it's shown in the diagram on the right (below).

If you feel that your fingers are leaving your hand in protest, don't panic. This is a difficult chord shape even for an experienced player, but it will come with practice.

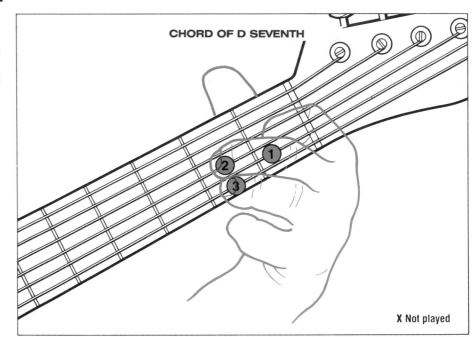

CHORD OF D SEVENTH

X Not played

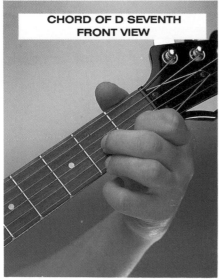

CHORD OF D SEVENTH FRONT VIEW

A four-string chord, where the third finger is 'pulled back' to the top **E** string. Keep the second finger nice and arched.

CHORD OF D SEVENTH AS YOU SEE IT

A common set-up, which is used for a variety of chords. Keep the hand looking like a werewolf's claw, and you're in business.

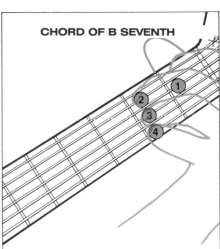

CHORD OF B SEVENTH

B7 is an awkward you-know-what because once learnt, it is not a position that is repeated anywhere else on the fretboard. But it is good discipline, so press on.

THE TREMOLO arm is a device for raising or lowering the pitch of a note, giving a slurring sound. Combined with different pedals and tone controls, it can produce a range of effects from screeching feedback to a sleepy twang.

Sometimes known as a vibrato system or 'magic wand', the tremolo arm is linked to the bridge of the electric guitar.

As you push or pull the tremolo arm, the bridge pivots, causing the strings to go slack or taut.

With old tremolo systems, this often put your guitar out of tune, but that no longer happens with modern tremolos such as the one on the Yamaha RGX 211 featured in this book.

While playing, you can either bounce the whole hand against the tremolo arm to give a quick, not too tremulous effect, or you can link your little finger round the arm in order to depress it when the time is right. But be warned: over-use will probably depress the audience.

Pulling a tremolo arm can help you get feedback. Used with an overdriven amplifier, it can give you extra noise, distortion, whirring sounds and other interesting things.

BY NOW, your fingers should be almost 'thinking' for themselves in constructing chords, particularly those using a barre.

There are two main seventh chord shapes which can be turned into barre chords: the **E7** and **A7** shapes.

The barred **F7** shown here is a derivation of the open **E7** shape, raised one note.

Place your first finger across all six strings on the first fret, with the second finger just behind the second fret on the third (**G**) string, and the third finger just behind the third fret on the fifth (**A**) string.

As we've explained previously, by raising or lowering a barre position, you can go through the entire scale with one chord shape.

In the case of **F7**, by raising the position two frets we form **G7**, two more is **A7**, and so on.

Don't be confused by variations in chord shapes. On page 44, we showed you a half-barre **F7** – a four-string chord. Using the full barre gives you a six-string chord. Neither is necessarily better: they are just different options. The barre chord gives a fuller sound.

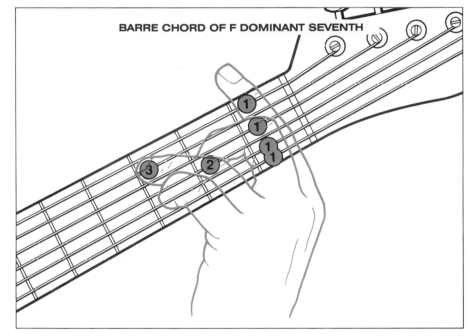

BARRE CHORD OF F DOMINANT SEVENTH

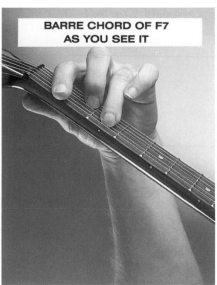

BARRE CHORD OF F7 FRONT VIEW

This F7 barred shape is built around the barred **F** major. You just take your little finger off the **D** string.

BARRE CHORD OF F7 AS YOU SEE IT

One advantage of barre chords is extra control. Unlike open chords you can stop the sound instantly just by raising your hand.

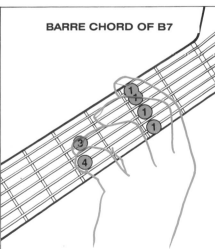

BARRE CHORD OF B7

Perhaps the most popular of all barred seventh shapes is this A7 derivative. You may find it more comfortable to support the first finger with the second.

MINOR SEVENTH CHORDS

MINOR SEVENTH chords are interesting, because they emphasize the relationship between relative major chords and minor chords.

Take a look at **E** minor **7** and its relative major, **G**:

Starting from the bottom **E** string, open **G** has the notes **G B D G B G**.

Em has the notes **E B E G B E**
Em7 has the notes **E B D G B E**.

As you can see, **Em7** is almost an exact cross between **G** and **Em**.

The same is true for other minor sevenths—in fact, by a strange coincidence, you can go from each of the three major chords in our **CFG** three-chord trick to its relative minor seventh simply by lifting two fingers off the fretboard (that is, from **C** to **Am7**, from **F** to **Dm7**, and from **G** to **Em7**).

Because of this close relationship, a minor seventh chord has many subtle uses, as it gives strong overtones of both the minor chord and its relative major.

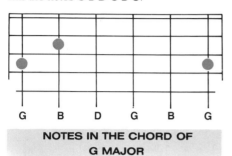

G	B	D	G	B	G

**NOTES IN THE CHORD OF
G MAJOR**

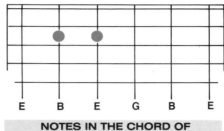

E	B	E	G	B	E

**NOTES IN THE CHORD OF
E MINOR**

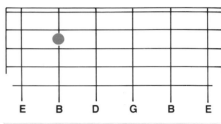

E	B	D	G	B	E

**NOTES IN THE CHORD OF
E MINOR SEVENTH**

MINOR SEVENTH CHORDS

MINOR SEVENTH chords can be used in a variety of situations. If a major or minor primary chord sounds too definite or forceful, try slipping in a minor seventh.

You can use a minor seventh instead of the minor chord it's formed from, or instead of its relative major. So if you're looking for a substitute for **F** minor, try **Fm7**. But if you want a substitute for **F** major, try **Dm7**. It may not turn out to be what you want, but it's worth a try.

PROBABLY THE most used minor seventh chord is **Am7**, which sounds great either as a barre chord (see above), or as the open chord shown here. It is mostly used in conjunction with its relative major, **C**.

Am7 is formed with just two fingers: the first just behind the first fret on the second (**B**) string, and the second just behind the second fret on the fourth (**D**) string. In other words, it's **Am** with one finger removed.

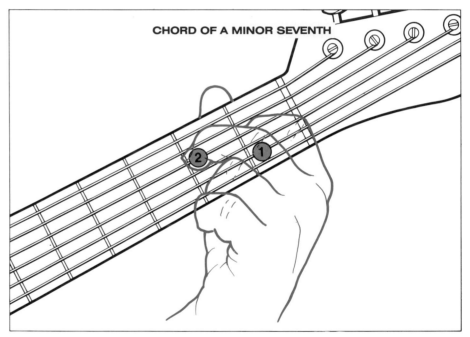

CHORD OF A MINOR SEVENTH

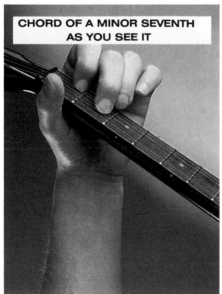

**CHORD OF A MINOR SEVENTH
AS YOU SEE IT**

Like many minor seventh chords, **Am7** has a nice, spacious sound and feel.

CHORD OF F MINOR SEVENTH

What could be simpler? A half-barre position, with the first finger doing all the work. This **Fm7** shape can be moved along to form any minor seventh chord—four strings only.

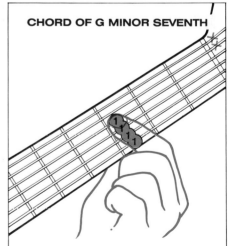

CHORD OF G MINOR SEVENTH

In both the **Fm7** and **Gm7** positions, remember to use the second finger to support the first if it feels more comfortable. Here's where our barre exercise comes into its own.

IT IS of course possible to barre a minor seventh chord – and it's often preferable, too, because the barre brings in the bass notes which give these chords their rich sound.

As you can see below, many of the 'open' minor seventh chords have bass strings which are not played.

There are two minor seventh shapes which readily lend themselves to being barred – the **Fm7** and **Bm7** shapes. The **Fm7** shape in particular is much improved when barred. Ironically, it's the easiest barre chord in the book.

As with many of the other barre chord shapes we've encountered, the fifth fret is where much of the action goes on, because you can form a closed **Am7** on the fifth fret using the **Fm7** shape, and a closed **Dm7** using the **Bm7** shape.

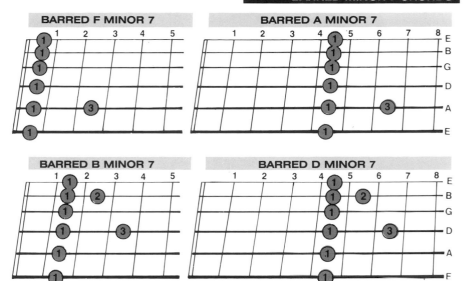

BARRED F MINOR 7

BARRED A MINOR 7

BARRED B MINOR 7

BARRED D MINOR 7

CHORD OF E MINOR SEVENTH

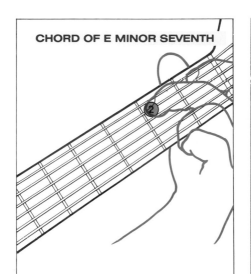

Em7 is a simple chord, with the second finger placed just behind the second fret on your fifth (A) string and the remaining strings played open.

CHORD OF E MINOR SEVENTH AS YOU SEE IT

Probably the easiest chord in the book, **Em7** is more like a tuning exercise than a chord shape!

CHORD OF B MINOR SEVENTH

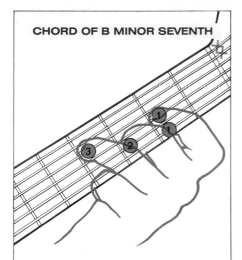

Note the relationship between **Bm7** and its relative major chord, **D**. The difference is just one extra finger. The bottom two strings are not played.

CHORD OF D MINOR SEVENTH

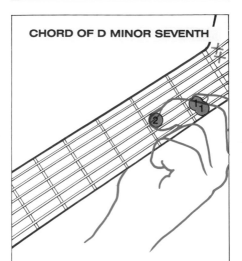

Dm7 is a four-note chord with the bottom two strings left unplayed. The first finger holds down the **B** and top **E** strings on the first fret, with second finger on second fret, **G** string.

CHORD OF D MINOR SEVENTH AS YOU SEE IT

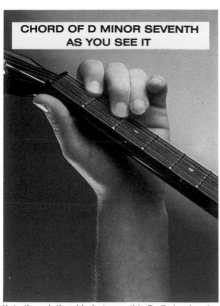

Note the relationship between this **Dm7** chord and its relative major, **F** – they're very similar.

CHORD OF C MINOR SEVENTH

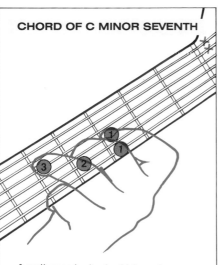

A really moody chord, which can be a challenge because of the spacing of the fingers. As with the **Bm7** chord, the bottom two strings are not played.

MAJOR SEVENTH CHORDS

MAJOR SEVENTH chords are easy to define: you simply take the major triad (root/third/fifth) and add the seventh note in the major scale.

So C major 7 will have the notes CEGB, and G major 7 will have the notes GBDF#.

What is less easy to define is their sound, their appeal and their uses. This is because they vary so. They also employ some very flexible chord shapes: move them along the neck, and you find you've got something completely different.

Take our three-fingered version of A major 7 – the one with the top E string left open. Try playing that chord, then moving your hand shape up one fret – but leaving the E and A strings open. You are now playing a chord of D minor ninth.

Move the chord shape up again, five frets from its original position – keeping those E and A strings open – and you've got what sounds like an alternative version of A major 7. In fact it's an A major sixth chord. (We explain sixths and ninths on page 66.)

There is, however, a genuine alternative A major 7 in close proximity.

Form an open A minor shape (as shown on page 31), and move it five frets along the neck – and hey presto, another A major 7, with those E and A strings ringing out the same as before.

NOW TAKE a look at F major 7. You can play it as a straightforward four-string chord, or you can try a nifty alternative by adding the fifth string, third fret as in a conventional F major – and then hooking your thumb round the neck to fret the bottom E string on the first fret.

That way you get the best of both worlds:

a solid root note F on the bottom string, with a nice twangy seventh note (E) on the top string.

Now move this chord two frets up the neck, to the G position – still leaving that top E open. You are now playing a G sixth chord.

Now move the chord on again, up to the fifth fret – still with the top E string open. There's another fine chord: A major with an extra E note.

THESE ARE just a few ideas for ways you can play around with chords – major sevenths are particularly adaptable. Make the most of them, because they're the last new chords you'll meet before the Chord Directory (pages 67–80), where you can investigate sixth, ninth, thirteenth, augmented and diminished chords. You'll

MAJOR SEVENTH CHORDS

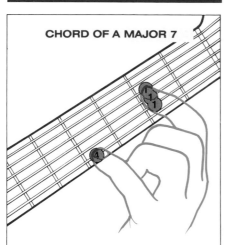

CHORD OF A MAJOR 7

A major 7 is formed from A major – the first finger holding down the D, G and B strings on the second fret, with the little finger or third finger stretched to the fourth fret, top E string. The A string is played open. The bottom E string is optional.

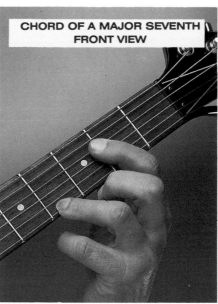

CHORD OF A MAJOR SEVENTH FRONT VIEW

A short stretch for the third finger here – note the slight change from A7 to A major 7.

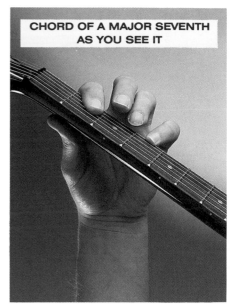

CHORD OF A MAJOR SEVENTH AS YOU SEE IT

You can move up the neck to play other major 7 chords, but it then becomes a four-string chord.

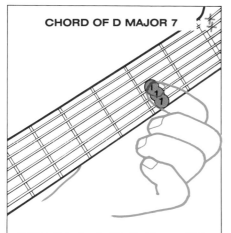

CHORD OF D MAJOR 7

D major 7 requires just the first finger, which holds down the G, B and top E strings on the second fret. The D string is played open. The bottom two strings should not be played, but it won't hurt if the open A string creeps in accidentally.

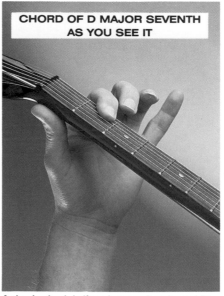

CHORD OF D MAJOR SEVENTH AS YOU SEE IT

A simple chord, halfway between D major and D7 – and an interesting sound too.

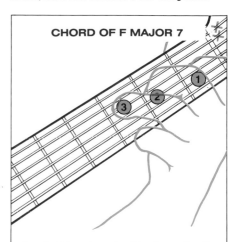

CHORD OF F MAJOR 7

F major 7 is a nice natural hand spread, with the first finger placed on the first fret, B string, the second finger on the second fret, G string and the third finger on the third fret, D string. The top E string is left open. The bottom two strings are not played.

also find lots of different ways of playing the chords you've already learnt.

If you can't wait till page 67, by all means jump ahead and try out some of the chords on display. Your fretboard is waiting to be explored – and the Chord Directory is your map.

Get as much out of it as you can. Don't just use the Chord Directory as a reference; use it for inspiration as well as information.

And keep trying new tricks. Now that we've shown you the basic chords, don't just fall back on them time after time. Forge ahead, and forge your own style.

Meanwhile, if you've taken in the majors, minors, sevenths and so on – the essentials of rhythm guitar – then you should be ready for the next step . . . how to play rock lead guitar.

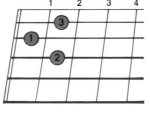

CHORD OF A MAJOR 7

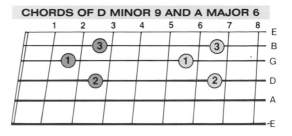

CHORDS OF D MINOR 9 AND A MAJOR 6

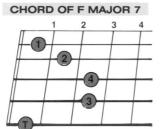

CHORD OF F MAJOR 7

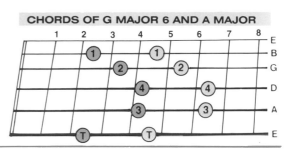

CHORDS OF G MAJOR 6 AND A MAJOR

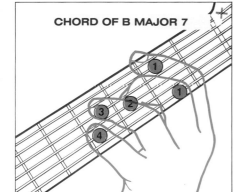

CHORD OF B MAJOR 7

B major 7 requires a barre across the second fret, with the second finger placed on the third fret, G string, the third finger holding down the fourth fret, D string and the fourth finger on the fourth fret, B string. The bottom E string is not played.

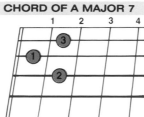

CHORD OF B MAJOR SEVENTH AS YOU SEE IT

B major 7 is nearly a full barre chord, and so can be used to form different major seventh chords.

CHORD OF E MAJOR 7

E major 7 has a tricky little set-up on the first fret, where the first finger is placed on the D string, and the second finger holds down the G string. The third finger is pushed across to the second fret, A string. The bottom and top E strings and B string are played open.

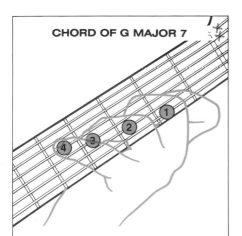

CHORD OF G MAJOR 7

G major 7 is the same chord as F major 7, but 'up' the fretboard two notes. The first finger holds down the second fret, top E string, second finger on the third fret, B string, third finger fourth fret, G string, whilst the little finger holds down the fifth fret, D string.

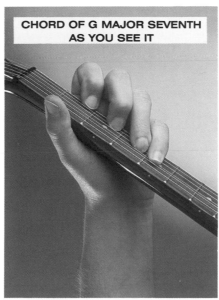

CHORD OF G MAJOR SEVENTH AS YOU SEE IT

You can slide this chord up the neck to form other major 7 chords.

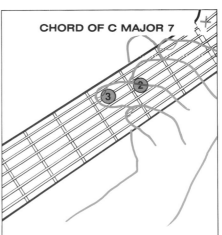

CHORD OF C MAJOR 7

C major 7 is a five-note chord, with the second finger holding down the second fret, D string and the third finger on the third fret, A string. The G, B and top E strings are played open. You can, for a variation, play the bottom E string open, or fretted at the third fret.

TRANSPOSING KEYS

TO 'TRANSPOSE' is the technical term for moving a piece of music from one key into another.

A song doesn't have to be played in the key it was written in. You can take a song in the key of G major, for instance, and change the chords so that it can be played in C. This is called transposing the key.

But why should you want to do this?

When the song was originally written or recorded, it was set in a key that suited that particular band or singer's style. If you are straining to sing the chorus, or find it difficult to finger a certain chord, you can transpose the key to suit yourself.

THERE ARE two methods of transposing. Both of them are quite easy.

Let's say you want to transpose to a key fairly close to your original key – for instance from C to D. You simply check how far apart the root notes are (from C to D is two semitones), and then move all the chords in the song the same distance. So if your original chords were C, Am, F and G, you add two semitones to each, giving D, Bm, G, A.

THAT METHOD is fine if the two keys are close together. But if you want to transpose

CAPO

THIS WEIRD looking device is called a capo, and it makes transposing keys easy. For example, if the capo is clamped on the first fret, all your standard chords such as E, C and Am are raised one note. So in the picture we have a chord of B♭ minor, played like Am.

Suppose you need to play a song in E♭ – three semitones up from C. By clamping the capo on the third fret, you can play it as if the song was in C.

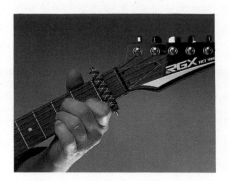

'THE BOYS ARE BACK IN TOWN'

TRANSPOSING THE SONG

AS PROMISED, here is our new, improved version of 'The Boys Are Back In Town', incorporating some of the seventh chords we've been looking at.

What's more, in the light of the information above about transposing keys, we've decided to transpose it. On page 40 we learned how to play it in C major. Now we're going to play it in the key of G major.

So let's just take a look back at the grid on page 40. The chords used were C, Dm, Em, F, G, Am and A♭. Of these, the only chord which doesn't fit naturally into the key of C is A♭. All the others can be tranposed easily using the table on page 35.

We've reproduced the relevant section of that table at the top of the page opposite, and we've marked the original key, C major, and the new key of G major. Just check across the columns:
C is replaced by G;
Dm is replaced by Am;
Em is replaced by Bm;
F is replaced by C;
G is replaced by D;
Am is replaced by Em.
As for our A♭, if A is replaced by E then it should be obvious that we replace A♭ with E♭.

SEVENTH CHORDS

IF YOU compare this grid with the one on page 40/41, you'll see that those transpositions have been made. But you'll also see that we've replaced some straightforward major and minor chords with the sevenths and minor sevenths which Thin Lizzy used in the original.

In the fourth line of the verse, in the key of C we had F and G. If we transpose those chords, it should give us the chords of C and D. Instead, we'll be using Am7 and D7.

That D7 is repeated in the last bar of the verse, and the last bar of Bridge 1. Note that each time it's used, it leads to the root chord, G.

Notice also the second bar in Bridge 1. In the key of C, that was an Am chord. Directly transposed it would give Em. Instead, there's that simplest of chords, Em7.

TITLE	KEY	TEMPO
'THE BOYS ARE BACK IN TOWN'	G MAJOR	QUITE FAST

VERSE							
G	G	G	G	Bm	Bm	Bm	Bm
C	C	C	C	Em	Em	Em	Em
Bm	Bm	Bm	Bm	Em	Em	Em	Em
Am7	Am7	Am7	Am7	D7	D7	D7	D7
G	G	G	G	Bm	Bm	Bm	Bm
C	C	C	C	E♭	E♭	E♭	E♭
D	D	D	D	Em	Em	Em	Em
Am	Am	Am	Am	D7	D7	D7	D7

CHORUS							
G	G	G	G	G	G	G	G
Am	Am	Am	Am	C	C	C	C
G	G	G	G	G	G	G	G
Am	Am	Am	Am	C	C	C	C

LYRICS

The words fall in the same place as on page 40/41. We haven't included the intro as it's just the chorus without words.

CHORD OF G/B

In Bridge 1 there's a chord marked G/B. It means G major with a B bass note. Play an open G but miss the bottom E string.

52

from, say, **C** to **G**, it's not that easy. So here's another method.

As you know, the notes in a scale can be numbered from root note to seventh note (or, in Roman numerals, from **I** to **VII**).

All you have to do is number the chords of the song in its original key, then put in the appropriately numbered chords from the new key.

The easiest way to do this is by using our indispensable scales and chords table from page 35.

You can just read straight across from one key to another.

ANY SONG can be transposed. Obviously, if a song is in a major key it can only be transposed *to* a major key. A minor key song can only be transposed to another minor key.

The table below highlights how to transpose from **C** major to **G** major.

	NOTE IN SCALE		PRIMARY TRIAD CHORD	SCALE (READ DOWN FROM ROOT NOTE)										
MAJOR KEY	Root	(I)	Root major chord	C	Db	D	Eb	E	F	F#	G	Ab	A	Bb	B
	Second	(II)	Minor chord	D	Eb	E	F	F#	G	G#	A	Bb	B	C	C#
	Third	(III)	Minor chord	E	F	F#	G	G#	A	A#	B	C	C#	D	D#
	Fourth	(IV)	Major chord	F	Gb	G	Ab	A	Bb	B	C	Db	D	Eb	E
	Fifth	(V)	Major chord	G	Ab	A	Bb	B	C	C#	D	Eb	E	F	F#
	Sixth	(VI)	Relative minor chord	A	Bb	B	C	C#	D	D#	E	F	F#	G	G#
	Seventh	(VII)	----	B	C	C#	D	D#	E	E#	F#	G	G#	A	A#

It's easy to transpose keys using this table – you just read across from one scale to another. You can transpose minor keys too, by checking the table on page 35.

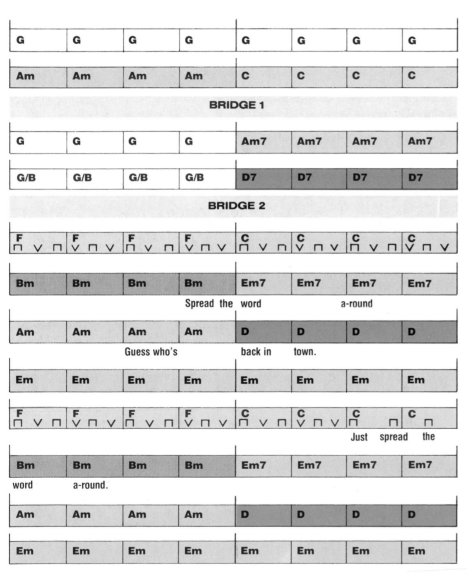

BRIDGE 1

BRIDGE 2

Spread the word   a-round

Guess who's   back in town.

Just spread the

word   a-round.

CHORD OF Eb MAJOR

You'll need this chord – it takes the place of the Ab we used when we played this song in **C**.

RHYTHM

YOU'LL SEE that we've left out the DOWN, down-UP. . . down rhythm we used on pages 40/41. As we said then, it was a simplified rhythm to help you through the song.

The fact is, there isn't a consistent rhythm guitar part on the record. Instead, guitarists Scott Gorham and Brian Robertson sketch in the bare bones, leaving plenty of holes for vocals, bass and lead guitars.

The one consistent rhythmic pattern they use is to hit the first beat of each bar with a resounding chord, and if you were playing this with a band that would be the essential element of the rhythm guitar part.

The other important facet of Thin Lizzy's rhythmic approach to this song is the way the guitarists hit a lot of their chords slightly 'early' – half a beat before the start of the bar.

This is generally known as 'pushing' the beat. It's very tricky to get right, and we're not expecting you to manage it just yet. If you want to try it out, you can. But if you want to stick to a regular rhythm pattern, you can do that too.

BRIDGE 2

YOU'LL NOTICE that we've added the final part of the grid: Bridge 2. Refer to page 41 to see where it occurs in the running order.

Perhaps now you can see why we've held it back – the section is full of triplets.

If you cast your mind back to 'That'll Be The Day', you may remember that a triplet is where three notes are played in the space of one beat: da-da-da, da-da-da, da-da-da, da-da-da. On record, these triplets are played as single notes hammered out by the lead guitarist, but if you want to try it with the chords, be our guest. Otherwise, stick to your regular rhythm.

KEY TO SYMBOLS AND COLOURS

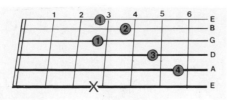

⊓ Downward stroke   ∨ Upward stroke
□ **G** major   ▪ **A** minor
▪ **B** minor   ▪ **D** major/**D7**
□ **C** major/**A** minor 7   □ **F** major
□ **E** minor/**E** minor 7   □ **Eb** major

LEAD GUITAR

WE HAVE now explored the world of basic guitar chords pretty thoroughly. We've looked at major chords, minor chords and three different types of seventh chord – how they are constructed, how to play them, and how they work together.

In other words, you have the essential ingredients of rhythm guitar. Later, we'll return to the subject, with more unusual chords such as sixths, ninths and thirteenths. But right now it's time for something completely different: lead guitar.

THE TWO terms, lead guitar and rhythm guitar, tend to conjure up very different images. Lead guitar equals glamour; rhythm guitar means drudgery.

As with all stereotyped images, this isn't strictly true. Some of the world's greatest guitarists are rhythm specialists – for instance Nile Rodgers, whose rhythm guitar was the force behind a whole musical movement. His work with Chic had far-reaching effects, and some would claim that he was the most influential guitarist of the '80s.

More to the point, few major guitarists play only lead or only rhythm. The two go hand in hand, and ideally you should have a good grasp of both.

THERE ARE, of course, almost as many definitions of lead guitar as there are lead guitarists. If we say that lead guitar entails playing single notes, then there are numerous different ways in which single notes can be used within a song.

Most common is the guitar riff – the repeated pattern of notes which holds a song together. Riffs are most used in heavy metal: two of the more famous examples would be Led Zeppelin's 'Whole Lotta Love' and Deep Purple's 'Smoke On The Water'.

Other uses for single note playing include 'fills' and embellishments – either planned or spontaneous little additions which enhance the song rather than being central to it in the way a riff usually is.

'The Boys Are Back In Town' provides good examples of this. Having two guitars gives one of them the luxury to 'sit back' and choose his moments while the other provides the central backbone (the same can equally be true if you have a keyboard player).

If, on the other hand you haven't got another guitarist or keyboard player to share the role of giving melodic meat to a song, you may want to develop a style that

BLUES RHYTHM GUITAR

THE BLUES is the main foundation of rock music today. Rock developed directly out of the blues, and there has probably never been a major rock guitarist who was not influenced to some extent by blues players or blues music.

So let's look first at blues rhythm guitar.

In our section on sevenths, we briefly mentioned 12-bar blues. No doubt it's a term you already know. What you may not realise is that, with what you've learnt to date, you can now play a 12-bar blues in just about any key.

All '12-bars' are based on our original three-chord trick – which in the key of **C** would be **C, F, G.**

If you check the chart on page 35, you'll see that they are the chords formed from the first, fourth and fifth notes of the scale – which we can refer to in Roman numerals as **I, IV** and **V.**

These are the three chords used in a basic 12-bar blues. The song grid shows how it goes.

Here are the chords **I, IV** and **V** in some popular keys for blues. You can use any of these three-chord tricks with our 12-bar grid:

CHORD I	C	D	E	G	A
CHORD IV	F	G	A	C	D
CHORD V	G	A	B	D	E

TWELVE BAR BLUES

BAR 1	BAR 2	BAR 3	BAR 4
I	I	I	I

BAR 5	BAR 6	BAR 7	BAR 8
IV	IV	I	I

BAR 9	BAR 10	BAR 11	BAR 12
V	IV	I	I

KEY TO COLOURS   □ CHORD **I**   □ CHORD **IV**   □ CHORD **V**

Most 12-bar blues are in 4/4 time (four beats to the bar), and this one is no exception. Try it out in different keys – you'll soon realise that it's just about the most natural 'rock' chord progression there is. You can make a number of variations to this basic 12–bar. Here are some you may care to try:
Bar 2 Chord IV. Bar 4 Chord I7 (in C, this would be C7). Bar 6 Chord IV7. Bar 8 Chord I7. Bar 9 Chord V7. Bar 12 Chord V or V7.

Muddy Waters' best-known 12-bar was 'I Got My Mojo Workin''.

Status Quo paid tribute to the 12-bar with their 'Twelve Gold Bars' album.

mixes straight rhythm with riffs and 'fills'.

Perhaps the purest form of single note playing is the solo – the guitar break, usually in the middle of a song, where the spotlight shifts from the singer to the guitarist, and you get a chance to express yourself for the duration.

For our purposes, we'll assume that this is your goal as a lead guitarist. If it's not, and you just want sufficient skill and technique to play riffs and embellishments, you'll be able to get what you need from this section anyway. So let's look at soloing.

TO MOST beginners, and indeed to many people who've played guitar for years, guitar solos are one of the mysteries of life. Hopefully, this section can dissolve some of that mystery for you.

The content of a solo is, by definition, in the hands of the player. Some solos are improvised; some follow a set pattern; but all solos work within the context of the player's own style and skill – and that comes from a combination of experience, practice, instinct and knowledge. We can supply the last bit; the rest you'll have to develop for yourself.

You may not realise it, but if you've been practising the scales we showed you earlier – for **G** major and **C** minor – then you've already started that process.

Nearly all lead guitar styles are based on scales and a knowledge of chord structure, so you've already got a lot of the basics. This section aims to give you a context for them – plus, inevitably, a lot more hard work for you to do.

Our starting point, perhaps surprisingly, will be blues rhythm guitar.

Foreigner lead guitarist Mick Jones has a distinctive and influential hard rock style.

BLUES RHYTHM GUITAR

THE 12-BAR blues is where barre chords really come into their own. Try playing a 12-bar in the key of **A**, using all barre chords.
Chord **I**: **A**. An **F**-shape barre chord, fifth fret.
Chord **IV**: **D**. An **F**-shape barre chord, 10th fret.
Chord **V**: **E**. An **F**-shape barre chord, 12th fret.

AN AMAZING number of rock songs are played like this, from early Beatles to ZZ Top. And many of them employ the following variation, shown below as Riff 1:
Instead of **A** major, form a barred **A7** at the fifth fret. On each alternate beat, bring your little finger down on the ninth fret, fifth (**A**) string – in other words, two frets beyond your third finger. Keep your other fingers where they are.

Repeat the process at the 10th and 12th frets with **D7** and **E7**.

THERE ARE other variations on this theme which you can use when laying down a basic blues rhythm. Try Riff 2, below, again keeping your hand in the barred **A7** position, and concentrating on your bottom three strings:

Beat **1**: Barred **A7** (emphasize bottom **E** string).
Beat **2**: Little finger ninth fret, bottom **E** string.
Beat **3**: Barred **A7** (emphasizing **A** string).
Beat **4**: Little finger ninth fret, **A** string.
Beat **1**: Barred **A** major (emphasizing **D** string: flatten your third finger to get this effect).
Beat **2**: Little finger ninth fret, **A** string.
Beat **3**: Barred **A7** (emphasizing **A** string).
Beat **4**: Little finger ninth fret, **E** string.

THESE BLUES rhythm parts can be played fast or slow. Try not to speed up or slow down.

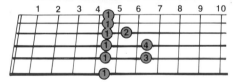

BARRE CHORD OF A MAJOR

BARRE CHORD OF A7 (RIFF 1)
* POSITION FOR LITTLE FINGER (ALTERNATE BEATS)

BARRE CHORD OF A7 (RIFF 2)
* POSITIONS FOR LITTLE FINGER

Eric Clapton was raised on 12-bar blues such as 'Crossroads'.

Dave Edmunds' biggest hit 'I Hear You Knocking' was a 12-bar blues.

Many ZZ Top hits such as 'Rough Boy' stick close to the 12-bar format.

LEAD BLUES SCALES

THE BEST way to begin playing lead guitar, and then to improve your lead playing, is to practise scales.

There are numerous different kinds of musical scales, and each offers some unique run or combination of notes which can contribute in some way to your repertoire.

You already know two basic scales – one for a major key, which appeared on page 25, and one for a minor key (page 41). We happened to show the scales of G major and C minor, but in fact they can be used in any major or minor key simply by moving them up or down the fretboard.

What makes those two scales so useful is the fact that they include all the notes pertaining to their particular keys, and no notes from outside the key. So if you are playing a song in the key of G, the scale of

G major gives you a fingertip map of the notes which will work in that song.

Other scales have different qualities. Some include notes from outside the key. Some leave notes out. The more scales you know, and the more contexts you try them out in, the greater your lead guitar armoury.

AMONG THE most useful are the three 'blues scales' shown on this page. These scales happen to be in A, but you can of

course move them up or down the fretboard for use in any key.

Technically speaking, the blues scale is a kind of minor scale, but it is mainly used in its major key. If you look at the table here you'll see the relationship between our blues scales in A, and the normal scale of A major.

Our blues scales contain three additional notes – C, D# and G. These are in fact the flattened third, flattened fifth and flattened seventh notes in the A major scale.

SCALE OF A MAJOR AND BLUES SCALES IN A																
SCALE OF A MAJOR	A	B	C#	D		E	F#		G#	A	B	C#	D		E	F#	G#	A
BLUES SCALE IN A (1)	G	A		C		D		E		G		A		C		D	E		G		A
BLUES SCALE IN A (2)	A		C		D D#	E		G		A		C		D		E F# G		A B C
BLUES SCALE IN A (3)			C		D		E		G		A		C		D D#	E		G		A C D

BLUES SCALES IN A

HERE ARE three blues scales to practise. They're all in the key of **A** and they are designed for use with a 12-bar blues sequence.

The best way to practise them is by playing them over a blues rhythm track supplied either by a friend or by recording yourself. But whether you practise your blues scales over a 12-bar or on their own, the same basic rules apply as for the other scales you've learnt.

Take them slowly at first, using all downward strokes. Then play alternate down and up strokes. Keep the left hand close to the fretboard, and aim for a crisp, clean, regular run through the scale, from bottom to top and back down again.

Once you're on top of them, try to play them less regularly, putting a firmer emphasis on certain notes, missing notes out, playing faster here, slower there, and so on.

In short, give them expression. This is the essence of successful lead playing, and as you practise you will gradually formulate your own approach and your own style.

LINK RUNS

YOU'LL NOTICE that each of our three scales is based around a couple of frets, in a particular part of the fretboard.

Scale 1 is the lowest, based around the second, third and fifth frets. Scale 2 centres on the fifth, seventh and eighth frets. And Scale 3 takes in the seventh, eighth and tenth frets.

You'll notice also that some notes appear in both Scale 1 and Scale 2, while others appear in both Scale 2 and Scale 3. It therefore stands to reason that the three scales can be linked together.

Our two link runs show you how to do this, but these are only our suggestions. Obviously, you can go from one scale into another at any point where they overlap – and as they're all blues scales in **A**, they fit together naturally.

In fact, as you'll soon realise, they are basically the same scale played in different parts of the fretboard.

Practise linking scales together, and before you know it you'll have the freedom of the fretboard.

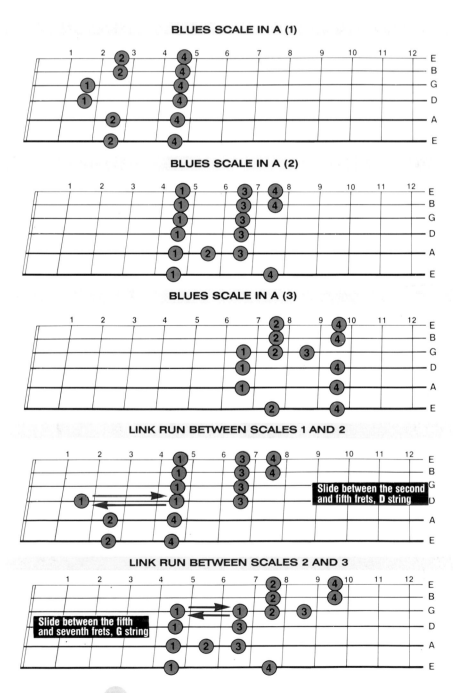

BLUES SCALE IN A (1)

BLUES SCALE IN A (2)

BLUES SCALE IN A (3)

LINK RUN BETWEEN SCALES 1 AND 2

Slide between the second and fifth frets, D string

LINK RUN BETWEEN SCALES 2 AND 3

Slide between the fifth and seventh frets, G string

You'll also notice that the blues scales miss out one note from the major scale – G#, the seventh note.

The overall effect is to create a less rounded, more 'bluesy' selection of notes which sound good in a guitar solo.

INCIDENTALLY, ALTHOUGH we haven't included them, the open E, G, D and A strings can also be incorporated into a solo based on the blues scale of A.

This won't necessarily be the case if you transpose these scales to another key – which, as we said before, can be done simply by moving the whole thing up or down the fretboard.

The most popular keys for blues are A major, E major, C major and G major. The blues scale of A is shown here – we'll leave you to work out E, C and G.

ONE FINAL point. We said that this blues scale is a kind of minor scale. Used in a bluesy context such as heavy metal, R&B, soul or blues, it works in its major or minor key. So the blues scale of A works in both A major and A minor.

But it does have other uses, of a less bluesy nature, and on occasion it can be used in its relative major key, C.

Bear in mind, though, that it contains notes that are not related to that key, and which could sound discordant.

Remember, at the end of the day, scales are only a guide. They should not be taken as a hard and fast rule.

With the knowledge they give you, you can work out your own riffs and runs. Don't be afraid to take risks, cut corners and break the rules—it's essential to create your own style.

Jimmy Page's fast fingerwork relies on blues scales and techniques such as hammer-on and pull-off.

HAMMER-ON AND PULL-OFF

AS YOU struggle to pick your way through all these scales, you may be wondering how your favourite guitarists manage to play so fast.

Naturally, the main factor is practice, practice and more practice. However, there are a couple of techniques you can use to increase your speed: hammer-on and pull-off.

Here is a simple hammer-on. Put your first finger on the fifth fret, top E string. Play this note and then hammer-on your third finger onto the seventh fret – but don't play this second note with your right hand.

This technique is always easier with a distortion or sustain pedal, but you should be able to get a good sound from the second note without the help of effects. The secret is in really pressing your third finger down hard.

NOW LET'S return to blues scale 2. Try playing it from the bottom E string to the top, but only picking with your plectrum on the red notes. A letter H means hammer-on.

When you do pick, use down strokes to start with. You'll find it harder to hammer-on with your little finger at first, because it's not as strong. After a bit of practice it becomes easier.

Once you can hammer-on with scale 2, try it on the other scales. You'll soon find it enables you to play them a lot faster. It also gives you more scope for phrasing your melody lines.

THE NEXT technique to try is pull-off. Put your third finger on the seventh fret, top E string, and your first finger on the fifth fret at the same time. Pick whilst your third finger is down, but as soon as the note has sounded, pull your third finger away from the fingerboard. Leave your first finger on, but don't play the string again.

You will find that the note at the fifth fret will sound as you lift your third finger.

ONCE AGAIN, let's put this to use on our second blues scale in A. This time, play the scale from the top string to the bottom, and only pick on the red notes. There is a P on the diagram at the points where you should pull-off.

BLUES SCALE IN A (2) WITH HAMMER-ON

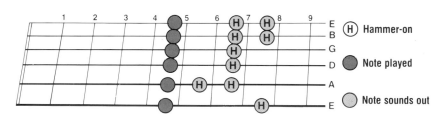

(H) Hammer-on

● Note played

○ Note sounds out

BLUES SCALE IN A (2) WITH PULL-OFF

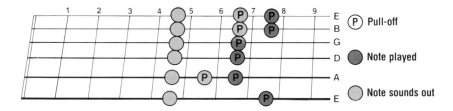

(P) Pull-off

● Note played

○ Note sounds out

USING PULL-OFF

TRY THIS embellishment which lead guitarists add to their solos using the pull-off technique.

Put your first finger across the top two strings on the fifth fret. Pick only on the red notes, starting at the eighth fret, top E string, then going to the second string.

After playing the second string, go back to the first. Repeat this several times. It will sound very impressive when you can play it fast.

BB King demonstrates pull-off.

(P) Pull-off

● Note played

○ Note sounds out

OPEN TUNINGS

LIKE SEAN Connery and James Bond, open tunings and bottleneck guitar are synonymous.

The idea of an open tuning is to create a chord without holding any strings down. This is achieved by re-tuning selected strings on the guitar.

The easiest open tuning is E. You smply tune your third, fourth and fifth strings up to give the notes G#, E and B. Instead of the usual **EBGDAE**, your open strings now play the notes **EBG#EBE**.

If you play right across the strings with your left hand off the neck, you'll recognise that this is the chord of **E** major.

It follows that if you barre all the strings on any fret, you'll have another major chord—**A** major at the fifth fret, **B** major at the seventh, and so on.

The interesting thing is that you can now barre a chord with anything that comes to hand—and create all kinds of different effects.

THIS IS where the bottleneck comes in. First lay your hands on a small bottle, then barre the strings with the bottle, and strum. You'll hear a whining noise that you should recognise, because you are now playing a rudimentary form of bottleneck or slide guitar—as practised by blues guitarists for over fifty years.

The style was popularised by country blues guitarists such as Robert Johnson and Son House. It was taken into the electric age by the likes of Muddy Waters and Elmore James, and has been refined in a rock context by Ry Cooder, Duane Allman, Johnny Winter and Ron Wood.

It's called bottleneck because one popular way of playing this style was to take the neck off a bottle and thread it over the little finger.

A good alternative is a length of steel or copper pipe—you can make one yourself or buy them in guitar shops. Less regular slide players use all kinds of things from bottles to cigarette lighters held in the left hand.

It's worth pointing out that you don't *have* to re-tune to use a slide—but of course you can't play slide guitar chords without an open tuning.

Whatever style of music you play, it's useful to know about open tunings and bottleneck guitar. Like fingerpicking, it's another string to your bow.

Like many techniques, it was developed by blues guitarists—but any imaginative player should be able to find a use for it.

OPEN TUNINGS

OPEN TUNING TO A CHORD OF E MAJOR

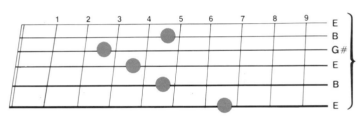

Notes on the open strings. The third, fourth and fifth strings are tuned higher than normal.

● Check your tuning at these frets. Seventh fret, bottom **E** string will give you the **B** note you need for your fifth string.

OPEN TUNING TO A CHORD OF G MAJOR

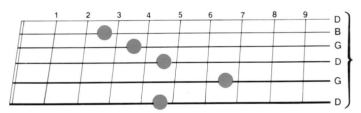

Notes on the open strings. The top, fifth and bottom strings are tuned lower than normal.

● Check your tuning at these frets. Fifth fret, bottom string will give you the **G** note you need for your fifth string.

THE MOST popular open tunings are **D, E, G** and **A**. Here you can see how to tune your guitar to open **E** and **G**.

To get an open **D** tuning, take the **E** tuning and tune all the strings down two semitones. To get an open **A** tuning, take the **G** tuning and tune all strings *up* two semitones.

The higher tunings in each case (**E** and **A**) are more suited to rock guitarists with light guage strings. Blues players often use heavier strings, and so prefer the **D** and **G** versions.

If you experiment with the two tunings shown here—**E** and **G**—you'll begin to notice that they have different characters.

The **E** tuning gives a harder attack. It was the one used by that fierce Mississippi bluesman Robert Johnson, and for the blues power chords of Elmore James. It's the one favoured by most rock players.

The **G** tuning is more of a country tuning. Used by Son House, Bukka White and Muddy Waters, it gives the mournful sound favoured by Ry Cooder on his film soundtracks.

George Thorogood carries on the Elmore James tradition at Live Aid, Philadelphia, 1985.

Rick Neilsen of Cheap Trick shows you don't have to play the blues to use a bottleneck.

BOTTLENECK GUITAR

FOR AN elementary R&B slide lick, tune to open **A** then try this, using whatever you've found for a bottleneck:

Open **E** (one four-beat bar);
Slide to fifth fret (**A**) for one bar;
Slide to seventh fret (**B**) for one bar;
Back to open **A**.

Having done that, you'll probably wonder what all the fuss is about. Well, here's the secret: the key to successful bottleneck guitar lies not in the slide, but in the expression you give it.

If you listen to Muddy Waters playing bottleneck, you can actually hear the bottleneck rattling against the guitar—this is beause he's trembling his hand furiously. That's how the slide guitarist achieves the different nuances in sound—not just by sliding, but by trembling!

ANOTHER CLUE to good bottleneck is where on the neck you play it. Generally, the higher the better. Elmore James, arguably the greatest bottleneck player of all, concentrated nearly all his famous riffs and phrases on the 12th fret.

The triplet riff he used on countless songs such as 'Dust My Broom'—dah-dah-dah, dah-dah-dah, dah-dah-dah, dah-dah-dah, DOW-dum—was achieved by sliding up to the 12th fret at the start of each triplet, playing just the first two strings. The DOW-dum was also played at the 12th fret, on the third and fourth strings respectively.

58

TABLATURE IS a method of reading music designed specifically for guitar. It's especially useful for showing solos, and there are many books available which feature famous solos transcribed note for note into tablature—it's usually written above the conventional music. These are the basics of tablature:

STAVE: Tablature is written on a 'stave' of six horizontal lines which represent the six guitar strings, from top **E** string (top line) to bottom **E** string (bottom line).

The tablature stave usually has the word **TAB** at the beginning. There are vertical 'bar lines' to indicate the end of each bar.

TIME SIGNATURE: Most rock is in **4/4** time, meaning four beats per bar.

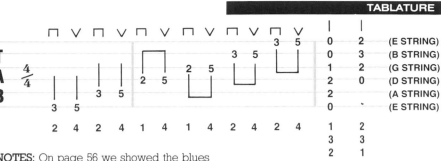

NOTES: On page 56 we showed the blues scale in **A** (1). The first two bars above show the 12 notes of that scale.

Each note is represented by a fret number, written on the string played. So our first note is third fret, bottom **E** string. Fingers to use are numbered below the stave. Down/up symbols are above it.

In the first bar, the notes are played one per beat. The second bar shows the next eight notes played *two* notes per beat.

CHORDS: The same rules apply, except that all the strings played have fret numbers, all stacked above each other.

The third bar of tablature above shows two chords. First comes an open **E** major. The figure **0** indicates an open string.

Next there's a **D** major chord, with only four strings played. No number on the stave line means don't play that string.

BLUES PLAYERS use notes called blue notes. These are created by bending strings so that their pitch is raised slightly. Put three fingers down and push the top **E** string towards the **B** string and back again. Alternatively, play a note on the **G** string and either pull it towards the **B** string or push towards the **D** string.

STRING BENDING

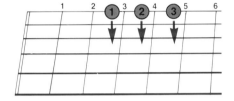

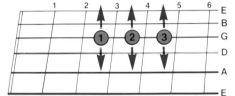

WHILE PLAYING a solo or a scale it's sometimes effective to drop in a chord. To save you having to form a full chord, there are some 'half-chords' which work just as well.

The three trebly chords shown here are often used by lead guitar players to break up their solos or to accentuate the rhythm guitarist's chords. We've shown them in **A**, but you can use them in any key by changing frets.

LEAD CHORDS

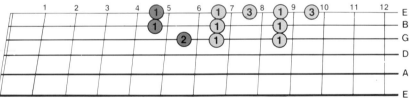

● Use in the key of **A** major over Chord I

○ Use in the key of **A** major over Chord IV

○ Use in the key of **A** major over Chord V

VIBRATO

VIBRATO IS one of the techniques lead guitarists use to give notes expression—the thing that makes each player unique.

Vibrato was developed by blues players such as BB King, to give certain notes in a solo more depth. It's achieved by the rapid sideways movement of the string—in short, the string vibrates.

Practising vibrato can be a little strange to start with, as the finger tends to slip off the string.

You only need your left hand to try it out. Place your first finger just behind the seventh fret, top **E** string. Move the string ever so slightly towards you, then allow it to return to its starting position. Now pull the string away from you, and ease it back again.

Vibrato is a combination of these two movements, but at quick-fire pace.

The next move is to play a string, then vibrate. Work up speed as you go along, but don't expect miracles overnight. In the course of time, as a lead guitarist, you'll find it takes its place automatically in your box of tricks.

Vibrato and string bending require strong fingers. Angus Young of AC/DC employs both techniques, making up for the lack of a tremolo arm on his Gibson SG by moving the strings physically.

ROBERT CRAY

AS AN example of lead guitar for you to play, we've selected a song by one of the world's most exciting guitarists, Robert Cray. Along with Stevie Ray Vaughan, he has put the blues back on the map and high in the charts.

Cray is a spare, unflashy player. His band has the tautness of Booker T And The MGs, with Cray's guitar as sharp as Steve Cropper on the rhythm, and as attacking as Buddy Guy on the solos.

'Phone Booth' is the best-known track on Cray's 1984 breakthrough album, 'Bad Influence'. Written by Cray with bassist Richard Cousins, sax player Mike Vannice and producer Dennis Walker, it's a 12-bar blues with some unconventional chords.

It gives you a new angle on the 12-bar blues, and a chance to use your blues scale in **A** in a solo.

In the spotlight: Robert Cray turns up the heat on his Stratocaster.

WHEN WE first played 'The Boys Are Back In Town', we used major and minor chords instead of the more complex seventh chords of the original. Robert Cray's 'Phone Booth' fits into the same pattern.

In essence it's a minor key 12-bar blues, with some neat little variations. Our diagrams on the right show the conventional major and seventh chords Cray could have used; instead, he makes it more interesting by introducing minor sixth and augmented seventh chords.

These chords aren't difficult, but if you do find them tricky, you can easily substitute the chords shown. Use **E** or **E7** instead of **E7+** (**E** augmented seventh). Use **F** or **F7** instead of **Cm6**. Use **G** or **G7** for **Dm6**.

Incidentally, Cray's use of **E7** in the key of **A** minor is an old blues trick—'House Of The Rising Sun' is a classic example.

'PHONE BOOTH' (CHORDS)

BEFORE YOU attempt the solo for 'Phone Booth', here are the chords and words. The chord names may be unfamiliar, but don't let that put you off. They're all fairly simple shapes which can be played near the nut of the guitar.

There are three new chords here: **E7+**, **Cm7** and **Dm7**. If you want, you can substitute more familiar chords—see above page 61.

If you need to remind yourself of the shapes for **Am7** and **Dm7**, see page 48.

RHYTHM

LIKE NEARLY all blues songs, 'Phone Booth' is in **4/4** time—four beats to the bar. The Robert Cray Band play it at quite a lick, with a heavy emphasis on every beat.

Cray uses a tricky 'shuffle' guitar rhythm, but it will sound fine if you just play a firm rhythm right on the beat, using sharp downstrokes.

As ever, take this song slowly at first. Once

you've got it working with open chords, you might find it effective to use the barre chords of **Am**, **Am7** and **Dm7** which you can play at the fifth fret.

If you can, record yourself playing the chord sequence over and over, so that you can practise soloing to your own accompaniment. Don't forget that you may struggle with the solo at first, so don't play too fast on the backing track!

TITLE	KEY	TEMPO
'PHONE BOOTH' (CHORDS)	A MINOR	QUITE FAST

BAR 1 Am / Am7 / **BAR 2** E7+ / / / **BAR 3** Am / Am7 / **BAR 4** / / / /
Phone booth baby, number's scratched on the wall. I'm in a

BAR 5 Dm7 / / / **BAR 6** / / / / **BAR 7** Am / Am7 / **BAR 8** / / / /
Phone booth baby, number's scratched on the wall. I'm

BAR 9 Cm6 / / / **BAR 10** Dm6 / E7+ / **BAR 11** Am / Am7 / **BAR 12** / / / /
New in Chicago, got no one else to call.

KEY TO COLOURS

■ A minor   □ A minor 7   □ E7 augmented   ■ D minor 7   ■ C minor 6   □ D minor 6

LYRICS

I'm in a phone booth baby, number's scratched on the wall.
I'm in a phone booth baby, number's scratched on the wall.
I'm new in Chicago, got no one else to call.

Been walking all day, old friends I can't find.
Heart's so cold, had to buy me some wine.
Calling you baby took my very last dime.

SOLO

I'm in a phone booth baby, number's scratched upon the wall.
I'm in a phone booth baby, number's scratched on the wall.
I'm new in Chicago, got no one else to call.

Said "Call me—Dorita—any time day or night".
You know I'm broke and I'm cold baby, and I hope you'll treat me right.
I'm in a phone booth baby, with the cold wind right outside.

SOLO (FADE)

'PHONE BOOTH' (CHORDS)

CHORD OF E MAJOR

CHORD OF E7

CHORD OF E AUGMENTED 7

CHORDS OF F AND G MAJOR

CHORDS OF F7 AND G7

CHORDS OF Cm6 AND Dm6

X Not played

'PHONE BOOTH' (SOLO)

OUR SOLO is based very loosely on Robert Cray's—and they're both based on the blues scale in **A** which we covered in page 56.

Learning a solo pattern is tough. Play the notes slowly until they fit together, then start putting your own rhythmic expression into it.

Obviously, this is just one possible solo that you could play over this chord sequence. Once you've tried ours, have a go at one of your own, using the blues scale as your basis.

HOW TO READ THE SOLO

WE'VE WRITTEN this solo out in tablature. Each line of tablature corresponds exactly to the grid of chords above it. We showed the basic rules of tablature on page 59, but there are a couple of new things here.

In Bar 3 you'll see three notes joined together in one beat. That's our old friend the triplet. Both here and in Bar 10, **H** means hammer on.

At the end Bar 3 there's a note with a tail, followed by a squiggle—that's a note lasting half a beat, followed by a half-beat rest or silence. In other words, if you're tapping your foot there's a gap as you bring the foot up.

A note followed by an arrow should be sustained or held for the length of the arrow. If there's no note on a beat, just hold your fire.

Tablature is broken up by vertical bar lines. We've added faint lines separating each beat.

TITLE	KEY	TEMPO
'PHONE BOOTH' (SOLO)	A MINOR	QUITE FAST

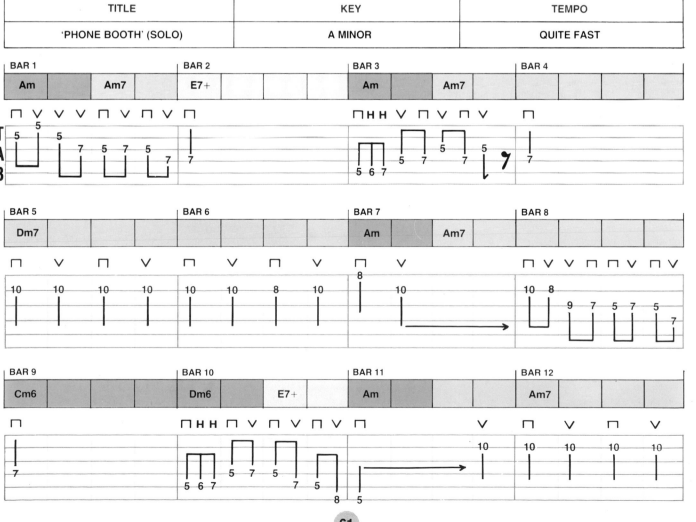

61

BASS GUITAR

WE'VE LOOKED fairly thoroughly at both ways of playing an ordinary six-string guitar—lead and rhythm. Briefly, for anyone interested, here's a basic rundown on playing bass guitar.

The transition from guitar to bass isn't as difficult as you might suppose, and it's possible to make your initial foray in bass technique on any six-string guitar.

The bass guitar has four strings, tuned in the same way as the bottom four strings of a guitar—G, D, A, E—but one octave lower.

So the riffs below can be practised using either a bass or a six-string.

YOU'LL SOON realise that a lot of what we said about lead guitar scales and techniques such as hammer-on can be applied to the bass.

Traditionally, while the lead guitarist is given free rein, the bass player 'chug-a-lugs' along in the background. This doesn't mean that the bass player's role is any less important.

The bass is a vital element of any song, giving it both a rhythm and a melodic guide. When playing bass you should always put your rhythm function first.

If you break up the rhythm, it must be for a reason. Our bassline for 'Phone Booth' illustrates this, setting a firm rhythm but deliberately changing it from time to time, to highlight certain bars.

Harmonically, you should follow the chord sequence. Some bass patterns have relatively few notes; others may be quite complex; but the one thing they usually have in common is that the root note of each chord is played on the first beat of the bar. Above all, keep it simple!

The best known bass player? Paul McCartney in days of yore with rhythm guitarist John Lennon.

BASS GUITAR

HERE ARE some possible basslines for a chord sequence of **C/F/G/C**.

In the first grid you simply finger the notes of **C**, **F** and **G** four beats at a time – 1, 2, 3, 4 (**C**), 1, 2, 3, 4 (**F**), 1, 2, 3, 4 (**G**) back to 1, 2, 3, 4 (**C**). Count each note as you play it.

WHILST THIS simple set-up is musically correct, and often used, it's hardly going to stretch your imagination. So let's introduce a four-note pattern for each four-beat bar.

In the second diagram we start on the **C** note, and add three other notes sympathetic to the **C** chord, **E**, **F** and **G**. For our first shot at this, we'll play all four notes on the **A** string.

You can repeat this exact same order on the string above **A**, the **D** string, although this time you will be playing notes sympathetic to the **F** chord. And you can use exactly the same line of notes for **G**, played on the **A** string. Revert back to the **C** sequence for the final chord.

FINALLY, INSTEAD of sliding along one string at a time, keep it nice and tight by following the third grid—it stays within one hand's span on the fretboard.

KEY TO GRID

C	Note played
A3	String and fret played
(2)	Finger used

BASSLINES

C	C	C	C	F	F	F	F
A3	A3	A3	A3	D3	D3	D3	D3
(2)	(2)	(2)	(2)	(2)	(2)	(2)	(2)

G	G	G	G	C	C	C	C
D5	D5	D5	D5	A3	A3	A3	A3
(3)	(3)	(3)	(3)	(2)	(2)	(2)	(2)

C	E	F	G	F	A	B♭	C
A3	A7	A8	A10	D3	D7	D8	D10
(1)	(1)	(2)	(3)	(1)	(1)	(2)	(3)

G	B	C	D	C	E	F	G
E3	E7	E8	E10	A3	A7	A8	A10
(1)	(1)	(2)	(3)	(1)	(1)	(2)	(3)

C	E	F	G	F	A	B♭	C
A3	D2	D3	D5	D3	G2	G3	G5
(2)	(1)	(2)	(3)	(2)	(1)	(2)	(3)

G	B	C	D	C	E	F	G
E3	A2	A3	A5	A3	D2	D3	D5
(2)	(1)	(2)	(3)	(2)	(1)	(2)	(3)

KEY TO COLOURS

☐ Played under a chord of **C major**   ▣ Played under a chord of **F major**   ☐ Played under a chord of **G major**

There are three distinctive methods for using your right hand while playing bass guitar. In the first picture, the first two fingers of the right hand pluck the strings, in an area just above the pick-up. The second illustration shows the relatively new 'slapping technique', when the thumb 'bounces' off the strings. In the final photograph, the right hand strikes the strings with a plectrum.

The best known bass stance? Bill Wyman holding his bass guitar like a portable double bass.

The best bass player in America? Jazz funk maestro Jaco Pastorius plucks his Fender Jazz bass.

The best bass player in Britain? Mark King of Level 42—note black band on his slapping thumb.

'PHONE BOOTH' (BASS)

NOW THAT you've tried some simple bass guitar exercises, let's put that to use in the context of a song you should know well by now—'Phone Booth' by Robert Cray.

This is a nice, stripped down bassline which follows two rhythmic patterns. For some bars, you play on the first, third and fourth beats. In others, you play on beats 1, 2½ and 3. This simple device stops the song becoming boring, and gives a different feel to different chords.

If you have recorded a rhythm track in order to practise the solo, you can put it to use again now, by playing bass to it. Better still, once you've mastered the bass part, record that onto your rhythm track and give yourself a really strong backing track for solo practice.

KEY TO GRID

F	Note played
D3	String and fret played
(2)	Finger used

0 = Open string

TITLE	KEY	TEMPO
'PHONE BOOTH' (BASS)	A MINOR	QUITE FAST

BAR 1

A A 0		A A 0	A A 0

BAR 2

| E
E
0 | | E
E
0 | E
E
0 |

BAR 3

| A
A
0 | | C
A3
(2) | E
D2
(1) |

BAR 4

| A
A
0 | | C
A3
(2) | E
D2
(1) |

Phone booth baby, number's scratched on the wall. I'm in a

BAR 5

| D
D
0 | | F
D3
(2) | A
G2
(1) |

BAR 6

| D
D
0 | | F
D3
(2) | A
G2
(1) |

BAR 7

| A
A
0 | | C
A3
(2) | E
D2
(1) | A
A
0 |

BAR 8

| | C
A3
(2) | E
D2
(1) |

Phone booth baby, number's scratched on the wall. I'm

BAR 9

| C
A3
(2) | | C
A3
(2) | G
G3
(2) |

BAR 10

| D
A5
(3) | | E
E
0 | G
E3
(2) |

BAR 11

| A
A
0 | | C
A3
(2) | E
D2
(1) | A
A
0 |

BAR 12

| | C
A3
(2) | E
D2
(1) |

New in Chicago, got no one else to call.

KEY TO COLOURS

☐ Played under a chord of **A minor**
☐ Played under a chord of **A minor 7**
☐ Played under a chord of **E augmented 7**
☐ Played under a chord of **D minor 7**
☐ Played under a chord of **C minor 6**
☐ Played under a chord of **D minor 6**

HOPEFULLY, THIS brief crash course in bass playing will have given you some understanding of what it's all about. We should point out, however, that although you can mess about on the bass strings of a six-string guitar, you won't really know whether it's right for you until you try out a real bass with four heavy strings.

As ever, if you do want to play bass, the bottom line is practice, practice and more practice. The only way to conquer any instrument is to *keep practising!*

HOW TO READ MUSIC

HERE AS promised is our crash course in reading music the traditional way. Please note, these are only the basics—a detailed study would fill many more pages.

An ability to read music is useful but by no means essential. Many rock musicians survive perfectly well without it.

Having said that, you will definitely need to read music if you hope to become a session musician, and it's useful if you want to send your songs to a publisher, or get other musicians to play them.

For most people, however, the crunch comes when they want to play other people's songs, because all sheet music uses traditional musical notation.

Chords are usually named on sheet music, but for the riffs, melody and bassline you'll need to read music. What follows should help you to do that.

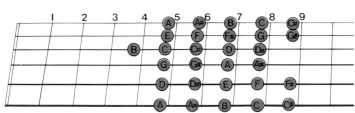

NOTES ON THE GUITAR AT POSITION I

NOTES ON THE GUITAR AT POSITION V

NOTES

WE HAVE divided reading music into two parts: notes (this page) and rhythm (opposite). This page tells you whether a note is **C** or **C#**, etc. The opposite page tells you how long it lasts.

When discussing lengths of notes, we show them in relation to our song grid. Please note that each grid is one bar in length. The divisions and the numbers **1, 2, 3, 4** show the beats.

MUSICAL STAVES

TREBLE CLEF

BASS CLEF

Here are two musical 'staves'. A stave consists of five horizontal lines, and is the traditional equivalent of our music grid.

The two staves are marked with 'clefs'. The treble clef is roughly equivalent to lead/rhythm guitar; the bass clef usually shows the bass guitar part. We won't be paying much more attention to the bass clef—but you read it in the same way as the treble clef.

NOTES ON A STAVE

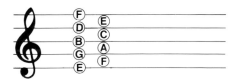

Musical notes can appear either on or between the notes on a stave. An easy way to remember the notes in the spaces is that, reading upwards, they spell **FACE**. As for the notes on the lines, they stand for that well-known phrase **E**very **G**ood **B**oy **D**eserves **F**un.

You'll notice that we have two **E**'s and two **F**'s on our stave. That's because those at the top of the stave are an octave above those at the bottom. In other words, this isn't any old **E** or **F**—they do in fact relate directly to precise notes on the guitar.

The diagram at the top of page 65 shows these notes on the guitar.

HIGHER AND LOWER NOTES

Obviously there are higher and lower notes than we can show on the stave. Lower notes are shown below the stave with short 'ledger' lines through or below them as necessary; higher notes are shown above the stave.

SHARP AND FLAT NOTES

By now you've probably noticed that there are no sharp or flat notes on any of the staves we've looked at. Sharps or flats are signposted by the sharp/flat symbols at the beginning of the stave. A sharp symbol on the top line of the stave means **F** is replaced by **F#**. A flat symbol on the bottom line means **E** is replaced by **E**♭, and so on.

KEY SIGNATURES

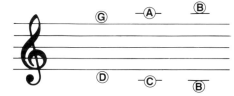

| C MAJOR | G MAJOR | D MAJOR | A MAJOR | E MAJOR | F MAJOR |
| A MINOR | E MINOR | B MINOR | F# MINOR | C# MINOR | D MINOR |

The sharp/flat symbols at the start of a stave are known as the key signature, since the presence of certain sharp/flat notes tells you what key you're in.

If there are no sharp/flat notes, the music must be in the keys of **C** major or **A** minor, as they are the only keys with no sharps or flats. If there's one flat symbol on the middle line of the stave, it means **B** is replaced by **B**♭—and that should tell you that the piece of music is in the key of **F** major or **D** minor, as they are the only keys with that one flat note.

Here (above) are the most common key signatures. If you have trouble working others out, refer to the chart on page 35, which shows which keys have which sharp/flat notes.

UNRELATED NOTES

| D SHARP | D FLAT | D NATURAL | C MAJOR | C MAJOR 7 | C 7 |

When a note unrelated to the key appears—for instance in a dominant seventh chord—the note is preceded by a sharp, flat or 'natural' sign.

CHORDS

A chord is shown by stacking all the notes on top of each other, because they are played together.

NOTES ON THE GUITAR

RIGHT AT the start of the Instruction Manual, we showed the 12 musical notes as laid out on one guitar string.

That's not how a guitarist would usually picture them. In the guitarist's eye, the notes form a cluster around each fret, so they can all be played within a short distance of one another.

THE DIAGRAMS on the left show how the notes lie around the first fret and fifth fret— known as Position **I** and Position **V**. Try and work them out on the seventh and tenth frets for yourself later.

THE DIAGRAMS on the right show where you can locate the notes on a music stave on the neck of your guitar.

HOW THE NOTES ON A STAVE RELATE TO POSITION I

Open top **E** string	Ⓔ	Ⓕ — 1st fret top **E** string
1st fret **B** string	Ⓒ	Ⓓ — 3rd fret **B** string
2nd fret **G** string	Ⓐ	Ⓑ — Open **B** string
3rd fret **D** string	Ⓕ	Ⓖ — Open **G** string
		Ⓔ — 2nd fret **D** string

HOW THE NOTES ON A STAVE RELATE TO POSITION V

5th fret **B** string	Ⓔ	Ⓕ — 6th fret **B** string
5th fret **G** string	Ⓒ	Ⓓ — 7th fret **G** string
7th fret **D** string	Ⓐ	Ⓑ — 4th fret **G** string
8th fret **A** string	Ⓕ	Ⓖ — 5th fret **D** string
		Ⓔ — 7th fret **A** string

BARS

Music staves are divided into bars by regular vertical lines.

TIME SIGNATURES

These are the most common time signatures. The top number is beats per bar. The number below describes the beat—**4** means it's a 'quarter note' beat. Most rock songs are in **4/4**.

DOTTED AND TIED NOTES

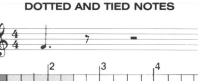

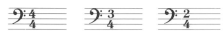

When a note is 'dotted', it lasts for its normal length plus half its length again.

LENGTHS OF NOTES

SEMIBREVE (Whole note, lasting full four-beat bar)
(Below: as seen on the music grid)

MINIM (Half note: two minims in a semibreve)
(Below: as seen on the music grid)

CROTCHET (Quarter note, one beat of four-beat bar)
(Below: as seen on the music grid)

QUAVER (Eighth note: eight to a semibreve)
(Below: as seen on the music grid)

SEMIQUAVER (Sixteenth note, a quarter of a beat)
(Below: as seen on the music grid)

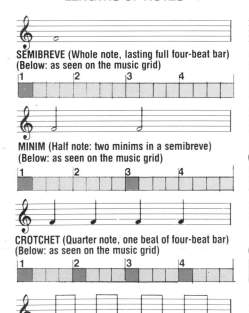

These (above) are the different note lengths, in relation to our music grid, and the names given to them.

SILENCES OR RESTS

SEMIBREVE REST
(Below: as seen on the music grid)

MINIM REST
(Below: as seen on the music grid)

CROTCHET REST
(Below: as seen on the music grid)

QUAVER REST
(Below: as seen on the music grid)

SEMIQUAVER REST
(Below: as seen on the music grid)

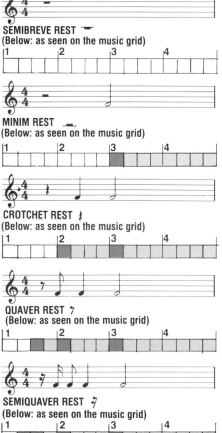

The symbols above represent 'rests' or silences. They also show how notes of different lengths can be used in one bar.

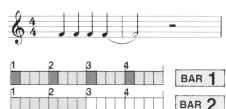

BAR **1**
BAR **2**

When two notes of the same pitch are 'tied' (linked by a curved line), the note is held for the total length of both notes. The note is not played twice, it is just sustained.

1 BEAT   1 BEAT   1 BEAT 1 BEAT

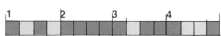

When more than one quaver or semiquaver occur on the same beat, unless there is a rest between them they are linked together. Unless they are 'tied' by a curved line, they are played separately.

Notes above the middle line of a stave usually have stems pointing downwards. Notes on the middle line can have either up or down stems.

SIXTHS, NINTHS, THIRTEENTHS

IN THE Chord Directory which begins opposite, there are three types of chord we haven't met before: sixths, ninths and thirteenths. These chords may sound complicated, but they are often remarkably easy to play. You can create added interest in a song by replacing some of the primary chords you already know with these 'jazz' chords. The trick is knowing when to use them.

Here are some basic substitution rules, to show which chords can replace which. And while we're on the subject, we might as well chuck in some ways of using major sevenths, minor sevenths and diminished chords too...

TO START with, experiment with each 'rule' by itself. Choose a song which has simple chords, and gradually substitute more difficult ones. You'll be surprised by the way these new chords give a song a much jazzier feel.

First, you need to work out what key the song is in. Then you should work out where each chord stands in relation to the root major chord, and number them like this:

Root chord = Chord **I**. Chord derived from second note = Chord **II**. Chord derived from third note = Chord **III**. And so on, remembering that in Roman numerals **V** is five, **VI** is six, and **VII** is seven.

Rule 1. A major chord can be replaced by a major seventh chord or a sixth chord. So **C** can be replaced by **C maj 7** or **C6**.

Rule 2. Chord **I** can be replaced by **III** minor **7** or **IV** minor **7** (which is of course the relative minor **7**).

So in the key of **C**, **C** major can be replaced by **Em7** or **Am7**. And in the key of **G**, **G** major can be replaced by **Bm7** or **Em7**.

Combining these first two rules together, in the key of **C**, **C** major can be replaced by **C maj 7**, **C6**, **Em7** or **Am7**.

Rule 3. Chord **V** is usually the dominant seventh chord. In jazzier pieces, it can be replaced by the ninth or thirteenth chords.

So in the key of **C**, the dominant seventh **G7** can be replaced by **G9** or **G13**.

Rule 4. Chord **VI** is usually the relative minor. It can be replaced by a relative minor seventh, or by **III**♭ diminished, or by **I** major 6.

So in the key of **C**, **Am** can be replaced by **Am7**, **E**♭ diminished or **C6**.

SIXTHS, NINTHS, THIRTEENTHS

SIXTH CHORDS

A SIXTH chord is formed by taking the major triad – the first, third and fifth notes in the major scale – and adding the sixth note.

In the key of **C** major, you take the triad (**CEG**) and add the sixth note, **A**. So **C6** has the notes **CEGA**.

In the key of **G** major, you take the triad (**GBD**) and add the sixth note, **E**. So **G6** has the notes **GBDE**.

NINTH CHORDS

A NINTH chord is a little harder to explain. It is in fact an extension of a dominant seventh chord.

As you know, a dominant seventh chord consists of the major triad, plus the seventh note in the minor scale.

So **C7** has the notes **CEGB♭**. And **G7** has the notes **GBDF**.

To form a ninth chord, we add in the ninth note of the major scale – that is, the second note from the next octave.

So **C9** has the notes **CEGB♭D**. And **G9** has the notes **GBDFA**.

If you look at some of the ninth chords in the Chord Directory, you'll notice that they don't all have all five of the required notes. But whatever notes may be missing from the chord, you'll always find the ninth note present.

THIRTEENTH CHORDS

A THIRTEENTH chord is formed in a similar way to a ninth. Again, we take the dominant seventh chord. But this time we add the thirteenth note in the major scale – that is, the sixth note from the next octave.

So **C13** has the notes **GEGB♭A**. And **G13** has the notes **GBDFE**.

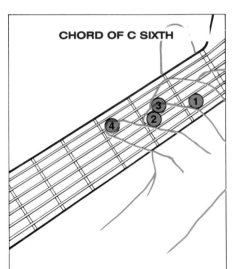

CHORD OF C SIXTH

C6 – or C major sixth, to give it its full title – is like A minor with the little finger added in a C position.

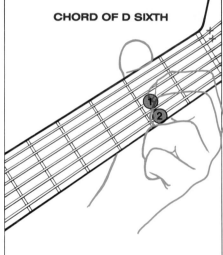

CHORD OF D SIXTH

Try this interesting sequence D, D major 7, D7 and D6. Like the others, D6 is a four or five-string chord.

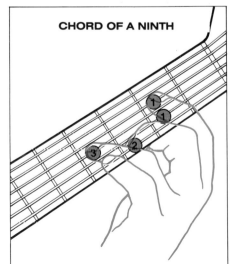

CHORD OF A NINTH

A major ninth is in fact A dominant seventh with the ninth note B added on the third string. The bottom two strings are optional.

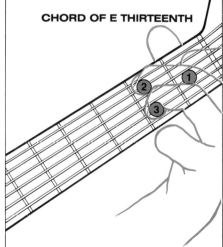

CHORD OF E THIRTEENTH

E major 13 is similar to E7. The thirteenth note C# is added on the second string. Play all six strings.

CHORD DIRECTORY

This 13-page Chord Directory shows you how to play most of the chords you are ever likely to need.

Each of the first 12 pages is devoted to one key. For each key, we show nine different chords: major, minor, seventh, major seventh, minor seventh, sixth, ninth and thirteenth.

Each chord is shown in three different formations, giving you the same chord in different parts of the fretboard. The three versions of a chord are displayed on one guitar neck, in different colour dots.

Dots of the same colour comprise one chord shape.

A coloured cross means *do not play* that string when forming the chord using dots of that colour.

A string with no dots or crosses of a certain colour is *played open*.

Finger numbers are marked in black on each coloured dot.

And that's it: a simple system giving over 300 chord shapes.

As you know, the chord referred to in the Chord Directory as the seventh is also known as the dominant seventh.

Finally, there's a page devoted to diminished and augmented chords.

CONTENTS

KEY OF C

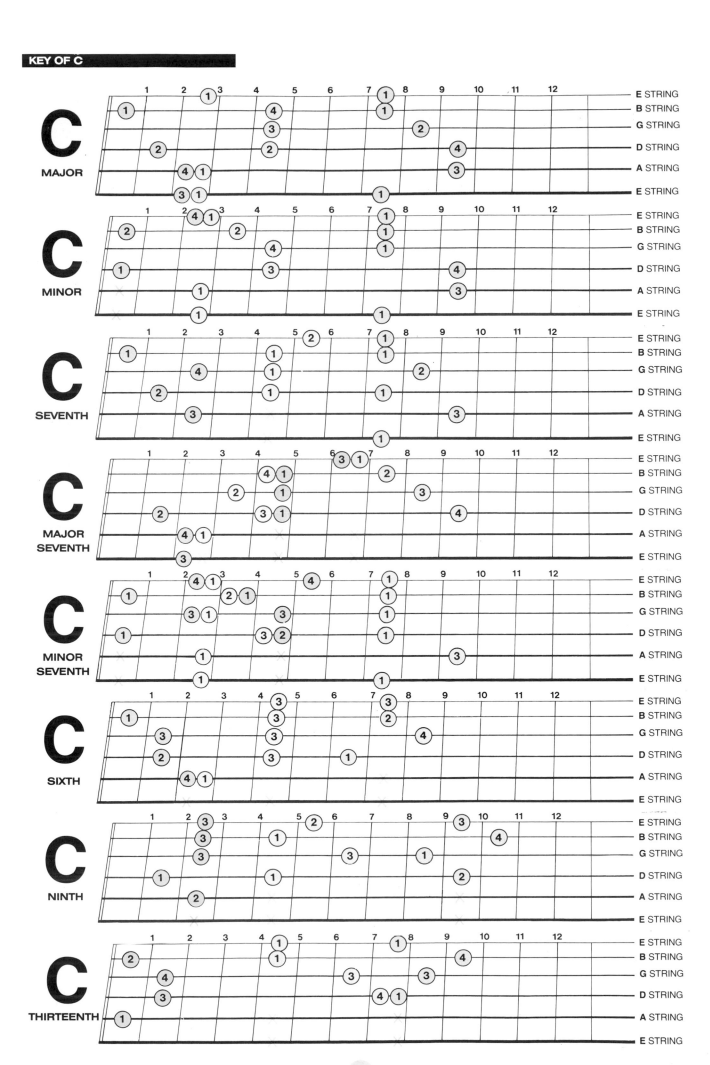

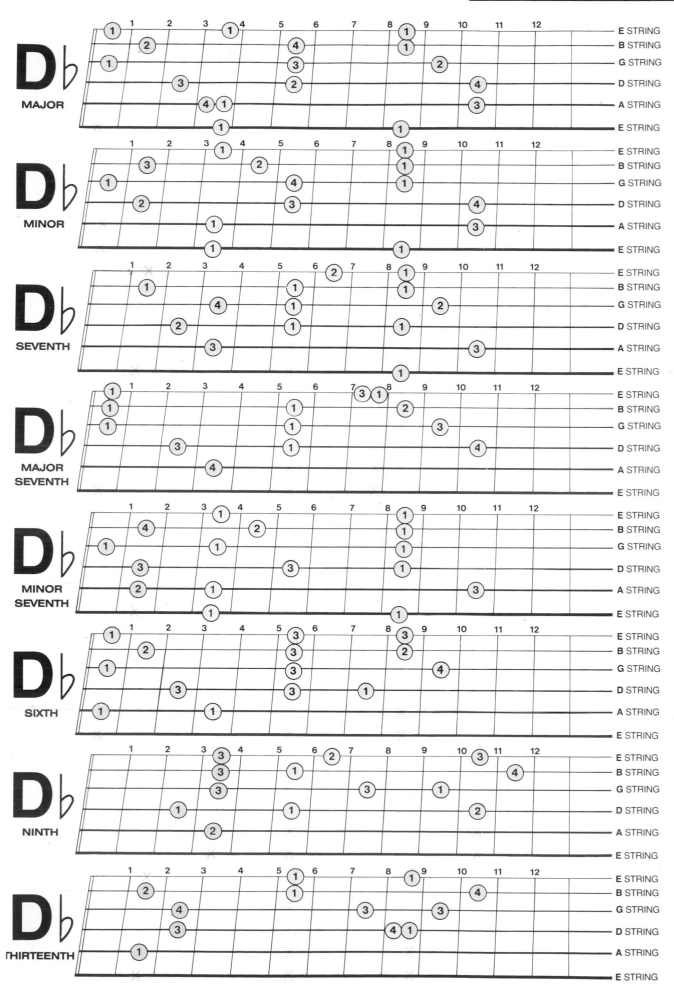

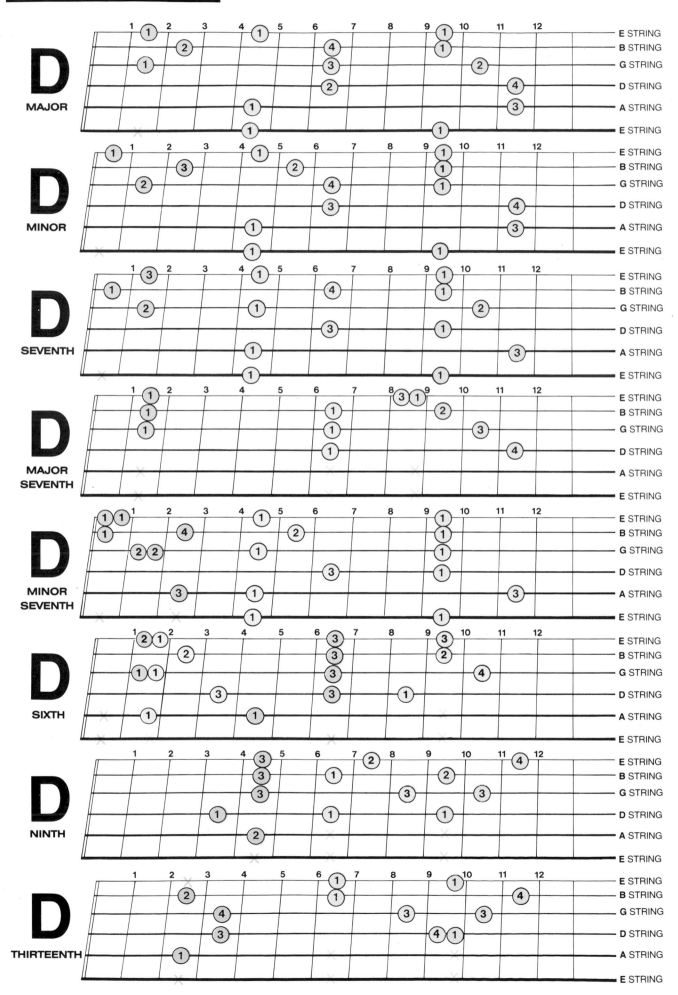

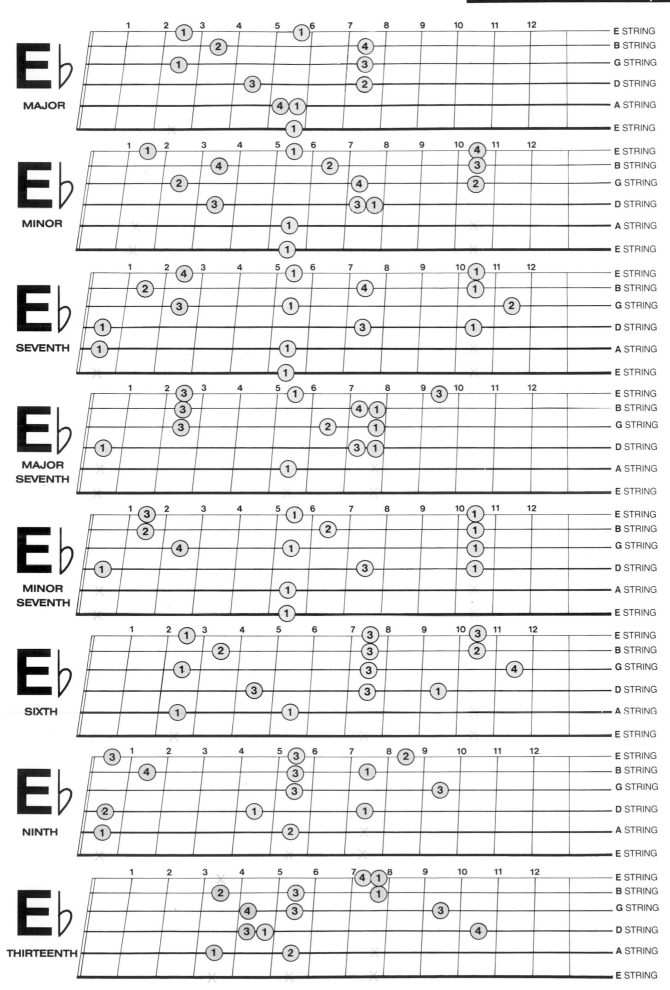

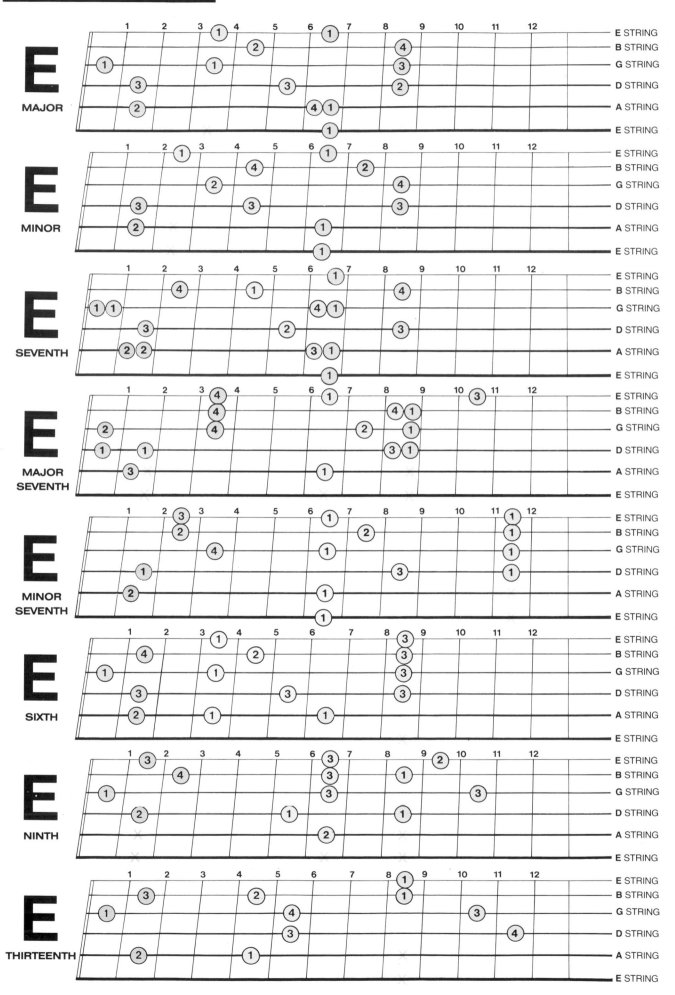

F MAJOR

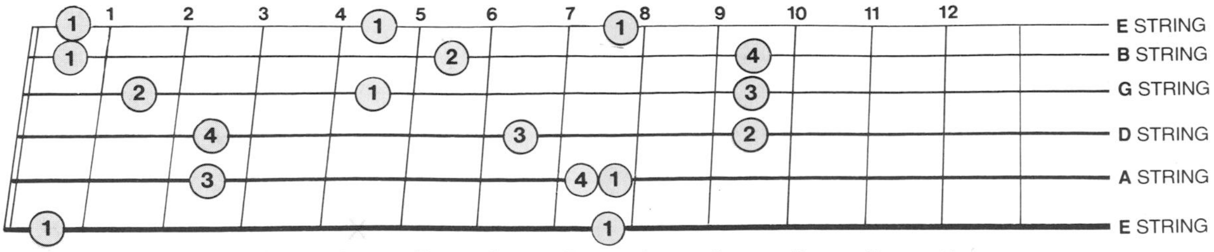

F MINOR

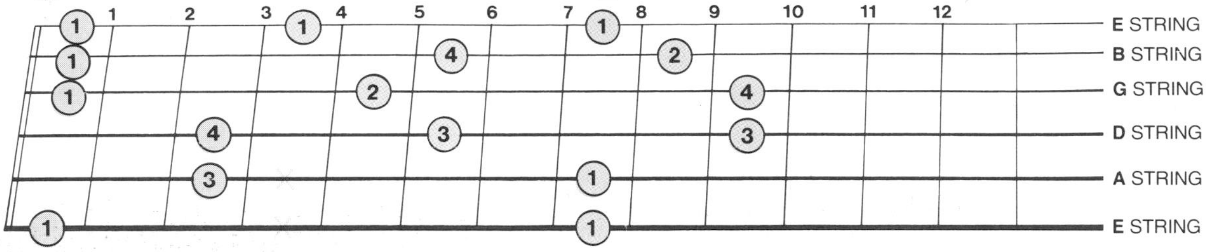

F SEVENTH

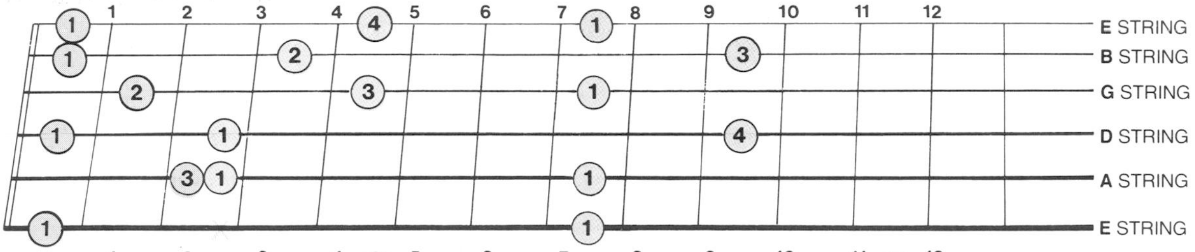

F MAJOR SEVENTH

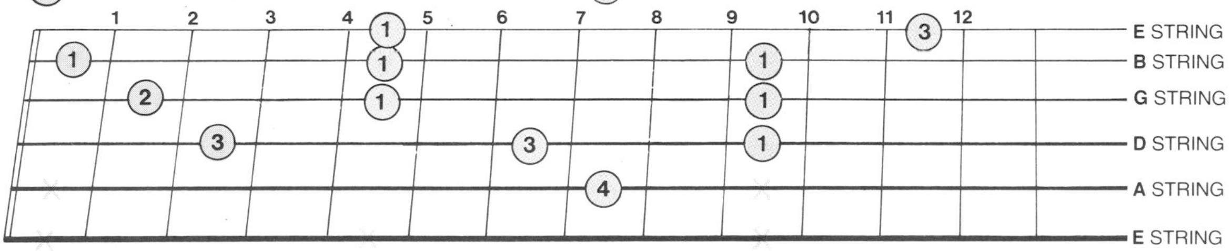

F MINOR SEVENTH

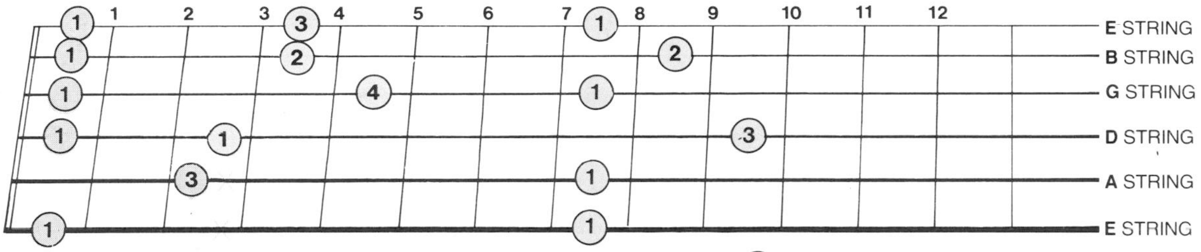

F SIXTH

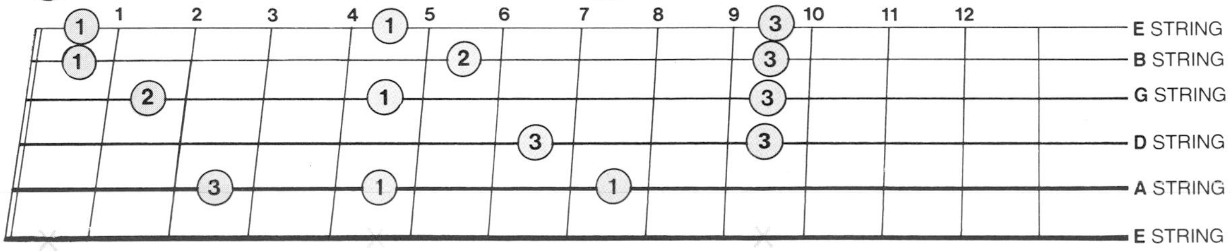

F NINTH

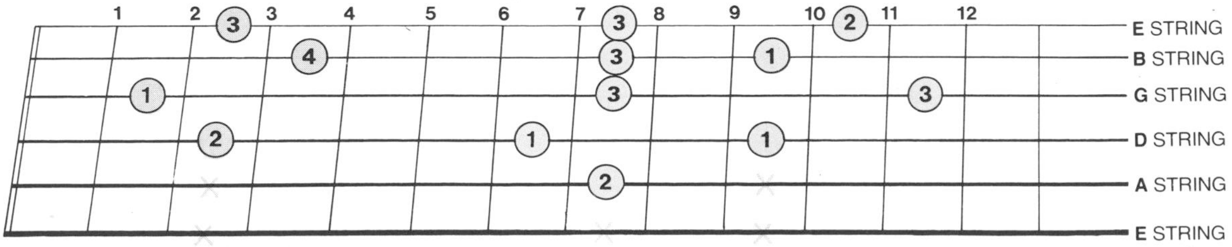

F THIRTEENTH

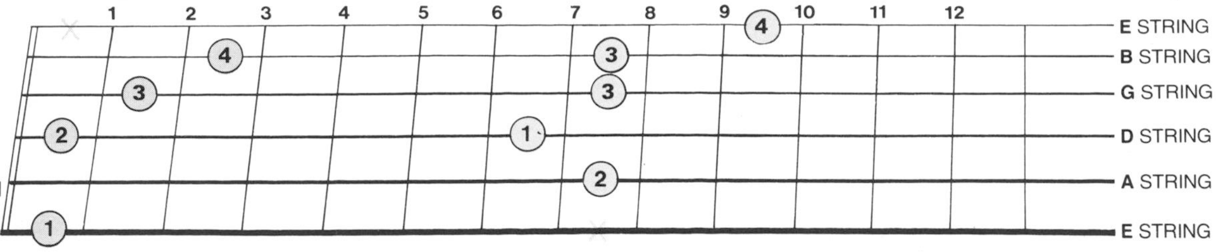

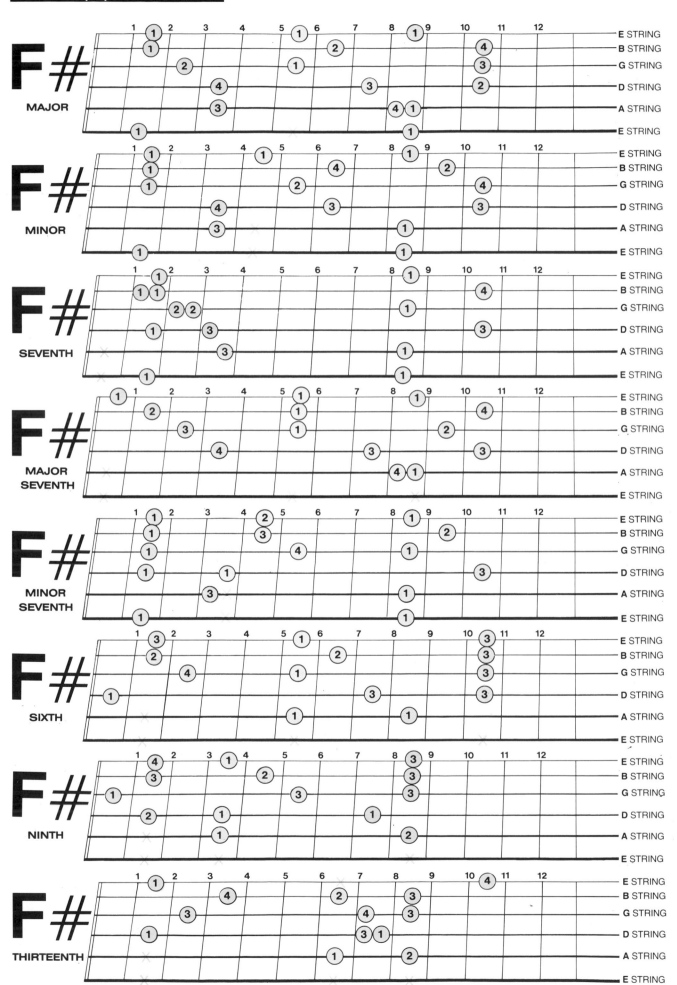

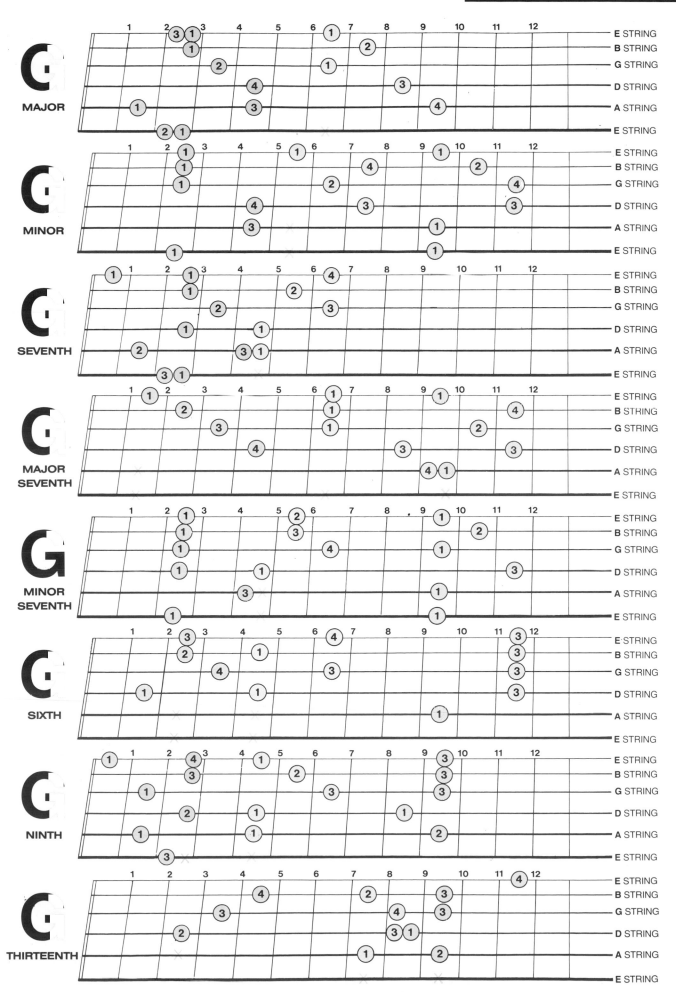

KEY OF Ab (G#)

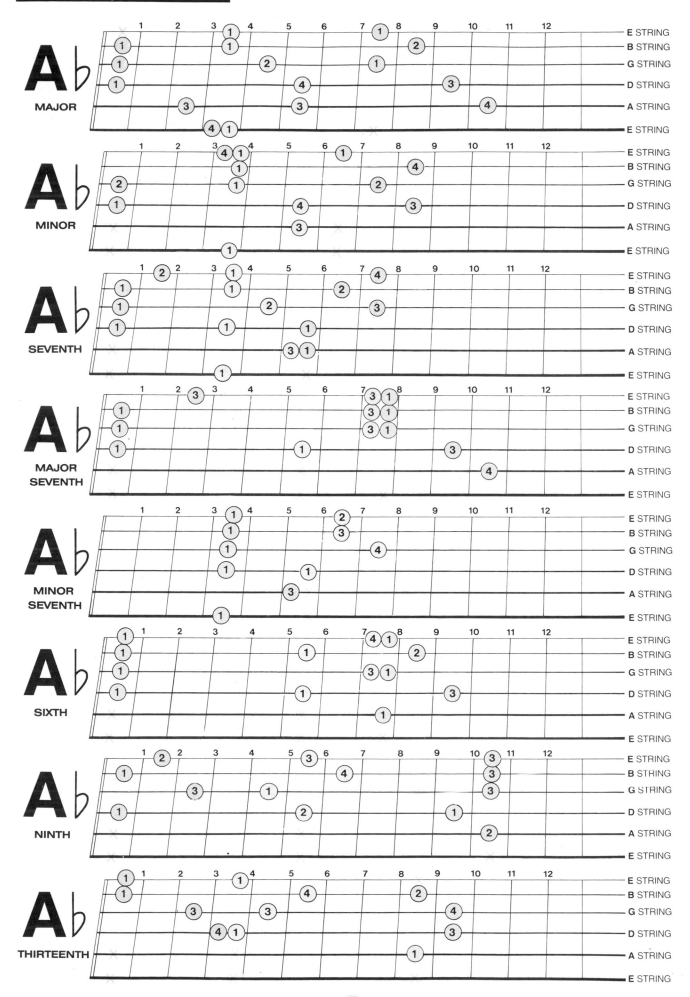

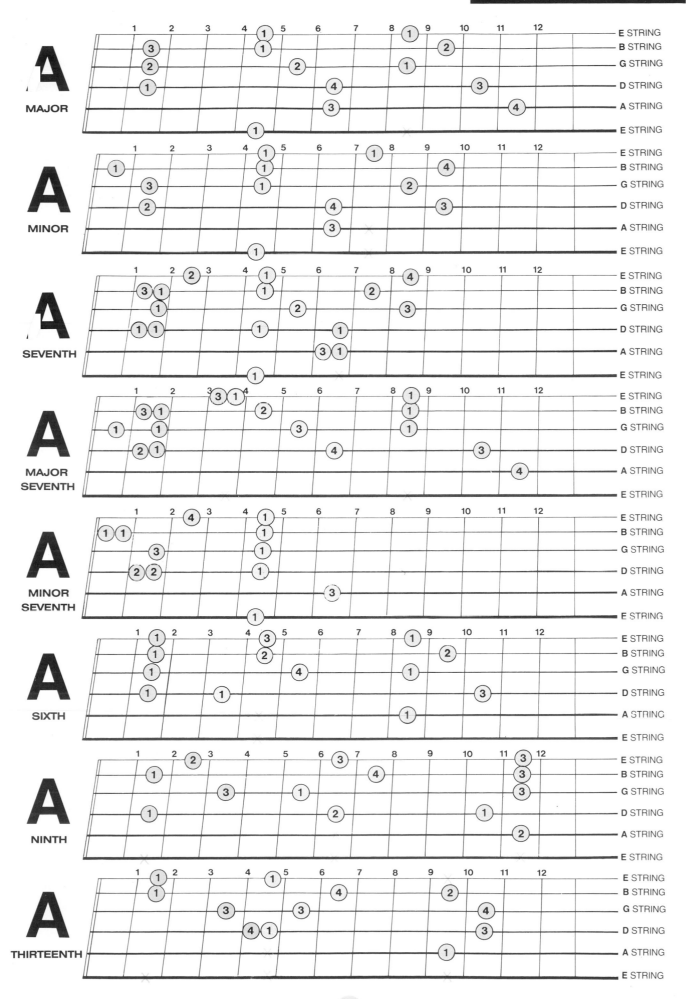

KEY OF Bb (A#)

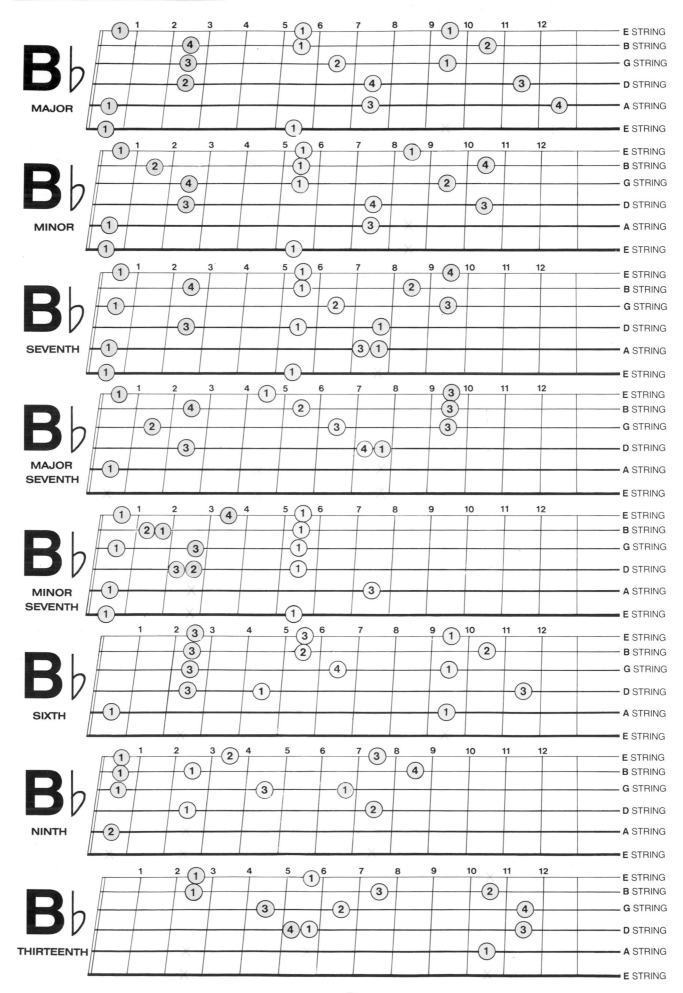

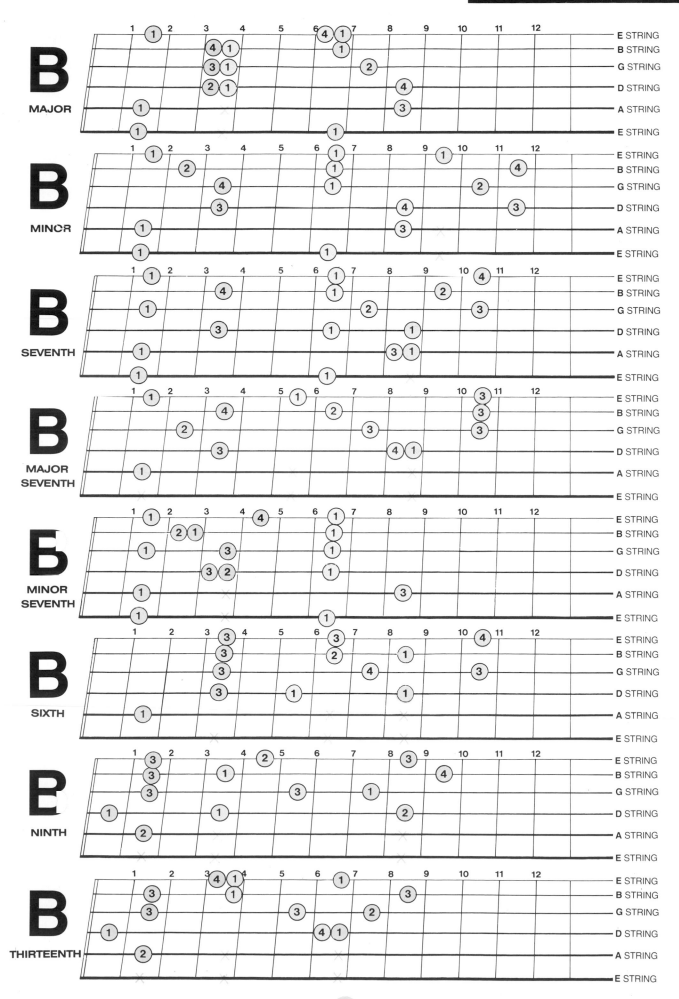

DIMINISHED AND AUGMENTED CHORDS

DIMINISHED CHORDS

IN THIS 'Strange But True' episode, we show the unusual situation of *one* chord shape with four different names. Believe it or not, there are only four diminished chords – so each has to serve for four of the 12 keys.

Here's how it works. Diminished chords are derived from the diminished scale. The diminished scale is a four-note scale which divides the 12 notes precisely in three.

Each scale gives us one chord, consisting of the four notes in that scale. And that chord can be named after any of those four notes.

So the first scale in our diagram gives us a chord which can be called **C** diminished or **D#/E♭** diminished or **F#/G♭** diminished or **A** diminished.

A DIMINISHED CHORD is normally used in a key for which it is the seventh note/chord. For instance, the seventh note in the scale of **C** is **B**. So **Bdim** is the diminished chord used in the key of **C**, even though it contains a **G#** note which is not in the key of **C**.

Try them out for yourself on a few chord sequences – for instance:
Bdim C Edim F
Bdim Am7 F#dim G.

You'll notice how, like dominant sevenths, they have an 'unfinished' quality. For this reason, they make good stepping stones between more important chords – try for instance **Gm7** to **G#dim** to **Am7**.

DIMINISHED SCALES			
C	D#	F#	A
C#	E	G	B♭
D	F	G#	B

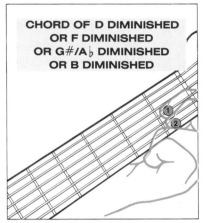

CHORD OF D DIMINISHED
OR F DIMINISHED
OR G#/A♭ DIMINISHED
OR B DIMINISHED

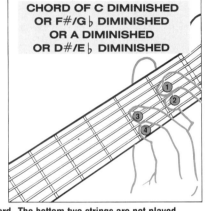

CHORD OF C DIMINISHED
OR F#/G♭ DIMINISHED
OR A DIMINISHED
OR D#/E♭ DIMINISHED

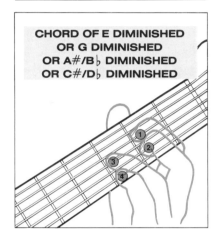

CHORD OF E DIMINISHED
OR G DIMINISHED
OR A#/B♭ DIMINISHED
OR C#/D♭ DIMINISHED

Each of these diminished chords is a four-note chord. The bottom two strings are not played.

AUGMENTED CHORDS

AUGMENTED CHORDS are the partners in crime to diminished chords. While the diminished scale cuts the 12 notes into quarters, the augmented scale chops them in six. This means that there are just two six-note augmented scales.

As with diminished chords, an augmented chord can have several names and work in several keys.

The augmented chord is a triad – first, third and fifth in the scale. But you'll notice that whether you start on **C**, **E** or **G#**, the first/third/fifth triad is always the same: **CEG#**.

This chord is known as either **C** augmented (**C+**) or **E** augmented (**E+**) or **G#/A♭** augmented (**G#+/A♭+**).

From which you may deduce that just four augmented chord shapes are required to cover all 12 keys.

Like diminished chords, augmented chords make good 'passing' chords between more important chords.

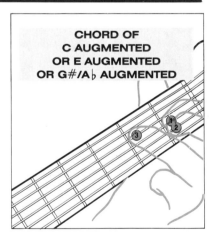

CHORD OF
C AUGMENTED
OR E AUGMENTED
OR G#/A♭ AUGMENTED

AUGMENTED SCALES						
C	D	E	F#	G#	B♭	C
C#	D#	F	G	A	B	C#

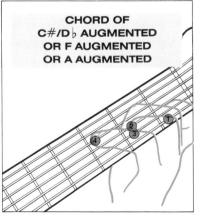

CHORD OF
C#/D♭ AUGMENTED
OR F AUGMENTED
OR A AUGMENTED

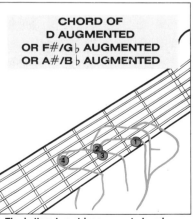

CHORD OF
D AUGMENTED
OR F#/G♭ AUGMENTED
OR A#/B♭ AUGMENTED

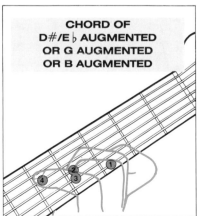

CHORD OF
D#/E♭ AUGMENTED
OR G AUGMENTED
OR B AUGMENTED

Each of these augmented chords is a four-note chord. The bottom two strings are not played.

BUYER'S GUIDE

Buying a guitar is a major purchase. Not only are they fairly expensive, but your guitar is vital to your progress as a musician. A second-rate instrument can hamper you, and may even put you off for life.

There are hundreds of electric guitars on the market. Most of them are good, but they may not be good for *you*. Different guitars suit different players with different styles and different needs.

For this reason, we've restricted our choice of recommeded guitars to a few good beginners' instruments, and concentrated on talking *about* electric guitars: their history, how they work, and what to look for when buying one.

After guitars, we take a look at amplifiers. Again, although we do recommend a few reliable start-up models, we concentrate on how amplifiers work, and how to decide what sort of amp is right for you.

Finally there's a section on effects pedals—important items for any rock guitarist. Here we outline the different types of pedal and what they can do for you, and recommend one good example of each.

Bear in mind, though, that these recommendations are just our opinion. You know far better what sort of guitar, amp and effects you're looking for, and it's always best to try them out for yourself in a shop and *then* make up your mind.

As with the Instruction Manual, the pages in this section are divided, so we have a general overview on guitars, amps or pedals at the top of each page, and other material below.

CONTENTS

GUITARS

ULTIMATELY ONLY you can decide which guitar is right for you. Of course, it is a good idea to listen to as many opinions as you can, but remember that to a large extent instrument appreciation is subjective. Your adviser's idea of a really great sound may not be what you have in mind at all.

In the same way, any player's opinion of a guitar is subject to certain physical considerations.

For example, nobody has exactly the same shape hands with the same capabilities. A person with large hands and long fingers will prefer a different guitar to someone with small hands and shorter fingers.

So we can't say which is the guitar for you. What we can do is tell you what to look out for, and where to begin.

FIRST, YOU need to find out as much as you can about the range of guitars available within your budget. There is actually quite a lot of research one can do before even entering a music shop.

Take a look at specialist magazines such as *Guitarist* (UK) or *Guitar Player* (USA), or the popular music papers. This is where most of the big guitar retailers advertise their stock and it's the quickest way to gain a broad idea of prices.

Whatever your price range there will be many different makes to consider. If you have the time, write to the distributors of the guitars which most interest you and ask them for a brochure and price list of their full range. The brochures have colour pictures and some details of design specifications of each guitar. For example, it will probably tell you the

number of frets, type and number of pick-ups, type of tremolo system, type of wood on the neck and body and the colours in which each guitar design is made.

This last point is useful because if you later find your local retailer has the exact guitar you would like but in a colour you dislike, you can ask your retailer to order one in the colour you want – if you can wait. Get your retailer to find out how long the delay will be – it might be six months!

Note, incidentally, that it is not possible for a member of the public to buy directly from the wholesaler/distributor. Most are helpful, however, and will give advice on prices, design specifications, availability in your area and spares. Your retailer can also find out these things for you.

Once you've done a little research at home, you can visit the music shops and

ELECTRIC GUITAR HISTORY

BEFORE WE talk about what is available in the market today, here is a brief account of the early history of the solid-body electric guitar.

It's useful to know a little about the subject because the companies who set the pace in the early days still have a marked influence today.

Up to the early 1920s guitarists either played into microphones or put microphones on or in their guitars. This was never ideal because there was always feedback or unwanted noise.

A device was therefore needed that could make loud music from the guitar strings only.

The first magnetic pick-up is thought to have been designed in America between 1920 and 1924 by Lloyd Loar, whilst working for Orville Gibson. This pick-up was not commercially available and when Loar left Gibson in 1924, the idea was dropped.

THE '30s

IN 1931 the Rowe-De Armand Company began manufacturing a magnetic pick-up that clipped onto the sound hole of a flat-top acoustic guitar.

The next ten years was a period of great experimentation with different designs of pick-up for use on various semi-acoustic resonator guitars (dobro-types) and Hawaiian steel guitars. The latter were the first commercially available guitars to be amplified totally electronically, rather than acoustically or semi-acoustically.

The most famous of these were developed by Adolph Rickenbacker in 1931. These were the A-22 and A-25, commonly known as the 'frying pan'. These were made of solid aluminum with a fairly basic but powerful pick-up.

The commercial success of this guitar prompted companies such as Gibson and Epiphone to produce similar designs.

THE '40s

THE FIRST solid body 'modern' electric guitar (as opposed to the Hawaiian Steel)

Two classic Gibsons. Carlos Santana (top) uses a Les Paul for the sustained notes that are his trademark. Angus Young of AC/DC gets a bluesy metal sound on his SG with customised lightning bolt fret markings.

start having fun. Try out as many guitars as you can. If you don't feel your playing is good enough, then make sure you go to a shop where the staff are willing to spend some time with you, without pushing you into a sale. Music shops are specialists, so there is usually not a problem.

If you only know two chords, then it will be better for you to just play those two chords on as many guitars as you can. You will notice the differences between them. Never be embarrassed by your lack of skill. We all had to learn once.

THE NECK
IN GENERAL, the quality control on guitars is good. Good, but not perfect, so hang onto your guarantee and make use of it if you need to. Normally, if you carry out a few basic common sense checks in the shop, you can be confident that nothing drastic will go wrong.

First, cast your eye over the paintwork. The paint and varnish should be immaculate on a new guitar.

Check that the neck is not twisted or bowed. If the neck is twisted, the strings will be too near the fretboard on one side of the neck and too far away on the other. The only simple way to check this is to look straight down the length of the neck towards the body so that the gaps between the frets disappear. Compare the straightness of each side. A twisted neck will reveal a dip on one side and a hump on the other.

This can be quite difficult to detect, so if you feel the neck *may* be twisted, get an expert to check it out. Actually, the chances are slim, especially with Japanese or American manufacturers.

The future? Ace Frehley (ex-Kiss) with the Roland G707 guitar synthesiser.

ELECTRIC GUITAR HISTORY

One of the most popular guitars of the '60s, and still widely used today: the Gibson SG.

was developed in 1947 by Paul Bigsby, with advice from guitarist Merle Travis.

This guitar was remarkably similar in appearance to the 'Broadcaster' invented nearby by Leo Fender and George Fullerton a year later.

The Broadcaster soon had its name changed to the Telecaster because Gretsch used the name Broadcaster on their drums and banjoes. The Telecaster was the first solid wood-bodied electric guitar to achieve economic and musical success.

THE '50s
ON THE advice of top player Les Paul, the Gibson company followed the trend for solids and produced the first Les Paul in 1952. There have since been numerous versions of Les Paul guitars made by Gibson – and even more copies.

The very first Les Pauls featured the single cutaway top, two tone and two volume controls and a three-way toggle pick-up selector switch with two single coil pick-ups.

The more sensitive and powerful humbucking pick-ups were invented by Seth Lover and Ted McCarthy for Gibson in 1956 and were added to the Gold Top Standard in 1957.

In 1956 in response to flagging sales the Flying V, the Explorer and the Moderne were introduced. The Flying V is still made by Gibson today. The Explorer was reissued as a limited edition in 1976 but is quite rare, although the shape has been copied by several companies.

Two classic Fender guitars—both well-worn personal favourites. Andy Summers (left) with the Telecaster whose trebly edge helps his reggaefied sound, and Stevie Ray Vaughan with his Stratocaster, flexible enough to take on roughhouse R&B and dramatic slow blues.

GUITARS

Heavy metal guitarists just love the attacking design of the Flying V: KK Downing of Judas Priest (right) plays a Hamer copy, while Rudolf Schenker of The Scorpions prefers a Gibson original.

The neck of a guitar is rarely dead straight. More often there is a slight dip so that the headstock bends fowards.

If the neck bends the other way, the strings will buzz against the frets. In this case, if the curve is not too great, it can be adjusted by use of the adjustable truss rod in the neck. Once again, this should really be done by an expert, but it is not a serious problem, and most retailers can take care of it on the premises.

Unfortunately neck problems are not confined to cheap guitars. They are usually caused by sudden changes in temperature. Sometimes a poor piece of wood may have been used.

Some guitars suffer from a lack of care in the finishing process. Sometimes the frets overlap the neck, which can make playing quite painful. Older instruments

ELECTRIC GUITAR HISTORY

In 1959/60 the SG (solid guitar) range was introduced to replace the Les Pauls. These had sharp double cutaways.

In the '50s Fender were equally active and innovative. In .1954 the Stratocaster was developed by Fred Tavares and Leo Fender.

It was the first guitar with three pick-ups. These were single coil and were wired to a three-way switch.

Later, guitarists discovered that the switch could be balanced between two positions to give an 'out of phase' sound. This proved so popular that Fender soon designed a five-way switch.

The Stratocaster was also the first guitar to have a double cutaway body and a tremolo unit built into a special 'floating' bridge design.

The Stratocaster has changed little over the years. It can now be obtained in a wide variety of colours, with a variety of pick-up combinations including hum-buckers.

Like Gibson, Fender experimented with different shapes such as the Jaguar, Mustang and Musicmaster, but Tele-casters, Stratocasters, Les Pauls and SG's were the guitars which set the standards in solid guitar design.

TODAY

EVEN TODAY these four types of guitar, particularly the Stratocaster and Les Paul, are the most copied of all guitars.

Most copies are considerably cheaper, and some are simply appalling. A few of the best copies are reviewed later in this section.

Manufacturing in the Far East has become increasingly popular because it keeps costs down.

For example, Gibson's Epiphones, Fender's Squiers, Vox and Washburn are all manufactured in Japan.

Actual Japanese companies tend to be best known for their copies, some of which are excellent. Many also make their own original guitars, many of which are of a high standard.

can also suffer from protruding frets due to slight shrinkage of the wood.

This is easily rectified by an expert. It should not be attempted by an amateur.

THE ACTION

YOU MAY find that on one or two of the frets you hear a rattling noise. Provided that the neck is not bowed or twisted, you've probably got one or two frets higher than the others. This causes 'fret-buzz', coming from a high fret in front of the fret played. This will need to be levelled with a fine file by an expert.

Fret-buzz can also be found on a guitar if the action (distance between the string and fingerboard) is too low.

The higher the action, the more pressure a player has to exert on the string for it to make contact with the fingerboard. For this reason, most lead guitarists like

the action to be as low as possible without fret-buzz, because it enables them to play faster. Rhythm players often prefer a slightly higher action because fret-buzz is more likely when strumming and a higher action gives you more volume. It's really a matter for you to decide for yourself.

If a guitar has a good action, it will be as easy to play at the twelfth fret as the first.

If you are considering buying a guitar but are not totally happy with its action, then you should discuss it in the shop. Many inexperienced players buy a new guitar with an unsatisfactory action and become discouraged with their playing, not realising that a guitar can be adjusted.

All competitive guitars these days are fitted with adjustable bridges, but few leave the factory with their action set to the optimum level.

THE ELECTRICS

THE NEXT item to check is the guitar's electrics. At the same time you can introduce yourself to the confusing world of pick-ups.

Acutally the subject is more straight-forward than most people imagine. All pick-ups are transducers, that is they convert forms of physical energy into electrical energy. A vibrating guitar string produces an energy which is converted by the pick-ups into an alternating current which is fed to an amplifier. The amplifier then magnifies the pulses which are transformed into sound waves by the loudspeaker.

Electric guitars have between one and three pick-ups and usually a selector switch which enables a player to use a different combination of pick-ups accord- ▶

With the advent of solid guitars, manufacturers realised they could make them any shape at all . . . and they did! Here are a few of the more bizarre shapes that have appeared over the years. Clockwise from top left:

● Original weird guitar player Bo Diddley with box-shaped guitar made specially for him by Gretsch.
● Frank Zappa strolling though London's Hyde Park in the '70s with a pencil-thin Vox guitar.
● Eric Bloom of Blue Oyster Cult with his custom-built guitar in the shape of the band's logo, alongside lead guitarist Buck Dharma.
● Rick Nielsen of Cheap Trick does a double-take with his double-neck guitar built in his own image.
● Randy Piper (then with WASP) gets his BC Rich guitar in a twist.
● Just to show that bass players can customise their instruments, Nikki Sixx of Motley Crue gives his Hamer the popular dripping blood look, also used by Chris Holmes of WASP.
● And finally, a man who really likes his Jack Daniels—Van Halen bassist Michael Anthony with matching guitar and bottle.

GUITARS

ing to what kind of sound is required. For example, the lead pick-up (which is usually situated nearest the bridge) emphasises the treble frequencies.

There are two main types of pick-up: the single coil, and the twin coil or hum-bucker.

The single coil, at its most basic, consists of a bar magnet with very thin copper wire wrapped around it several thousand times, so that it forms an electrical coil. The magnet generates a magnetic field. Every time a string vibrates, the shape of the magnetic field is altered. This generates pulses of electrical energy in the coil which travel to the amplifier in the form of alternating current.

Some of these magnets a 'fin' which extends one pole of the magnetic field, taking it closer to the strings.

The most famous type of single coil pick-up is that associated with Fender Stratocasters and Telecasters. These contain six individual magnetic pole pieces, the height of each slightly staggered to equalise the volume of the thicker bass and thinner treble strings. These pick-ups produce a distinctive, clear 'trebly' sound.

The main disadvantage of single coils is that they tend to 'hum' when placed near other electrical equipment.

Humbucking pick-ups prevent this by having two coils instead of one, out of phase with each other, so that the hum is cancelled out. However, this design reduces the responsiveness to high frequencies (treble) and produces a more mellow and 'fatter' sound, so many rock

The Fender Stratocaster—probably the most used guitar in rock—with its three single coil pick-ups.

PICK-UPS

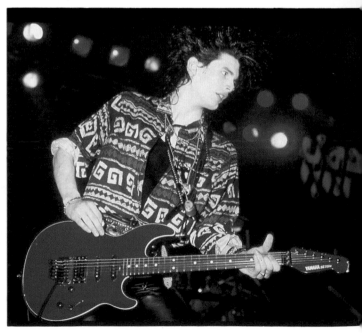

The Gibson Les Paul—probably the second most used guitar in rock—with its two twin coil pick-ups.

Pick-ups can vary immensely, depending on what sound you prefer. Susanna Hoffs of The Bangles (far left) plays a Rickenbacker with three humbuckers. Andy Taylor (above left) uses a Yamaha with two humbuckers with their casings removed: you can see why humbuckers are also known as twin coil pick-ups. Lou Reed (above) prefers three single coil pick-ups, while Charlie Sexton (below left) has a mix of one humbucker and two single coils on his Yamaha.

Right: Brian May of Queen shows off his famous self-built guitar, which is now copied fairly accurately by Guild using DiMazio pick-ups. May's guitar has a very distinctive thick sound with lots of sustain and a treble which can really cut through on lead work. You'll notice that he plays with a coin—an old silver sixpence—instead of a plectrum, because it gives a sharper attack on the strings.

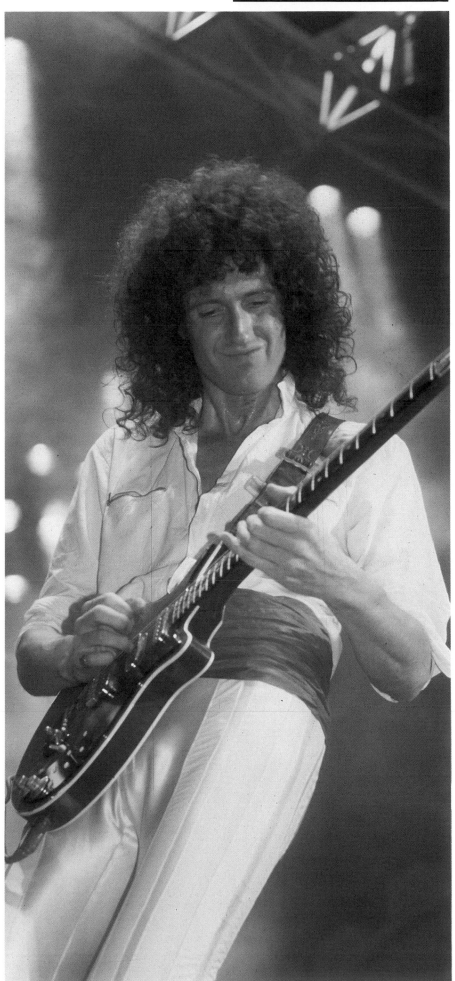

GUITARS

guitarists prefer single coils.

All this will become apparent if you simply try out a few guitars with these different types of pick-up in a music shop. Remember to play them through the same amplifier with the same settings. Always take time in the shop to experiment with the pick-up selector switch to discover exactly what the tonal range of the guitar is.

To check if a pick-up is working, all you need to do is tap it lightly with something metallic. If you can hear the tapping sound through the speaker, it's working.

If you are in any doubt about a pick-up, get it checked in the shop before you buy it. It is rare for a new guitar to have a serious electrical problem. Any fault is likely to be due to careless soldering or dust and can easily be fixed.

PRICES

THE PRICES of guitars vary from the cost of a pair of shoes to the price of a car. Generally, the more you pay, the better quality your guitar will be. The market is too competitive for it to be any other way.

However, this competitiveness has raised standards across the board, resulting in some of the cheaper guitars being surprisingly good. So what increases the price of a guitar?

APPEARANCE

THE OVERALL appearance and finish on a guitar will make a considerable difference to its price. An expensive guitar should have no visible flaws in the paintwork or varnish and there should be no sinking of lacquer into the wood grain.

Most guitars have a hardwood fingerboard – ebony, rosewood or maple. Lower quality guitars sometimes have fingerboards of mahogany or plywood which have been stained black or veneered to look like the real thing. Whether the inlays on the fretboard are plastic or pearl will also affect price.

Even an inexperienced eye can usually tell by looking at a guitar if it has been designed with care and imagination by craftsmen who consider the player's needs. If not, this will certainly become apparent on playing it. Good guitars are described by reviewers as having 'great playability' and 'character'.

MACHINE HEADS

THERE SHOULD always be top quality machine heads on an expensive guitar. In other words, they should be pleasing to look at and reliable. A guitar should not

TREMOLOS

Masters of tremolo: Jimi Hendrix (left) bent the arm on his Stratocaster so that he could touch the strings with it for 'slide' effects (he also used his rings). Eddie Van Halen uses a Floyd Rose tremolo on a Kramer guitar fitted with just one Gibson humbucker pick-up—and started a trend for matching stripes and strides.

have to be tuned every five minutes.

The machine heads should turn smoothly without being too loose or too tight. Good quality machine heads are self-lubricating and are designed to last years without wearing out. Two famous names to look out for are Grover and Schaller, though they are by no means the only good makers.

Many machine heads have a tightening screw in the middle, which adjusts the tension and feel of the head in use.

TREMOLO SYSTEMS

IF YOUR playing style does not require a tremolo arm, then you would be well advised to buy a guitar without one or with one that can be detached easily, because they can really get in the way.

Some companies are now offering them as an option and charge quite a lot more for them. Cheap tremolo systems can be more trouble than they are worth.

The traditional problem with tremolos was that they put the guitar out of tune. Recent designs have overcome this by adding locking nuts which keep the strings in a totally stable position after basic tuning. Fine tuners are then placed on the bridge for minor adjustments.

You should seriously consider whether, for you, the tremolo system justifies the extra expense. If you do decide it is essential, then look for one which is neither stiff nor squeaky and returns easily to an inactive position. Also, if you choose a locking nut system, consider how easily it can be locked and unlocked.

Two big established names to look out for are Fender and Kahler. Fender ▶

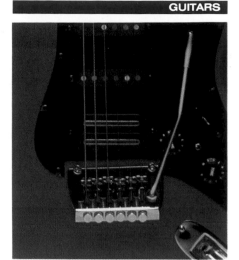

The Marlin K34 (reviewed below) has a sophisticated locking nut tremolo system.

PRICES AND quality in the guitar business vary considerably. There are bad buys and good value items at both ends of the market. This is not a comprehensive list but it should give you a few reliable models within your price bracket, which you can go and try out yourself. The four price groups do not take into account special discount or sale prices.

Low price up to £150 ($225).
Low-mid price £150–£300 ($225–$450).
Mid-high price £300–£500 ($450–$750)
High price £500–£700 ($750–$1000).

LOW PRICE

HOHNER SE604
EXTRA THICK contoured laminated birch body. Maple neck with rosewood fingerboard. Adjustable truss rod. 22 nickel silver frets. Three (very powerful for the money) single coil pick-ups. One volume control, two tone controls and a five-way selector switch for different combinations of pick-ups. Chrome plated hardware, including tremolo. White scratch plate. Body available in tobacco sunburst, white, black, cream, ice blue and pink. An ideal beginner's guitar.

YAHAMA RGX 110
LIGHTWEIGHT LAMINATED basswood body. Detachable mahogany neck. Adjustable truss rod. 24 nickel silver frets. One ferrite coiled pick-up. One volume, one tone conrol. Basic tremolo arm. Individual machine heads. Standard synchronized bridge. Black scratch plate. Body colours available: white, red, black. The RGX 110 is featured throughout *Play Rock Guitar*. We liked the easy action and lightweight 'feel' and would recommend it as a good first electric guitar.

MARLIN K34
STRATOCASTER SHAPE body with a gloss finish maple neck and a rosewood finger-board and colour matched headstock. All have two single coil pick-ups with a twin blade humbucker at the bridge with a coil tap (which gives a three single coil set-up). A sophisticated locking tremolo system with fine tuners and locking nut – very good for the price: see close-up picture at top of the page. Available in seven metallic finishes with black scratch plates.

GUITARS

Midge Ure of Ultravox with his favourite guitar, a Yamaha AE2000 semi-acoustic.

tremolos can be found on many of the guitars in their range, whilst Kahlers can be bought separately.

BRIDGE

ALL GOOD quality bridges should be capable of adjusting both string height and string length, both of which affect the intonation of a guitar.

Some expensive bridges (with or without tremolo) have fine tuners which enable you to make very precise adjustments of pitch. The better the guitar, the more sense there is in having fine tuners because the intonation is good and stable anyway.

ELECTRICAL CIRCUITRY

WE'VE ALREADY discussed what pick-ups are, how to check if they actually work, and the two main types – single coil and humbucker. So we can now consider

how they vary in quality.

If you look through a few brochures you'll soon discover that many manufacturers claim their pick-ups are hot. This does not mean they have been stolen but rather that they are loud, because they generate a high voltage output. The two main factors to affect the voltage output are the strength of the magnet and the number of turns of wire around the coil. Unfortunately, an increased number of turns of wire also filters out much of the treble (high) frequencies.

Pick-ups made of poor quality materials which generate a low output or are slow in responding will be cheaper than the really hot type.

Cheap guitars can often be vastly improved if the pick-ups are replaced. This has become a very popular practice

GUITAR GUIDE

LOW–MID PRICE

TOKAI TST 50
A CONTOURED alder body with three single coil pick-ups and a five-way selector switch. Comes with either a maple or rosewood neck in 1964 or 1958 vintage models. A traditional tremolo. A high quality Fender copy with an authentic sound – some people actually prefer it to the original. Available in a wide range of colours.

SQUIER TELECASTER
A GOOD basic guitar with two single coil pick-ups with one volume and one tone switch with a three-way selector. A trebly sound is easily obtainable. The fretboard is maple and the body is available in blond and black. A very comfortable guitar to play, and it gives a good variety of sounds.

ARIA PRO II RS-CAT 3K
AN INTERESTING and original shaped guitar, with a neck reminiscent of a Gibson. It has two single coil pick-ups and one humbucker plus a coil tap and a five-way selector switch. It also has one tone and one volume control. A Kahler locking tremolo system. Available in black, white and candy apple red. Well made.

YAHAMA RGX 211
AS THE RGX 110, but with sophisticated vibrato system incorporated in bridge, which also has individual 'fine-tuning' controls. Two ferrite coiled pick-ups, with twin blade humbucker at rear. Additional tone control and pick-up selector switch. Available in red, white or black.

This has become a very popular practice over the last few years and quite an industry has grown up around it. Names such as Seymour Duncan, Di Marzio, Schechter, EMG are firmly established. These all make a wide variety of pick-ups; in general they will either be loud or will boost a particular frequency range.

Selector switches enable you to play with different combinations of pick-ups. The more selections you have, the more sounds you can get.

Many guitars today are being fitted with coil taps. These have the effect of cutting off one half of a humbucker to give it the qualities of a single coil. Coil taps are often found on guitars with a pick-up configuration of two single coils and one humbucker. This gives you the advantages of both types of pick-up.

All the circuitry in guitars has traditionally been passive—in other words, it changes the sound by cutting things out. However, for more money you can now have some active circuitry. This means you can have a device which increases the volume and tonal output of the signal from your guitar before it reaches the amplifier. It is, in fact, a pre-amp.

This has several advantages. For a start, you can obtain a consistently high output from a guitar which may have unresponsive pick-ups. The high signal level also reduces any noise interference in your guitar lead, and makes it easier to get a distorted sound or sustain.

The more complicated the circuitry in your guitar, the higher the quality and the more variety of sound and tone available. It also costs more.

Guitar gonzo Rick Nielsen of Cheap Trick plays just four from his huge collection of guitars.

GUITAR GUIDE

MID–HIGH PRICE

WESTONE PANTERA X300
A SOLID maple body with a Canadian hard wood maple neck and a rosewood fingerboard. A volume switch with a push/pull coil tap and five-way pick-up selector. It features a Bendmaster FT fine tune tremolo (with a carbon graphite locking nut). The hardware is all black. Body available in pearl pink, candy red and pearl white. Good sustain – a real rock guitar.

IBANEZ RG 525
A BASSWOOD body (which is lighter than average) with a maple neck and rosewood fingerboard. The fingerboard has an oil finish which makes it extra smooth. It has 24 frets and two powerful humbuckers. The hardware is white and gold or black. Available in gun metallic, pearl or silver. It's got class.

HIGH PRICE

GIBSON LES PAUL STANDARD
A MAPLE and mahogany body with a mahogany neck and rosewood fingerboard. The hardware is chrome. There are two 'Patent Applied For' humbucking pick-ups with separate volume and tone controls. A tune-o-matic bridge and stop bar. One of the best.

FENDER CONTEMPORARY STRATOCASTER DE LUXE 275700
TWO SINGLE coil pick-ups and one humbucker. A five-way selector switch plus a coil tap. One volume and one TBX (active) tone control. The new System III tremolo. Available in Lake Placid Blue, Metallic Pewter. Metallic Frost White, Burgundy Mist and Emerald Mist. The guitar that most people would like to own.

Westone Pantera X300

Gibson Les Paul Standard

AMPLIFIERS

CHOOSING AN amplifier is similar to choosing a guitar, in that you have to decide for yourself the kind of sounds you like best and the requirements of your ideal product.

Once again, there are good and bad value for money items throughout the price spectrum, so read as many brochures as you can and then go along to your retailer and try out as many different types as you can.

If this is a first-time experience for you, then I suggest you try some from all price brackets to start with. Even if you can't afford the expensive ones, it should help to give you an overall picture.

If you can, try them all out with the same guitar. Ideally this would be your own or one very similar to it. A good retailer shouldn't object to you bringing your own guitar along. By doing this, you will know exactly what to expect from the amplifier when you take it home and there will be no unpleasant surprises.

A few other points to consider. How heavy is it? How easy is it to carry? Will it fit into the back of your car? Simple questions, but if you are gigging or even practising with a friend on the other side of town, they could become surprisingly important.

This is one reason why combos have become more important than stacks. Combos combine the amplifier and the speaker in one unit. Stack systems have a separate amplifier and speaker cabinets.

Can the shop support its sales with service? Do they have a resident amplifier repairer? If not, can they send it away and how long will the average repair take? Will you be offered a replacement during repair?

When treated correctly, the average transistor amplifier will last several years before it requires attention. It is, however, better to know where you stand from the outset.

If you do not know much about amplifiers, the quickest way to find out what a control does is to play with each dial at '0' and then 'full'. If it is a fairly small amplifier, you could turn the volume up to full to check the speaker is working properly.

You should also decide if the amount of background noise is acceptable, particularly at low volume. How noisy is it when the treble dial is on 'full'? Some amplifiers are noisier than others. If you normally play with a distortion pedal, any background noises will bother you less.

AMPLIFIER GUIDE

HERE ARE some amplifiers available today which represent good value for money. This is not a comprehensive list; you could also look out for such names as Music Man, Sunn, Mesa Boogie, Ampeg. Many players prefer older amplifiers such as Marshall, Orange and Sound City. The amps we've selected range from about £65 ($100) for the Ross Fame Practice Amp, to around £230 ($350) for the H.H. L50 and Laney Linebacker, with one more expensive product – the Session S.G.75 at around £350 (£500) – thrown in.

The Squier 15: flexible and inexpensive.

The Peavey Backstage Plus: later model reviewed.

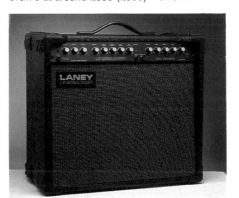

The good value Laney Linebacker: 100-watt model.

5–20 WATTS

ROSS FAME 10 PRACTICE AMPLIFIER
THIS IS a single channel ten-watt practice amplifier with channel and master volume controls. It has tone controls for bass, middle and treble. It also has a 'tube booster' overdrive switch for extra volume and distortion, and a headphone and line out socket for recording purposes.

MARSHALL 12 WATT PRACTICE COMBO MODEL 5005
THIS has two inputs, gain, volume, treble, middle and bass controls. The two inputs have different sensitivities when used in conjunction with the gain and volume controls: this will give you a wide range of sounds. The high input socket should give you a good sustain.

SQUIER 15
THIS 15-WATT amplifier has a single input with volume, gain and master volume which enables you to achieve a wide range of clean and distorted sounds. The treble, middle and bass controls are 'active', which gives you much more tonal control. This also has a headphone jack and looks very attractive.

30–50 WATTS

35 WATT PEAVEY BACKSTAGE PLUS
THIS IS a very sophisticated little amplifier with one input. A variety of levels of overdrive and distortion are attainable. It has a good tonal range with a three band graphic equaliser with pre-set 'bright' (treble) and 'thick' (mid-range) sounds. The reverb is excellent. It also has a headphone jack and an optional dual button footswitch for reverb and saturation (which imitates the distorted sound of a heavily driven valve amp).

H.H. L50 COMBO
THIS HAS two channels with bass, middle and treble controls. Channel one is designed to deliver a clean sound and features a 'bright' switch on the gain control which you pull out to boost the treble frequencies. Channel two is designed for heavy rock and sustain sounds. It has a distortion control with a 'heavy' facility for a heavy metal sound and a 'smooth' control on the gain for smoothing the high frequency edge.

You can change channels by using a foot switch which is available as an optional extra. There is good reverb and headphone and line output sockets.

65–100 WATTS

LANEY LINEBACKER 65R
THIS HAS two channels with a foot switch to select channels. Channel one is clean but can be overdriven for distortion; channel two has a pull-boost for wider overdriven sounds. It has full tone and gain controls for each channel and a master volume. It also has a presence dial, headphone and D.I. sockets.

SESSION S.G. 75 (2 × 12")
THIS HAS two foot switchable channels for clean or distorted sound. Channel A has one gain switch which sets the amount of overdrive and sustain and another gain switch for volume. Channel B is the clean channel which has one gain control.

It has treble, middle and bass controls, plus a filter switch which alters the quality of sustain. It also has reverb, headphone and effects send and return sockets.

Try and have a clear idea on how many inputs you need. If you wish to sing through the amplifier whilst playing, then two inputs are essential. Do check that both inputs will work together and also that the second input does not 'steal' too much volume from the primary one. It is also worth considering whether you need a headphone socket.

Finally, does the amplifier sound how you want it to? Can you make subtle changes of tone and volume as well as drastic ones? Let's look at ways in which amplifiers vary their sound and other capabilities.

VALVE OR TRANSISTOR

MOST PROFESSIONAL guitarists prefer valve (tube) amplifiers to transistor (solid state) amplifiers.

The transistor adds little to the sound being produced by your guitar, and if you overdrive the amplifier to get distortion you will hear some unpleasant harmonics. In contrast, a valve amplifier adds depth to the sound and when overdriven produces harmonics which are pleasing to the ear.

Valve amplifiers tend to be more powerful and more pleasing, but they are more expensive, less compact and need replacement parts, usually the valve itself, more often. If you are just beginning your playing career, the subtle differences in sound will probably matter less to you than the somewhat less subtle differences in price and so a reliable transistor amplifier would be a better choice for you. Some transistor amplifiers today even have circuits which imitate valve sound.

POWER

THE BEST and most common method of rating the power of an amplifier is RMS (Route Mean Square). This tells you the sustained power load that the amplifier can handle at various frequencies.

Practice amplifiers are the smallest and least powerful of amplifiers and as the name suggests, are meant for use at home or backstage.

Most have fairly rudimentary controls, because they are not meant for performance. It also keeps the price down so that people can afford to buy a performance amplifier as well.

If you are just starting out and do not plan on giving any concerts for a while, you may want to consider a practice amplifier. There are many makes. They tend to be rated at between 5 and 20 ▶

Extremes of amplification: Paul Weller (inset) in his Jam days, revisiting the '60s with a Gretsch guitar and Vox AC30—the original good value amp—and Ritchie Blackmore with a powerful Marshall stack, probably the most used amps in rock over the past twenty years.

AMPLIFIERS

watts RMS. As with all amplifiers, they are not meant to be played with the volume on full and will probably distort if you do.

Mr or Ms Average will have an amplifier rated somewhere between 30 and 65 watts. These are ideal for use in school halls, bars and other smallish venues.

It may be a few years before you are doing gigs that require 100 watts or more of power. Having an over-powerful amplifier can be as much of a problem as having one that is under-powered because you may not be able to overdrive it at a sensible volume.

CONTROLS

AT THE most basic level you will have a volume, bass and treble dial. These are essential and speak for themselves. Any dials marked 'gain' will also affect the volume. Amplifiers with 'gain' also have a

master volume dial. A clever combination of these two can give you overdrive and distortion.

You will be paying extra for any control other than volume, bass, middle and treble so be wary of gimmicks and decide if you will use them regularly.

The most popular and useful of extras is reverb. If you are thinking of singing through your amplifier, it's an essential control.

Without reverb the sound is flat. With reverb the tone has an echoey quality, as if the instrument is being played in a church or large hall. The more reverb you have, the larger the hall appears to be. As with most amplifier controls, it is a subtle effect whose benefits can be felt long before the dial reaches '10' or 'full'.

Amplifiers look robust but they should

be treated with respect and always put down gently – particularly amplifiers containing a reverb unit. This device is often mechanical rather than electronic, using the vibrations of a delicate metal spring to create the echo effect.

Other popular features on amplifiers are Presence, Tremolo and Chorus. The Presence switch enhances the treble and middle frequencies; the Tremolo produces a vibrato-like effect by emitting regular changes in volume; the Chorus gives you a much fuller sound and can make it seem as if several guitarists are playing at one time.

Foot switches are another useful extra which allow you to operate amplifier effects such as reverb, distortion, chorus, without having to run back to the amplifier mid-solo to turn them on or off.

PEDAL GUIDE

DISTORTION/OVERDRIVE

PROBABLY THE most popular pedal of all. The kind of distortion you can obtain varies enormously from smooth and fuzzy to coarse and rough. If you want to play heavy metal, some kind of distortion is essential.

Many distortion pedals work by electronically emitting a square sound wave at the same frequency as the input from the guitar. The two are then blended together. The proportion of square wave to normal sound is then adjusted by a dial labelled distortion – the more square wave you have, the more distorted it will sound.

DOD AMERICAN METAL FX56
THIS HAS three controls:
  Level adjusts the volume.
  Presence produces bright high frequencies and fat low ones.
  Distortion adjusts the amount of distortion.

PHASING AND FLANGING

A PHASER works by splitting the sound signal which comes from the guitar pick-up into two. The two sound signals are then put out of phase with each other. This process is known as phase shifting, and is the basis of both phasing and flanging.

The signals are put out of phase by altering

the speed of one signal, this affects the pitch. The overall result if you play a chord is a rich sound which seems to bend up and down.

BOSS HF 2 FLANGER PEDAL
THIS HAS four controls:
  Manual sets the delay time.
  Depth adjusts the sweep range – how far the sounds go 'out of phase'.
  Rate determines the sweep speed.
  Resonance controls the amount of feedback.
  This unit has FET electronic switching. The flanging effect is only applied to harmonics and does not affect the note itself. This should make the effect extra clear and light.

NOISE GATES

NOISE GATES cut out background noise and are essential for serious recording. If you use several pedals it is useful to install a noise gate as the last pedal before the amplifier.

We would recommend the Korg KNG-101 noise gate. It has three controls, most important being the Release Time. This affects the speed with which the noise gate opens and closes. A fast release could create a more punchy sound by cutting the decay (the time it takes for a sound to fade), giving brief clipped notes.

CHORUS

CHORUS EFFECTS are also arrived at through phase shifting, which can create delay and changes of pitch. Slight changes in both can make one instrument sound like several playing in near unison – known as chorus. This gives a very full effect when strumming.

ARION SCH-1 STEREO CHORUS
THIS HAS three controls:
  Rate varies the intensity.
  Depth controls the sweep width.
  Tone boosts the treble.
  Many chorus pedals have a poor high frequency but that this has a tone control which will boost high frequencies when needed.

DELAY/SAMPLING

DELAY FOOT pedals create delay digitally. This is a very versatile effect. It is possible to obtain resonant, echoey sounds as with reverb, but you can also gain an audible echo. The volume and pitch of this echo can be adjusted, as can delay time between echoes.

The echo is a digital recording, held temporarily in the machine's memory. Many delay pedals take this one step further with a 'hold' facility which enables them to record or 'sample' a riff or chord. It is then possible to play over the top of the sample.

EFFECTS PEDALS give guitarists far more tonal freedom than any amplifier could produce by itself. They are small, compact units and most run on one nine-volt battery or an A.C. adaptor.

As with all equipment, the price range is considerable – from about £30 ($50) to £100 ($150) – and pedals which are capable of creating more than one effect cost almost double. But your sound can only be as good as the worst piece of equipment, so make sure your pedals are as good as your guitar and amplifier.

A quality pedal should be robust and hard wearing. It should have some kind of battery power indicator. The dials should be easy to read and use.

A more expensive pedal should have a wide range of sounds available, from subtle to extreme: you should not have to turn the dial halfway around before you notice a change. The tone of the effect should also be better.

Many pedals are now being made with a stereo capability which means you can use the effect whilst playing through two amplifiers. Some also have a device built in which eliminates the 'click' noises when they are turned on and off – look out for FET switching.

Below are some of the most popular types of pedal. There is a brief technical explanation for each one and we have attempted to describe the sound they produce. But the best thing is to visit a music shop and try them all out – you will soon recognise the sounds that your favourite professional guitarists use, and you may be pleasantly surprised by what they can do for your own playing.

Jimi Hendrix: the man who turned using foot pedals into an art form.

ARIA DDX10
THIS HAS five controls:

Delay Level affects the volume of the delay. When set on maximum, the echo level is the same as the original. Turn it down and the echo goes down.

Feedback adjusts the speed at which the signal is repeated.

Delay Time is a fine tuner for the delay time used in conjunction with range.

Range has four pre-set delay ranges which govern how pronounced the echo effect is.

Hold has three positions: off, unlatched and latched. When on 'off' the foot pedal switches delay on or off. When on 'unlatched', the signal will be repeated as long as the foot is held down, then lost. When on 'latched', the delay signal is stored in the memory and repeated indefinitely once the pedal is tapped lightly.

This pedal has an LED monitor which shows if the effect is on, when the memory function is in operation and the battery power level. It also has FET switching.

It is also possible to 'layer' the sound. This means you can place an additional phrase in the memory over signals which it already holds, and in effect have three guitars playing at once.

WAH WAH

THIS DEVICE emphasises a specific band of frequencies. Any musical note has both high and low frequencies. The movement of the pedal control moves the band of frequencies up or down the audio spectrum, so the same note can sound 'fat' or 'thin'.

A very popular pedal in the late '60s, the most famous is the Cry Baby which is still much sought after today. Its most famous user was Jimi Hendrix.

A wide variety of sounds can be achieved.

The Cry Baby wah wah pedal.

COMPRESSORS/LIMITERS

COMPRESSORS AND limiters are used to reduce the dynamic range of a sound signal before it reaches a loudspeaker. An unsubtle form of manual compression would be to pull down a fader control during loud passages in a studio. The advantage of electronic devices is that they respond much quicker than the human ear to variations in volume.

Limiters are used in studios or in situations where excessive volume could damage the human ear, loudspeakers or other equipment. They enable you to set a maximum volume threshold so that at high volumes the output level remains constant.

Compressors work along a similar principle. Instead of altering gain to preserve a fixed output level, the compressor changes the amplifier's ratio. For example, before compression, the ratio is 1:1. This means that if the input voltage rises by one volt (of volume), the output voltage rises by one volt. If a compressor changes the ratio to 2:1, the output voltage would only rise by half a volt for each one volt rise in input.

In terms of playing, compressors help sustain without distortion and reduce differences in volume between strings, low and high notes, harmonics and real notes. It also gives a very 'gutsy' rhythmic sound.

BOSS CS-3
THIS HAS four controls:

Sustain Control determines the sustain time. The further it is rotated clockwise, the longer the sustain time. The further it is rotated counterclockwise, the stronger the compression – shorter sustain but less distortion. This allows the pedal to act as a limiter.

Tone Control gives a variety of tone colours on the effect sound.

Attack Control determines the time the compressor takes to react to any excessive volume, so that even notes of a quick passage can be compressed.

Level Control adjusts the volume balance between the effect and normal signals.

This also has FET switching and easy battery withdrawal.

GUITAR MAINTENANCE

STRINGING THE GUITAR

On an acoustic guitar, insert the ball end of the string into the recess on the bridge. Replace the peg.

Some electric guitars have a set of holes at the back of the body. Thread the string through the hole.

Other electric guitars have a fixing point at the bridge. Again, you simply thread the string through the hole.

Pull the string taut and thread it through the hole in the machine head. Turn the tuner handle away from you.

Make sure the string has enough overlap to get a firm grip on the machine head. Route the string through the grooves on the nut.

Tighten slowly, particularly the top three strings which are more liable to snap. Tie the end of each string in a loop or trim it off neatly.

ELECTRIC GUITAR BRIDGE

MOST ELECTRIC guitars have a two-way adjustable bridge. The example used here—a Fender Telecaster—has a system common to many models.

Using a small screwdriver, turn each horizontal screw at the end of the bridge, until the note at the 12th fret is the same as the note on the open string, but one octave higher. The 12th fret should be exactly halfway between the nut and the saddle (the metal groove on the bridge where the string sits).

EACH STRING has an individual screw which raises or lowers the string. If you set the action too low, you will get the dreaded fret buzz. But don't over-adjust, because that will make your guitar more difficult to play.

If you are new to electric guitar technology, the best advice is to get advice. Guitars are like cars when it comes to maintenance. The better prepared they are, the better the service they will provide.

TRUSS ROD

THE TRUSS rod is a relatively modern development of guitar technology. Located in the neck, it's an adjustable metal bar which can literally straighten out the little kinks and twists which may develop due to atmospheric conditions, or lack of care and attention.

Fiddling with the truss rod is no job for a beginner. Take professional advice, and only get involved when you feel confident.

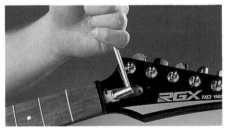

Most modern electric guitars are fitted with a truss rod, which adjusts the neck by means of the key provided. Don't try it unless you're sure of what you're doing.

ACOUSTIC GUITAR BRIDGE

IF YOUR guitar has a separate tailpiece and movable bridge, your adjustment is limited to pitch. In other words, you can move the bridge along the body in order to establish the point where the note on the 12th fret is exactly one octave above the note on the open string.

The fixed bridge is more common. It requires little or no attention. Occasionally, however, this type of bridge may have a pair of small rollers at the sides of the bridge, to raise or lower the strings.

This arrangement is also found on some electric guitars.

Some acoustic guitars have a similar set-up to their electric brothers. Others have an adjusting screw at the base of the neck.

WHO'S WHO

From legends like Hendrix to little-known session stars such as Tommy Tedesco, from rock and roll veterans like Link Wray to tomorrow's guitar heroes such as Yngwie Malmsteen, these are the performers who've made the guitar rock's greatest instrument.

Listening is an important part of learning any instrument. Take note of the work of any of the artists in this section: there's a lot that you can pick up, as long as you don't copy them too closely. Listen, learn, then do your own thing.

CONTENTS

STUART ADAMSON

AN ANGLO-SCOTTISH band, Big Country produces a sound which evokes rugged romanticism and the wide open spaces. The group's trademark is the plangent, ringing dual lead of founder, frontman and songwriter Stuart Adamson and his colleague Bruce Watson.

Raised in Fife, on the east coast of Scotland, Adamson is a refugee from late '70s punk. He was a member of The Skids – one of the first groups to try to fuse punk with glamour, art and rock power, as epitomised now by Simple Minds. But Adamson and singer Richard Jobson couldn't make it work, and Adamson left to form Big Country as a deliberate return to straightforward, guitar-based rock.

The band played its first gig in Adamson's home town of Dunfermline in 1982. Their fiery sound – not a million miles removed from Thin Lizzy's – soon brought them success with singles such as 'In A Big Country' and 'Look Away' from their albums 'The Crossing', 'Steeltown' and 'The Seer'.

Onstage, Big Country's passionate, full-blooded delivery, coupled with the anthem-like quality of Adamson's songs, raises a fervent, fiercely partisan atmosphere amongst its followers. However, the band are finding it hard to progress beyond their initial impact, and will need to find fresh inspiration to prevent their Celtic warcry becoming a stale formula. Classic cuts: 'East Of Eden', 'In A Big Country'.

Stuart Adamson, in mid-solo, suddenly remembers the one about the Scotsman and the Stratocaster.

DUANE ALLMAN

ONE OF rock's many casualties – he died in a motorcycle smash aged only 24 – Duane Allman achieved more in his short career than most rock guitarists achieve in a lifetime.

Born in Nashville in 1946, Allman was working as a session man at the famous Muscle Shoals Studios by the late '60s, backing soul legends like Clarence Carter, Percy Sledge, Wilson Pickett and Aretha Franklin. His bluesy, soulful yet edgy style provided a perfect counterpoint to the muscular horn-based arrangements then in vogue.

Jeff Beck – the rock guitar maestro who got away (to jazz-funk).

With keyboard-playing brother Gregg, Duane put together The Allman Brothers Band in 1969. Duane's outstanding slide work, and the twin-guitar sound he formulated with Dickey Betts, brought almost immediate success.

During this period Allman also played with Eric Clapton on the classic Derek & The Dominoes album 'Layla'.

Allman's death in 1971 cut short a career that would have been even more glittering. Already acclaimed as *the* rock slide player, he would have gone on to achieve major guitar hero status. Classic cuts: 'Hey Jude' (Wilson Pickett), 'Statesboro Blues' (Allman Brothers).

JEFF BECK

JEFF BECK was one of a triumvirate of influential guitarists associated with '60s British band The Yardbirds – the others being Eric Clapton, who preceded him, and Jimmy Page, who played alongside Beck before taking over.

Brilliant but erratic, Beck has always been concerned with pushing back the boundaries of the electric guitar. Born in Surrey, England, in 1944, he joined The Yardbirds in time to play on most of their hits like 'Shape Of Things' and 'Heart Full Of Soul'.

Embarking on a solo career in 1966 – starting with the Jeff Beck Group which launched Rod Stewart to fame – Beck has embraced most aspects of rock including heavy metal and jazz fusion.

Whatever the context, Beck's untutored but often inspired playing is rarely less than exciting. Blending together influences from blues to jazz, from Eastern to psychedelia, Beck epitomises the true musician's search for new and fresh concepts. A seminal rock

player. Classic cuts: 'You Shook Me' (Jeff Beck Group), 'Over Under Sideways Down' (Yardbirds).

George Benson flakes out with his autograph model Ibanez.

GEORGE BENSON

GEORGE BENSON is that rare thing—the jazzman who has made good commercially.

Born in Pittsburgh, Pennsylvania, in 1943, Benson moved to New York in 1963 to join organist Brother Jack McDuff's jazz outfit. He quickly gained a reputation, and worked as house guitarist with the prestigious label CTI.

Switching to Warner Brothers in the early '70s, Benson hit paydirt with the album 'Breezin'' – a light jazz-funk outing which also featured his Stevie Wonder-ish vocals. It eventually sold double platinum.

From that time Benson has never looked

ERIC CLAPTON

EVER SINCE the mid-'60s, when London was decorated with 'Clapton Is God' graffiti, Eric Clapton has always personified the guitar hero. His taste, attack, timing and invention ensure that it is a tag he is unlikely to lose.

Born in Surrey, England, in 1942, Eric Clapton was hooked on the blues in his teens. An early member of the legendary Yardbirds, he quit as the band became successful to join the equally legendary John Mayall's Bluesbreakers.

With the Bluesbreakers Clapton forged a reputation as a blues colossus, drawing huge crowds of dedicated followers – many of them guitar players themselves.

Never a showman, Clapton concentrated on the music, moulding the influences of his teenage years – Muddy Waters, BB King and Freddie King amongst others – into something new and compelling. In a sense he reinvented the blues, using his astonishing technique and sense of dynamics to break down the barriers which surrounded the traditional form and drag it howling into the new rock era.

In 1966 Clapton left Mayall to form Cream – the first 'supergroup' – with bassist/vocalist Jack Bruce and drummer Ginger Baker. This groundbreaking trio combined blues feel with psychedelic sensibility and a loose, improvisatory concept – a format that catapulted the band, and Clapton, to superstardom.

After Cream, Clapton was involved in a number of projects, including supergroup Blind Faith and the pseudonymous Derek And The Dominoes (progenitors of the classic 'Layla'), before embarking on a solo career in the early '70s.

Since that time Clapton has survived a number of health and personal crises, while gigging and recording at regular intervals. His musical output has been patchy, veering towards blandness at times, but his playing has remained consistently remarkable.

Using a variety of instruments, but most often Fender Strats and Gibsons, Clapton still has the ability to surprise, to play a run so perfect in its logic, so immaculate in its execution, as to leave the listener breathless.

Never harmonically adventurous – he admits to being happiest in a basic rock/blues context – he is nevertheless a consummate stylist. There are few rock guitarists playing today who do not owe something to him. Classic cuts: 'Have You Heard' (John Mayall's Bluesbreakers), 'Crossroads' (Cream), 'Layla' (Derek And The Dominoes), 'Behind The Mask'.

CARLOS ALOMAR Ace session man who has played with artists as varied as John Lennon, Bette Midler and James Brown. Best known as leader of David Bowie's stage band. Classic cuts: 'Fame', 'Heroes' (Bowie).

Carlos Alomar with longtime boss Bowie.

CHET ATKINS Veteran guitarist who has achieved fame as MOR/easy listening soloist. Also producer and major Nashville industry figure. Classic cuts: 'Teensville', 'One Mint Julep'.

JEFF BAXTER Boston-born 'Skunk' Baxter was a founder member of Steely Dan, contributing regular and pedal steel guitar to their early classics before joining The Doobie Brothers, again adding fluid guitar to great albums. Classic cuts: 'Midnite Cruiser', 'Bodhisattva' (Steely Dan).

MIKE BLOOMFIELD Guitarist for Paul Butterfield Blues Band, Electric Flag, and Bob Dylan (on the pioneering folk rock LP 'Highway 61 Revisited'). Achieved near-legend status in late '60s, but lost his way amid numerous 'supersessions' – good for the ego, but not for the music. Died in 1981. Classic cuts: 'Like A Rolling Stone' (Dylan), 'East West' (Butterfield).

JAMES BURTON Session guitarist who played on Ricky Nelson's hits and went on to front Elvis Presley's band. Later became featured member of Emmylou Harris' Hot Band. Classic cuts: 'Hello Mary Lou' (Ricky Nelson), 'Las Vegas' (Emmylou Harris).

LARRY CARLTON Top session guitarist, particularly at home in the jazz-funk idiom. Former mainstay of The Crusaders, has recorded under his own name with some success. Classic cuts: 'Hill Street Blues' (Mike Post), 'Room 335'.

Bo Diddley with custom-made five-speed special.

BO DIDDLEY R&B pioneer and inventor of 'Bo Diddley beat'. Famous for strange oblong-shaped guitars, dynamic stage, and songs with titles like 'Bo Diddley', 'Hey Bo Diddley' and 'Bo Diddley's A Gunslinger'. Influence on Rolling Stones and other '60s blues/rock acts, still worth seeing. Classic cuts: 'Who Do You Love', 'Road Runner'.

Eric 'Slowhand' Clapton and his faithful Strat: a classic combination.

back, and has continued to consolidate his position as a major record-seller and international concert draw.

A phenomenal technician who is respected by the most exalted jazz names, Benson has made jazz-inflected music palatable to a mass audience. Classic cuts: 'Breezin'', 'The Greatest Love Of All'.

BERRY/BLACKMORE/COODER

Classic rocker Chuck Berry with cherry red Gibson, Bigsby tremolo arm and one heck of a suit.

CHUCK BERRY

ONE OF the founding fathers of rock'n'roll, Chuck Berry has exerted incalculable influence as a performer, songwriter and instrumentalist.

Born in San José, California, in 1926, Berry played local gigs before recording 'Maybelline' for the Chess label in 1955. The record became a top five US hit, and was followed by a string of further smashes. Many Berry songs like 'Sweet Little Sixteen' and 'Johnny B. Goode' have become standards.

As a player Berry was technically limited but brilliantly individualistic, originating many of the stylistic devices which have become part of the language of rock – most notably his spiky two-note riffs and phrases, and the characteristic back-and-forth 'Chuck Berry beat', hammered out on his red Gibson 335 and accompanied by his famous 'duckwalk'.

Chuck Berry has influenced countless bands and performers including The Beatles, The Rolling Stones and The Beach Boys, and even now no budding guitarist is fully equipped without his repertoire of Berry riffs. Classic cuts: 'Carol', 'No Particular Place To Go'.

Ritchie Blackmore with the Strat that launched a thousand heavy metal riffs.

RITCHIE BLACKMORE

THE PROTOTYPICAL heavy rock guitarist, Ritchie Blackmore (born in Weston-Super-Mare, England, in 1945) has been stunning audiences with his fast, loud and flashy playing for almost two decades, and shows no signs of letting up.

Blackmore was a founder member of Deep Purple, the British aggregation which became

RY COODER

ANYONE WHO can cover hits by Jim Reeves ('He'll Have To Go') and Ben E. King ('Stand By Me') on one album ('Chicken Skin Music') is obviously no run-of-the-mill artist. But Ry Cooder has a great deal more to offer than musical nerve – like technique, creativity, originality and a finely-tuned ear for unusual material. Happily blending together jazz, country, blues, R&B, rock and any number of other forms in his playing, Cooder has become the guitarist's guitarist.

Born in Los Angeles in 1947, Cooder was showing dexterity with folk, blues and ragtime styles in his teens. He cut his musical teeth with a local band called The Rising Sons, which featured another eclectic fretboard man by the name of Taj Mahal. Work on film scores (*Candy*, *Performance*) followed, and The Rolling Stones brought him to a wider audience by featuring him on 'Let It Bleed'.

In 1970 Cooder embarked on a solo career in wilfully uncommercial fashion with an album ('Ry Cooder') which featured finger-picked guitar and material culled from the '30s. It was just a taster of things to come.

Ensuing albums showed Cooder as an artist of staggering versatility, able to handle material from every nook and cranny of American popular music and turn it into something new and fresh.

As befits a man with his ragbag approach to musical styles, Cooder is eclectic in his choice of guitars. He has played Fenders, Washburns and Martin and Ovation acoustics, but he also loves junk guitars, often gigging and recording with cheap Oriental hardware.

Stylistically, Cooder touches every base, from jazz and ragtime ('Jazz'), through Tex-Mex and country ('Chicken Skin Music') to R&B ('Bop Till You Drop').

His slide guitar soundtracks for *Paris, Texas* and *Southern Comfort* brilliantly captured the menace and mournfulness of America's wilder places.

Cooder may be a moderate record-seller, but he plays to sold-out audiences all over the world.

Something of a law unto himself, Cooder is not a guitar hero in the Clapton/Page sense – but his knowledge, musicianship and unerring taste continue to consolidate his reputation with audiences and musicians alike as a musical archivist and explorer.

Classic cuts: 'Little Sister', 'He'll Have To Go'.

Robert Cray: the '80s blues master packs a mean Strat.

one of the most successful 'heavy' outfits in the world in the early '70s. Along with piledriver rhythms and Ian Gillar's shrieking vocals, Blackmore's guitar was a prime attraction, making up in impact what it lacked in originality. Some would say he invented

heavy metal.

Blackmore left Deep Purple in 1975 to form his own band, Rainbow, a more pop-orientated heavy outfit which also scored considerable success.

Neither the most subtle nor the most

Ry Cooder: a man for all guitars . . . this one's a Spanish style 12-string.

Duane Eddy: still twanging' his Guild.

RICK DERRINGER Have guitar, will travel – talented player/producer who's worked alongside Johnny Winter, Edgar Winter and Cyndi Lauper as well as solo work ranging from pop-rock to power trio Derringer. Classic cuts: 'Change Of Heart' (Cyndi Lauper).

DUANE EDDY Originator of 'twanging' guitar style (made by tuning strings down) which brought many major hits at turn of '60s. Classic cuts: 'Rebel Rouser', 'Peter Gunn Theme' (1986 remake with Art Of Noise).

DAVE EDMUNDS Like his former Rockpile partner Nick Lowe, Welsh wizard Edmunds is a producer/player/ songwriter whose re-creations of the styles and spirit of the '50s and early '60s are often more authentic than the real thing. Classic cuts: 'I Hear You Knocking', 'I Knew The Bride (When She Used To Rock And Roll)'.

ROBERT FRIPP Leading light of British 'progressive' outfit King Crimson, an innovative, exploratory guitar player known for his experiments with electronics. Played on Bowie's 'Heroes' and 'Scary Monsters' LPs, and two albums with Police guitarist Andy Summers. Classic cuts: 'God Save The King' (King Crimson), 'I Advance Masked' (with Andy Summers).

ERIC GALE New York session player who has adorned records by everyone from Marvin Gaye to Paul Simon. Releases tasteful MOR/funk albums under his own name and plays live with sessioneers' supergroup Stuff. Classic cuts: 'Ginseng Woman', 'One Trick Pony' (Paul Simon).

RORY GALLAGHER Hard-working Irish blues-rocker whose dazzling fingerwork continues to impress live audiences worldwide, despite lack of major record success. Classic cuts: 'Laundromat', 'Bullfrog Blues'.

inventive player, Ritchie Blackmore has nevertheless inspired countless young 'air guitar' players to take up the instrument in earnest. At the time of writing Blackmore is once again pacing the stage with Deep Purple, proving that old rockers never die – they simply re-form. Classic cuts: 'Smoke On The Water', 'Black Night' (both Deep Purple).

LARRY CORYELL

A HIGHLY respected musician who has always operated somewhere between jazz and rock, Coryell has had consistent critical acclaim but moderate commercial success.

Texas-born in 1943, Coryell first achieved recognition with vibraphone player Gary Burton's jazz-rock outfit. Since the early '70s Coryell has fronted a series of his own bands, most recently Eleventh House, and has recorded with a long list of jazz-rock luminaries – most notably John McLaughlin.

One of the prime movers of fusion music, Coryell continues to blend the energy of rock with the subtlety and range of jazz. Classic cuts: 'First Things First', 'Birdfingers'.

ROBERT CRAY

LEADER OF a new breed of young, progressive bluesmen, Robert Cray has injected new excitement into blues-based music with his heartfelt vocals and stinging, inventive guitar playing.

Born in Columbus, Georgia, in 1956, Cray was brought up on the music of greats like Sam Cooke, Ray Charles and Bobby Bland. After early experiments with the piano he turned his attention to the guitar and formed his first band in Tacoma. He put the Robert

Cray Band together in 1974.

After early encouragement from comedian and blues fan John Belushi (who based his *Blues Brothers* band in part on the Cray outfit), Cray put out his first album 'Who's Been Talking' in 1978.

Since then he has moved to the forefront of the music scene. He was responsible for the highest-selling blues album of all time ('Strong Persuader'), and has become a major live attraction, working extensively with Tina Turner.

A Bobby Bland-like singer who plays fluid guitar with resonances of BB King, Cray proves that there's still plenty of mileage in the blues when it's handled with taste and imagination. Classic cuts: 'I Guess I Showed Her', 'Nothing But A Woman'.

Rory Gallagher leaves the stage but his Fender doesn't want to go.

STEVE CROPPER

DESPITE HIS limited fame, Steve Cropper (born in Missouri in 1942) inspired a generation of musicians weaned on the great Stax/Volt soul records of the '60s.

With Booker T Jones (organ), Duck Dunn (bass) and Al Jackson (drums), Cropper was a member of Booker T & The MG's, Stax's house rhythm section.

The band stepped out of the studio to achieve fame in 1962 with 'Green Onions', a slice of rock-solid funk that became a huge US hit. Cropper's solo on 'Onions' is a classic of its type. Simultaneously raw and laidback, it demonstrates conclusively that you don't need flashy technique to create a great solo – and Cropper repeated the feat on a stream of sublime instrumental singles.

Cropper continued to record and perform with The MG's until the early '70s. Now a session musician, he was responsible for the soundtrack of *Blues Brothers*, Dan Aykroyd and John Belushi's comic celebration of soul. Classic cuts: 'Soul Man' (Sam & Dave), 'Mustang Sally' (Wilson Pickett).

BUCK DHARMA

AS GUITARIST for US superheavy outfit Blue Oyster Cult, Donald 'Buck Dharma' Roeser played a leading part in pushing the band to its position of eminence as the '70s sonic overlords – part biker, part demon, part intellect, and three parts metal.

With Eric Bloom (vocals/guitar), Allen Lanier (keyboards/guitar), Joe Bouchard (bass guitar) and Albert Bouchard (drums), Dharma formed the band in the late '60s.

The breakthrough came with their third album, 'Secret Treaties', which established them as one of the US' top heavy attractions. Their metallic peak came with the awesome aural assault of their live 1976 double album 'On Your Feet Or On Your Knees', full of titles like 'Hot Rails To Hell', with Dharma's savage fretboard pyrotechnics acting as the eye of the hurricane. Shortly after, BOC introduced a new concept – melody – and added it to their brooding power to cut one of the finest rock sets of the '70s, 'Agents Of Fortune', with their classic '(Don't Fear) The Reaper'.

ZZ Top's Dusty Hill and Billy Gibbons model matching caps, shades, jackets, beards and Gibson Explorers.

BOC still draw the raving hordes, but it's not the same since drummer Bouchard left. You no longer get that glorious moment which defined them as the ultimate guitar group – when all five played guitar at once! Classic cuts: '(Don't Fear) The Reaper', 'Cities On Flame.'

AL DiMEOLA

ONE OF the most accomplished guitarists in any field today, Al DiMeola (born in New Jersey in 1954) started learning the instrument at the age of seven. Initially interested in rock and then country music, DiMeola was drawn into the jazz/fusion fold after hearing the work of Larry Coryell.

In the mid-'70s DiMeola's remarkable abilities came to the attention of Chick Corea, who invited him to join his successful fusion outfit Return To Forever.

Critically acclaimed solo albums followed, showcasing DiMeola's acoustic skills alongside his electric playing.

In the '80s DiMeola joined forces with jazz-rock pioneer John McLaughlin and flamenco legend Paco De Lucia to form a highly successful acoustic supertrio.

An innovative player who brings out the full possibilities of his instrument, DiMeola is a real musicians' musician. Furthermore, his record sales have shown that there is a substantial market for intelligent, demanding, often technically difficult guitar music. Classic cuts: 'Short Tales Of The Black Forest', 'Mediterranean Sundance/Rio Ancho' (with Paco De Lucia).

Jazz-rock star Al DiMeola with Gibson Les Paul.

BILLY GIBBONS

GUITARIST AND prime mover behind long-lived Texas boogie band ZZ Top, Billy Gibbons is a relentlessly propulsive rhythm player and a soloist of great force and inventiveness.

Gibbons first tasted success with Houston band Moving Sidewalks, who had a local hit with '99th Floor' in the late '60s. After the Sidewalks fell apart, Gibbons cast in his lot with Dusty Hill (bass, vocals) and Frank Beard (drums) to form ZZ Top.

The band recorded its first album (actually entitled 'First Album') in 1970, and a couple of albums later had achieved star billing. In the following years the band became firm hard rock favourites with an unassailable reputation as an all-stops-out live attraction.

As the '80s progressed and Hill and Gibbons' beards grew longer, ZZ Top fused sly good ol' boy humour and sci-fi hi-tech in a series of brilliant videos which propelled them out of a strict hard rock market, into CD superstardom. 'Eliminator' was the album that cracked it; 'Afterburner' followed,

Blue Oyster Cult's Eric Bloom and Buck Dharma in one of their more restrained moments onstage.

The Edge: an epic guitarist whose Gibson Explorer puts pride and power into the music of U2.

THE EDGE

THE LOOSELY structured, epic nature of U2's work has earned them the double-edged distinction of being known as an 'albums' rather than a 'singles' band, but it has also allowed room for the infinite textural variations and sustained guitar heroics which have earned Dave 'The Edge' Evans a worldwide reputation.

Formed in Dublin in 1978 by school friends Bono (vocals), Edge, Adam Clayton (bass) and Larry Mullen (drums), the band broke onto the English scene with their signing to Island Records two years later. By 1983 they were established as one of the world's top touring bands, and their album of that year, 'War', achieved the distinction of entering the UK charts at number one.

Their 1985 live LP and video 'Under A Blood Red Sky', recorded in Utah, showed them to be a stage band to rival Springsteen: Bono exhorting the crowd to feverish heights as The Edge's soaring guitar rang out magnificently around the Red Rocks canyon. U2's live pre-eminence was confirmed by their devastating 20-minute set at 1985's Live Aid concert, when a global audience watched them turn Wembley Stadium into a moving spiritual experience.

On record, meanwhile, U2 have forged a link with producers Brian Eno and Daniel Lanois which has added subtlety to their fire. The fervent attack of 'Gloria' (1981, from the 'October' LP) has been moulded via the ringing tones of 'New Year's Day' (1983, from 'War') and the anthemic 'Pride' (1984, from 'The Unforgettable Fire'), into a wide vision which on 'With Or Without You' (1987, from 'The Joshua Tree') admits both tenderness and power.

The Edge's sound, one of the most recognisable in rock, is the musical focus of what many now consider the world's top rock group. Classic cuts: 'Sunday Bloody Sunday', 'Where The Streets Have No Name'.

Jerry Garcia, king of San Francisco rock.

JERRY GARCIA Brave, bizarre and sometimes simply boring, San Francisco's Grateful Dead were the leaders of '60s acid rock, and remain a huge stadium draw in the '80s. For twenty years now Garcia's quicksilver guitar has led them through stumbling improvisations, corny country, heartbeat rock and roll and a mess of other musics. A truly inspirational musician. Classic cut: 'Dark Star'/'St Stephen'/'The Eleven'/ 'Lovelight'.

Peter Green: a guitar genius who lost his way.

PETER GREEN Brilliant British blues guitarist/singer who played with John Mayall's Bluesbreakers and went on in 1967 to form original Fleetwood Mac, UK's top '60s blues band. Cut classic sides including 'Albatross' before leaving to become recluse. Has since made a couple of albums of modest musical ambition but rare sensitivity. Classic cuts: 'Black Magic Woman', 'Need Your Love So Bad'.

ALAN HOLDSWORTH Semi-legendary British fusion guitarist acclaimed by musicians like Eddie Van Halen. Has played with Tony Williams' Lifetime, UK and Soft Machine amongst others. Classic cuts: 'Devil Take The Hindmost', 'In The Dead Of The Night'.

ERNIE ISLEY Hendrix-style player who combined rock and soul influences to power Isley Brothers to massive success in the '70s. Talented multi-instrumentalist. Classic cuts: 'That Lady', 'Hope You Feel Better Love'.

STEVE JONES Laddish punk star of The Sex Pistols, his wall of sound power chords on 'Anarchy In The UK' signalled the start of a new era. Rarely heard or seen since 1979, Jones now co-writes, produces and plays with ex-Duran Duran guitarist/singer Andy Taylor. Classic cuts: 'Anarchy In The UK', 'God Save The Queen'.

featuring synths judiciously mixed in with the guitars; and the extensive Top back catalog began moving as well.

As a guitar player Gibbons aims for excitement, but his witty approach gives him an edge most rock guitarists lack. There are moments of high invention which show that he would be a force to be reckoned with in a less constricting context, but he prefers to be the man who made boogie-rock an art form. Classic cuts: 'Gimme All Your Lovin'', 'Rough Boy'.

JIMI HENDRIX

IT WAS late in 1966 that James Marshall Hendrix first exploded onto the rock scene, making a debut of unparalleled impact.

In a world not short of guitar heroes – Clapton, Page and Beck had all established strong reputations by this time – Hendrix was nevertheless immediately recognized as something else: a phenomenon, a megastar, even a rock genius. In four short years before his death in September 1970 he would revolutionize the art of rock guitar.

Born in Seattle, Washington, in 1942, Jimi Hendrix cut his musical teeth on the R&B circuit, backing stars like Sam Cooke, Little Richard and The Isley Brothers.

The crucial break came when he was spotted playing in a New York club by Chas Chandler, former bass player with The Animals.

Chandler realised he had stumbled across a potential superstar. He took Hendrix to England and teamed him with Noel Redding – a guitarist turned bass player – and drummer Mitch Mitchell. The Jimi Hendrix Experience was born.

The Experience's first single 'Hey Joe' was a major UK hit, and instantly established Hendrix as a new star with enormous personal charisma. The inventive guitar solo on 'Hey Joe' was however only a taste of things to come.

Albums like 'Are You Experienced' and 'Axis – Bold As Love' showed Hendrix to be the complete rock player, able to mesh the bluest of blues lines with slashing, stuttering rhythmic patterns and a staggering variety of effects.

An eclectic listener with a taste for everything from Bach to country, Hendrix synthesized the whole history of rock in his apparently wild but actually closely controlled guitar style.

But above all he was the master of electronics. Using a Stratocaster fed through a fuzz-box, wah-wah pedal and other devices, he was able to set up a barrage of shriek, sustain and feedback sounds at will, making them an intrinsic part of the music.

By the end of 1968 he had made his double-album masterpiece 'Electric Ladyland'. A heady combination of psychedelic drugs, bursting talent and a frenetic lifestyle had taken Hendrix out into the unknown. The compositional scope was breathtaking, the range of guitar styles and sounds almost supernatural.

On stage he had progressed from playing his guitar with his teeth and behind his back, to burning it, and later to simply playing it – if that's how you'd describe the ten-minute version of 'The Star Spangled Banner' wrenched entirely from feedback which climaxed the Woodstock festival movie.

It was Hendrix's command of electronics, coupled with his unflagging powers of invention, that placed him in a class of his own.

His personal magnetism and sense of style were inimitable, but his playing influenced a whole generation of musicians, including Townshend, Clapton, Page and Beck.

He remains one of the greatest guitarists rock has ever produced – some would say *the* greatest. Classic cuts: 'All Along The Watch Tower', 'Voodoo Child (Slight Return)'.

STEVE HOWE

AS GUITARIST with Yes and latterly Asia, Steve Howe has achieved a reputation as an all-round master of rock, progressive and semi-classical forms.

Replacing founder-member Peter Banks in 1971, Howe made a major contribution to Yes's classic mid-'70s period. His virtuosity was an integral part of the band's long, complex and often quasi-orchestral outings.

Despite continuing international popularity, Yes collapsed at the end of the '70s and in 1981 Howe went on to form Asia with John Wetton (bass), Geoff Downes (keyboards) and Carl Palmer (drums).

Massive success was almost immediate, consolidating Howe's position as a superstar

Yes man Steve Howe, classically trained, with his hollow bodied electric Gibson.

guitarist. He's since left for another 'supergroup', GTR with guitarist Steve Hackett (ex-Genesis).

A perennial poll-winner, Howe is a highly accomplished musician who has explored many innovatory techniques for recording the guitar. Classic cuts: 'I've Seen All Good People' (Yes), 'Going For The One' (Yes).

ALBERT KING

WITH HIS namesakes BB and Freddie, Albert King has been one of the greatest blues influences on rock guitarists.

Born in 1923 in Indianola, Mississippi, Albert King played small-time gigs and recorded sporadically before signing to Stax Records in 1966. Teamed with house musicians Booker T & The MG's, King cut a series of albums like 'Born Under A Bad Sign' and 'Live Wire – Blues Power' that cut across the divide between blues and rock to find wide acceptance.

A left-handed player who plays 'backwards', King uses an unorthodox 'E minor chord' tuning to achieve his distinctive mellifluous sound and menacing lead runs. Rock players influenced by him include Hendrix, Clapton, Stevie Ray Vaughan and the late Mike Bloomfield. Classic cuts: 'Cold Feet', 'I'll Play The Blues For You'.

JOHNNY MARR

ALONG WITH Morrissey, Johnny Marr was the guiding light behind the 1982 formation of The Smiths.

Between them they propelled the band and

Johnny Marr, left, with fellow Smith Morrissey – a combination of style and intellect.

its highly idiosyncratic music to international acclaim, dividing fans and critics into 'love' and 'hate' camps along the way.

An eclectic musician, Marr has absorbed the sounds of artists from The Beatles and Pentangle (Bert Jansch in particular), via Don Gibson and Emmylou Harris to Jerry Donahue and the New York new wave of Television.

The key to Marr's style is its bright, crisp clarity, providing the perfect counterpoint for Morrissey's dramatic lugubrious persona. Marr's Rickenbacker-powered guitar patterns have characterised a string of hits all over the world, bringing a '60s direct drive to bear on Morrissey's artful words and vocals.

The Smiths' immense popularity stems from their integrity and their consciousness

FREDDIE KING With BB and Albert, third 'King' of blues. Famous for instrumentals like 'Hide Away' and 'Driving Sideways' which became showcases for young British bluesers like Eric Clapton, Peter Green, Mick Taylor. Died in 1976. Classic cuts: 'Hide Away', 'Have You Ever Loved A Woman'.

EARL KLUGH Former George Benson alumnus who has made speciality of jazz-funk played on acoustic guitar. Lightweight approach has ensured wide commercial success. Classic cuts: 'See See Rider', 'Living Inside Your Love'.

ALBERT LEE British player who started with '60s rocker Chris Farlowe. Has played with everyone from Dave Edmunds to Emmylou Harris, and is now regarded as *the* country guitar player. Classic cuts: 'Country Boy', 'Rock'n'Roll Man'.

Nils Lofgren, now a Springsteen sideman.

NILS LOFGREN Stylish guitarist who worked with Neil Young in early '60s and went on to successful solo career. Latterly member of Bruce Springsteen's E Street Band. Classic cuts: 'Keith Don't Go', 'I Came To Dance'.

Yngwie Malmsteen: funny name, funny boy.

YNGWIE MALMSTEEN Ex of Steeler and Alcatraz (replaced by Steve Vai), this Swedish expatriate is now pursuing a solo career. One of the most rated young heavy metal players around today. Classic cuts: 'You Don't Remember, I'll Never Forget', 'Hiroshima Mon Amour' (Alcatraz).

Jimi Hendrix: one of rock's many left-handed guitarists, with his right-handed Strat restrung.

of traditional rock values and virtues – their espousal of guitars over synths, their clear-cut song structures, their bold lyrical approach (typified by 'Meat Is Murder'), their sexual ambivalence, the Marr/Morrissey ying/yang in which the cool, aloof Marr plays Richards to Morrissey's effete Jagger – and Marr is just as essential to all this as the better known Morrissey.

At the time of writing The Smith are about to quit Rough Trade Records for the giant multinational EMI, but they are certain to remain Britain's most popular 'independent' band for years to come, because they embody the spirit of independence. Classic cuts: 'The Queen Is Dead', 'What Difference Does It Make'.

BRIAN MAY

AS GUITARIST with Queen, Brian May has been in the top echelon of rock guitarists for a decade and a half. Unusually among rock players he has carved out a reputation for both individuality and versatility.

Born in Middlesex, England, May came together with Freddie Mercury (vocals), John Deacon (bass) and Roger Taylor (drums) to form Queen in 1972. The band's combination of glam-rock theatrics and sub-Zeppelin dynamics propelled them to almost immediate success. The definitive pomp-rock single 'Bohemian Rhapsody' achieved classic status, and the band has gone on to consolidate its position as a global draw into the '80s, switching styles from disco-rap ('Another One Bites The Dust') to rock

anthems ('We Are The Champions') to rock'n'roll ('Crazy Little Thing Called Love') as the time seems right.

Generally playing the 'May Axe' guitar which he built himself, May is equally at home with rampaging metal solos or honeyed melodies that play off the group's dense harmonies. One of the few rock guitarists whose style seems to owe nothing to the blues, he has a unique sound.

His battery of effects includes delay, phase and echo, all of which he uses with great skill in the long guitar solo which is part of Queen's stage act. Classic cuts: 'Killer Queen', 'Crazy Little Thing Called Love'.

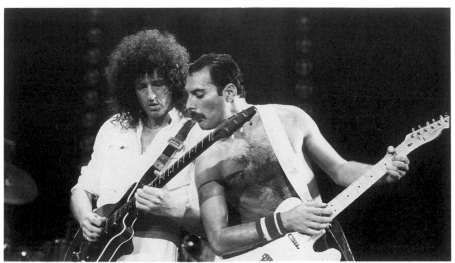

So that's how he does it . . . Queen singer Freddie Mercury takes notes from Brian May.

PRINCE/RICHARDS/McLAUGHLIN

John McLaughlin plays double speed on his double-necked Gibson.

JOHN McLAUGHLIN

BRITISH-BORN (Yorkshire, 1942) virtuoso McLaughlin has a phenomenal technique which has enabled him to make his mark in a number of musical contexts.

After working in British R&B outfits in the mid-'60s, McLaughlin decamped to the USA and became involved in the burgeoning jazz-rock scene. He recorded with the legendary Miles Davis ('In A Silent Way', 'Bitches' Brew') and went on to front a number of bands of his own, including numerous incarnations of The Mahavishnu Orchestra and the Indian-influenced Shakti.

Recent acoustic collaborations with Paco De Lucia and Al DiMeola have highlighted McLaughlin's stunning speed and lucidity. Although much of his music is an acquired taste, McLaughlin has opened up new possibilities for the electric guitar as an improvising instrument. Classic cuts: 'East Side West Side' (Mahavishnu Orchestra), 'Frevo Rasgado' (with Al DiMeola and Paco De Lucia).

PRINCE

TO MANY, Prince is the greatest rock musician of the '80s. A highly individualistic writer/singer/producer/actor and multi-instrumentalist, Prince was a fully-formed talent by the time he signed his first record contract at the age of 18.

His first three albums 'Prince', 'Dirty Mind' and 'Controversy' were all his own work, combining his experimental keyboards style with a hard funk guitar sound and lascivious vocals to produce a potent sexual mix — all but one of the 'Controversy' tracks were banned from US airplay.

Prince's career went into overdrive with the 1983 LP '1999' featuring the memorable guitar break of 'Little Red Corvette'. Although he now had a band (The Revolution), their contribution was minimal and Prince almost certainly played that break, for instance.

Prince's crossover into mainstream rock was completed by 1984's 'Purple Rain', which cast him both on record and on film as (among other things) a reincarnation of Hendrix, with outrageous guitar heroics on showstoppers like 'Let's Go Crazy'. At one point he had America's top movie, top single and top album simultaneously.

Since then, Prince has reaffirmed his genius by refusing to follow the hit formula that beckoned, preferring instead to take on '60s psychedelia ('Around The World In A Day', a dense blend of keyboards and guitar), electronic funk ('Parade', chattering keyboards offset by spare stripped guitar as on 'Kiss'), and a more guitar-oriented rock funk on the 1987 double LP 'Sign Of The Times'. A man of extremes, epitomised by classic cuts: 'Let's Go Crazy', 'Kiss'.

KEITH RICHARDS

ALTHOUGH NO ONE'S idea of a guitar virtuoso, Keith Richards has provided the musical cornerstone for 'The World's Greatest Rock And Roll Band' – The Rolling Stones – for over two decades.

Born in Kent, England, in 1943, Richards and schoolfriend Mick Jagger put together the Stones line-up that included Brian Jones (guitar), Bill Wyman (bass) and Charlie Watts (drums) in 1963.

Early recordings emphasized Richards' debt to Chuck Berry, but his role quickly evolved to embrace lead, rhythm and chordal work.

A pragmatic player equally at home with a powerhouse fuzztone riff or filigree acoustic accompaniment, Richards is one of rock's greatest rhythm players – an influence on nearly every young guitarist looking to play fast, loose and dirty.

As someone once remarked when 'Keef' swaggered into a room: "Rock and roll just walked in." Classic cuts: 'Start Me Up', 'Brown Sugar'.

Keith Richards shows off the self-portraits on his ring and his guitar body.

Prince with the bizarre custom-built guitar he's used since 'Purple Rain'.

Phil Manzanera with exotic Gibson Firebird.

PHIL MANZANERA Inventive guitar player who contributed a wide range of styles to Roxy Music classics such as 'Virginia Plain', 'Street Life', 'Love Is The Drug', 'Dance Away'. Has recorded solo and with groups 801 and Explorers. Classic cuts: 'All I Want Is You', 'Take A Chance' (both Roxy Music).

HANK MARVIN Leader of The Shadows, Britain's top pre-Beatles band who had 12 consecutive top ten instrumentals using Marvin's mellifluous tremolo action and Shads' patented shuffle. Classic cuts: 'Apache', 'Wonderful Land'.

Wendy Melvoin barres her Gibson semi-acoustic.

WENDY MELVOIN One of the few featured female guitarists in rock, former cornerstone of Prince's Revolution. Left to work with Revolution keyboard player Lisa Coleman. Classic cuts: 'Purple Rain', 'Little Red Corvette' (live).

PAT METHENY Former protegé of vibraphonist Gary Burton, Metheny has successfully brought rock sensibility to jazz guitar. Has recorded solo, with own Pat Metheny Group, and stars from Joni Mitchell to Ornette Coleman. Classic cuts: 'This Is Not America' (David Bowie), 'Phase Dance'.

SCOTTY MOORE Elvis Presley's first guitarist and influence on thousands of young rock'n'roll players. Classic cuts: 'Hound Dog', 'Heartbreak Hotel'.

TED NUGENT Flashy heavy rock stylist and self-proclaimed 'greatest guitarist in the world'. Certainly one of the loudest, he established major following in the late '70s. Classic cuts: 'Dog Eat Dog', 'Cat Scratch Fever'.

MIKE OLDFIELD Multi-instrumentalist who achieved massive success with 'Tubular Bells' (used in *The Exorcist*), Oldfield started out as guitarist in late '60s. Initially a hippy, later a devotee of EST, Oldfield pioneered guitar as part of lengthy instrumental/orchestral works. Classic cuts: 'Moonlight Shadow', 'Tubular Bells'.

BB King coaxes sweet music out of his favourite Gibson 335, 'Lucille'.

BB KING

ROCK 'N' ROLL IS firmly grounded in the blues. Drawing on every facet of the tradition, from the horn-based R&B of Louis Jordan to the electric menace of John Lee Hooker, rock gathered its strength from the blues.

To rock audiences, the blues is represented by one man above all – a man whose career has spanned every decade of modern music: BB King.

Born Riley B. King near Indianola, Memphis, in 1925, BB took up guitar in his early teens. Following army service in World War II, he began to perform professionally, developing the individualistic guitar style which was to prove so influential.

He began recording in 1949, and scored his first major R&B hit with 'Three O'Clock Blues'. More hits followed, and it wasn't long before King had become America's number one blues draw. As debonair as a '50s movie star, he maintained a large orchestra and played to sell-out crowds who came to hear not just his searing guitar, but also his soulful singing and wickedly bitter-sweet songs.

In the early '60s he signed to the major Paramount label, a move which was to result in the broadening of his appeal with classic albums like 'Live At The Regal' and 'Completely Well'. By the early '70s he commanded a wide following amongst rock and even MOR fans, and he has maintained his position as boss of the blues right up to the present day. As recently as 1985 he cut one of his greatest records, 'Into The Night', as the theme for the John Landis movie of the same name.

It's not hard to see why this dignified, unassuming man has such a broad-based appeal. His heartfelt vocals and sinuous spare guitar lines are irresistible to anyone with an ear for emotional, adult music.

As a guitarist, King is instantly recognizable, having blended a number of diverse influences – electric blues pioneer T-Bone Walker and jazz virtuoso Charlie Christian among others – into a compellingly individual style.

A long-time user of the Gibson 355 semi-solid, BB King pioneered many stylistic devices which have become part of the rock guitarist's vocabulary – the finger-style vibrato, for example, and the practice of hitting a note a fret lower than required and bending it upwards.

King's influence on other players has been incalculable. Amongst his devotees can be counted Eric Clapton, Peter Green and Mike Bloomfield.

Like Chuck Berry's licks and Bo Diddley's beat, King's timeless style has become part of the vocabulary of popular music. There will never be a better blues guitarist. Classic cuts: 'The Thrill Is Gone', 'Everyday I Have The Blues'.

Richie Sambora: his blend of raw riffs and pop power have taken Bon Jovi into the world's charts.

RICHIE SAMBORA

AS GUITARIST with Bon Jovi, Sambora is leader of a growing trend, combining the catchiness and instant appeal of pop with the bone-crushing rhythmic attack of heavy metal.

Sambora and the other members of Bon Jovi – David Bryan (keyboards), Alec John Such (bass), Tico Torres (drums) and Jon Bon Jovi (vocals) – had all worked on the East Coast club circuit before putting together Bon Jovi in early 1984. Sambora was the last to join.

Their debut single 'Runaway' achieved chart success, and paved the way for adulation on an international scale, which reached massive proportions in 1986/87. Their third album 'Slippery When Wet' and single 'Livin' On A Prayer' (featuring Sambora's neat use of the Vocoder) were both US number ones, and audiences around the world rocked to live classics like 'Wild In The Streets'. At the last count 'Slippery When Wet' had sold six million in the USA alone.

Sambora provides much of the appeal, both musical and visual, of this massively successful outfit. Classic cuts: 'Livin' On A Prayer', 'You Give Love A Bad Name'.

TOM SCHOLZ

GUITARIST AND keyboards player Scholz was the mastermind behind one of the most successful first albums in pop history – the 1976 debut album by Boston.

Entirely composed by Scholz and largely featuring his own playing beefed up by multi-layer recording techniques, the album took him seven years to make. It went double platinum and spawned the international hit single 'More Than A Feeling'.

Boston's West Coast sound belied their Massachusetts roots – they offered melodic rock with layered harmonies, counterpointed by Scholz's echoing guitar.

The grand 'pomp pop' style of 'More Than A Feeling' has influenced dozens of bands and guitarists in the past ten years – in fact in the era of Bon Jovi, Europe and AOR, it's rock's most potent currency.

The second Boston LP 'Don't Look Back' was a conventional follow-up, but their third album 'Third Stage' was an epic of 'Boston' proportions in more ways than one. In dispute with his label CBS, Scholz financed it himself by launching an amplifier manufacturing company (Rockwell). In the end it took $1 million, 10,000 hours of studio time and six long years, but it was worth the wait: on release at the end of '86 it rocketed to No.1 on the US chart and sold four million copies in four months. Featuring Scholz's almost orchestral layers of sound, it also gave Boston a number one single with 'Amanda'. Classic cuts: 'More Than A Feeling', 'Cool The Engines'.

STEVE STEVENS

THE LEADING light of a new breed of guitar heroes – combining hi-tech, hard rock, punk and metal – Steve Stevens has been the partner in crime of peroxide rock rebel Billy Idol since Idol's breakthrough 1983 album 'Rebel Yell'.

On that album and its successor 'Whiplash Smile', Stevens emerged not only as a demon guitar slinger, but also as a musical arranger and co-writer.

As a guitarist, Stevens offers a staggering variety of sonic effects: piledriver chords on 'White Wedding', cascades of shimmering notes on 'Sweet Sixteen', explosive power on 'World's Forgotten Boy' . . .

Increasingly in demand for session work, Stevens played on the soundtrack of the hit movie *Top Gun*, and can be heard on Michael Jackson's 1987 LP.

At the time of writing, Stevens is planning his debut WEA album. Classic cuts: 'Rebel Yell', 'Don't Need A Gun'.

ANDY SUMMERS

ONE THIRD (with Sting, vocals/bass and Stuart Copeland, drums) of international supergroup The Police, Andy Summers served a varied musical apprenticeship before achieving stardom in the late '70s.

Born in Blackpool, England, in 1940, Summers cut his musical teeth with a number of major British bands, including Zoot Money's Big Roll Band, Soft Machine and The Animals. The variety of musical contexts – jazzy R&B, progressive rock, hard rock-blues respectively – laid the foundations for the eclectic style which would serve him so well with The Police.

The Police's bare-bones instrumentation meant that it fell to Summers to provide most of the musical meat. He did this by using the entire vocabulary of the guitar – chords, single-note fills, rhythmic patterns – combined with a wide variety of electronic effects. But his special talent lay in not doing too much: the simple understatement of many Police hits was the key to their success.

Not so much an instrumental virtuoso as a clever and innovative arranger for the guitar, Summers has broadened the role of the instrument in rock. Classic cuts: 'Every Breath You Take', 'Synchronicity II'.

Andy Taylor: even in Duran Duran he showed a yearning for a bolder guitar style.

ANDY TAYLOR

FORMER DURAN Duran lynchpin Andy Taylor has worked successfully in a variety of musical settings.

Born in Newcastle in 1961, Taylor joined Birmingham band Duran just before their rapid rise to international success. 'Planet Earth', released in 1981, was the first of a series of hit singles that established the band as major stars on both sides of the Atlantic.

Steve Stevens (left) and Billy Idol, with a rebel yell on their 1987 tour.

Mark Knopfler shows the finger-picking style that gives his sound much of its subtlety.

MARK KNOPFLER

ONE OF the most surprising bands to emerge out of the late '70s was Dire Straits, led by Mark Knopfler. His quirky songs, husky vocals and liquid guitar playing flew against the prevailing musical winds, but in the '80s led to the Straits becoming one of the biggest draws in the world.

Formed in Deptford, South London, Dire Straits were always a vehicle for Knopfler's musical vision. But although Knopfler cuts an authoritative figure, he is not one's idea of the typical rock star. He sings like a kind of Anglicized Dylan, his songs are individualistic and ironically observant, and his guitar playing is as far from the average rock flailings as it is possible to imagine. Nevertheless, he is now established as a genuine original and prized addition to star recording sessions – he has played with Dylan and Steely Dan amongst others.

Knopfler's individuality extends to virtually every aspect of his playing. He has revived the bluesman's art of call-and-response to make his guitar an effective counterpoint to his own vocals,

bridging the gaps between phrases with pithy runs and fills. Listen to the semi-classic 'Sultans Of Swing' for an example of his effortless skill in this respect.

He is the master of melodic invention, able to coax new and fresh patterns from his Stratocaster (or latterly Schecter) where a lesser player would have fallen back on cliché, often using finger picking as well as a plectrum. Although rock is a form of music which relies on the familiar, Knopfler rarely takes the easy way out.

Finally, there is Knopfler's *sound*, a glorious, luminescent tone that can reflect every mood from sensuality to menace. It is one of the most instantly recognisable sounds in rock.

His involvement in film work – including the uplifting Celtic theme to *Local Hero* – indicates one direction which Mark Knopfler might take in future. Right now as a rock guitarist he has few peers, and his work will continue to shine whether in or outside the context of Dire Straits. Classic cuts: 'Brothers In Arms', 'Money For Nothing'.

LES PAUL Regarded by many as father of the electric guitar, and progenitor of sound recording techniques that are now standard practice. With wife Mary Ford, enjoyed many US hits in '50s. Still active player on New York club scene. Classic cuts: 'Humming Bird', 'Vaya Con Dios'.

Johnny Ramone in unmistakable Ramones stance.

JOHNNY RAMONE Progenitor of raw, 'buzzsaw' guitar that was lynchpin of Ramones' classic garage-band sound. Not outstanding technician, but captured the spirit of rock'n'roll and formulated the sound of punk rock. Classic cuts: 'Blitzkrieg Bop', 'Sheena Is A Punk Rocker'.

LEE RITENOUR Highly rated session guitarist who has recorded with artists ranging from Seals and Crofts to Bobby Bland. Has also made impact with jazz-rock albums under own name. Classic cuts: 'Captain Caribé', 'Sugarloaf Express'.

Nile Rodgers and his Chic buddy Bernard Edwards.

NILE RODGERS Along with bassist Bernard Edwards, virtually invented disco music, using spare, choppy guitar sound to propel Chic to success in '70s. Has since shone as producer and guitarist for Bowie, Madonna and others. Classic cuts: 'Good Times' (Chic), 'China Girl' (Bowie).

CARLOS SANTANA Force behind mega-selling Latin-rock band Santana, and a major guitarist of late '60s and early '70s. Has latterly leaned towards jazzier side of rock. Classic cuts: 'Black Magic Woman', 'Caravanserai'.

ROBERT SMITH Sometime member of Siouxsie And The Banshees, and founder and guiding light of British experimental cult band The Cure. Wit and musical integrity have always held sway over commercial considerations. Classic cuts: 'Killing An Arab', 'The Lovecats'.

However, Taylor became dissatisfied with the band's pop-orientated sound and left in 1985 to form Power Station with Robert Palmer (vocals), John Taylor (bass) and ex-Chic drummer Tony Thompson. The outfit scored a major hit with 'Some Like It Hot'. Although the Taylors returned to Duran, Andy was never really happy until he quit completely for a solo career.

Other projects have included the

soundtrack for the movie *American Anthem* (which he worked on with former Sex Pistols guitarist Steve Jones) – including the US hit single 'Take It Easy' – and sessions for Robert Palmer and Belinda Carlisle.

Taylor's hard, synthetic guitar provides the perfect foil for the studio-orientated rock sound of today. Classic cuts: 'Hungry Like A Wolf' (Duran Duran), 'Some Like It Hot' (Power Station).

PAGE/VAUGHAN/TOWNSHEND

The boys are back in town – Lizzy from left: Phil Lynott, Brian Robertson, Scott Gorham and Gary Moore.

THIN LIZZY

THE FOREMOST British guitar band of the late '70s, Thin Lizzy brought a stream of prime rock guitarists to prominence with its twin-guitar attack on either side of Irish singer/writer/bassist Phil Lynott – including Irish metal star Gary Moore, Scots firebrand Brian Robertson, and American Scott Gorham. The Celtic blood and thunder Lizzy sound has inspired many since, notably Big Country and Moore himself.

Moore now has a successful solo career, including hits such as 'Out In The Fields' (with Lynott) and 'Parisienne Walkways (solo), and guesting on the likes of 'Warriors Of The Wasteland' by Frankie Goes To Hollywood. Robertson played the fiery rock Robertson played the fiery rock lead on

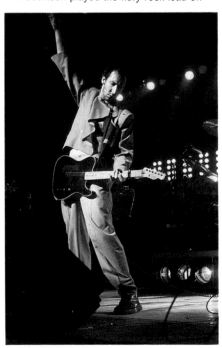

Pete Townshend windmills one of the power chords that regularly left his hand bleeding onstage.

Mike Oldfield's 'Moonlight Shadow' as well as lurching through Wild Horses and Motorhead, while Gorham vanished but now looks set to emerge with a new band. Classic cuts: 'The Boys Are Back In Town' (Robertson/Gorham), 'Still In Love With You' (live, featuring Robertson).

JIMMY PAGE

LED ZEPPELIN was always a band of extremes. They pioneered the bone-crunching heavy rock sound, they took it to commercial success on an unprecedented scale, and paved the way for hundreds of throat-wrenching, finger-busting imitators.

Founder of the band and architect of its uniquely powerful sound was Jimmy Page. Born in Middlesex, England, in 1944, Page took up guitar in his early teens. He was influenced first by the stylists of late '50s rock'n'roll – studio aces like Scotty Moore and James Burton – and later by the city blues of Elmore James, BB King and others.

Having established himself as a session man, playing for '60s names like The Kinks, Donovan and Tom Jones, Page went on to join the post-Clapton Yardbirds – at first splitting lead duties with Jeff Beck, who quit soon after.

But the turning point came in 1968 when Page, along with fellow session man John Paul Jones (bass), and unknowns Robert Plant (vocals) and John Bonham (drums), formed Led Zeppelin. Rock was never to be quite the same again.

Eric Clapton's Cream, on 'Crossroads', had taken the blues of Robert Johnson, stretched it out and cranked it up to 20,000 watts. Zep's first album 'Led Zeppelin' took the band's blues roots and stretched them to even more theat-

PETE TOWNSHEND

IF THE Who was one of rock's greatest band's, Pete Townshend was surely its most flamboyant perfomer. The foremost exponent of 'guitar as stage prop', Townshend on stage was a maelstrom of whirling arms, manic leaps and stunning power chords.

West London-born in 1944, Townshend and Roger Daltrey (vocals), John Entwistle (bass) and Keith Moon (drums) came together to play R&B-based power pop in the early days of mod, which they came to represent. The band quickly developed into one of the most important rock outfits of the late '60s and '70s, vying with The Rolling Stones for the title of The World's Greatest Rock And Roll Band.

Townshend was always the driving force behind the band, using the guitar as a source of power and dynamics rather than as a single-string solo instrument.

At one stage known more for smashing his intrument than playing it, Townshend remains an important role model for rock players. Classic cuts: 'My Generation', 'Won't Get Fooled Again'.

STEVIE RAY VAUGHAN

A MUSICAL blood-brother of fellow-Texan Johnny Winter, Stevie Ray Vaughan has taken hard blues-rock to new heights with his all-stops-out approach to guitar playing.

Born in Austin, the brother of Jimmy Lee Vaughan of The Fabulous Thunderbirds,

rical extremes. It made a huge impact with its raw power and instrumental pyrotechnics, and began a string of smash albums lasting until the late '70s.

The band's stage act was equally stunning, making them the third party in the Who/Stones battle for the title of The World's Greatest Rock And Roll Band.

Using an ever-changing variety of guitars including Gibson Les Pauls and Fender Telecasters, Page provided a riveting counterpoint to Plant's raw vocals. A slight but charismatic figure, Page was always in command on stage . . . using echo to build up multifaceted pyramids of sound . . . taking a violin bow to his strings to coax new and different textures from the guitar . . . or simply dazzling audiences with his sheer speed and dexterity.

Behind all the flash Page was a serious musician, willing to approach rock from a number of different angles – witness his acoustic work on the rock festival favourite 'Stairway To Heaven'. Lacking the inspired creativity of Hendrix or the subtle emotionalism of Clapton, he was nevertheless the premier heavy rock guitar hero.

Recent work with singer Paul Rodgers in The Firm has extended his playing career, but his finest hour was undoubtedly when he was the force behind heavy rock's greatest band. Classic cuts: 'Whole Lotta Love', 'Dazed And Confused'.

Vaughan plays with Double Trouble.

As well as Winter-style power blues, Vaughan draws on the Hendrix legacy, and is known for his stunning live versions of the master's 'Voodoo Chile' and Stevie Wonder's 'Superstition'. His 1987 'Live Alive' album, recorded at the Montreux Jazz Festival and the Austin Opera House, captures all the excitement of a Stevie Ray Vaughan live date.

An in-demand session player, Vaughan has played on records as varied as Bowie's 'Let's Dance' and James Brown's 'Living In America'. His perennial pulling power demonstrates the continuing appeal of powerful, straight-down-the-line guitar playing. Classic cuts: 'Cat People' (David Bowie), 'I'm Leaving You'.

AC/DC singer Brian Johnson comes over all excited at the sight of Angus Young's Gibson SG.

ANGUS YOUNG

CORNERSTONE OF Australia's heavy rock stalwarts AC/DC, Angus Young is the archetype of the headbanging metal guitarist. But his bizarre dress – usually a schoolboy outfit of shorts and blazer – and wild stage antics obscure the fact that he can be a fluent and exciting guitarist, capable of holding his own in the best of rock company.

Born in Sydney, Australia, Young formed AC/DC in Melbourne, with his brother Malcolm (guitar), Phil Rudd (drums), Mark Evans (bass) and Bon Scott (vocals). Having gained a local following, the band settled in Britain in 1976.

Their music was a serious shock to the system: heavy metal at that time was a lumbering beast, and AC/DC were so rabid and hi-energy that at first the Brits thought they were punk rockers. AC/DC could justly claim to have changed the face of metal, because it was their lead that the likes of Iron Maiden were later to follow.

Within a couple of years AC/DC had risen to eminence as heavy metal thrashers par excellence, a position they still occupy today. They survived the alcohol-induced death of singer Bon Scott by drafting in British-born singer Brian Johnson.

Angus Young is very much the focal point of the band, and provides the musical as well as the visual highlights of its performance. Classic cuts: 'Whole Lotta Rosie', 'Who Made Who'.

All-American boy Bruce Springsteen.

BRUCE SPRINGSTEEN Rock megastar, more than competent guitarist, but particularly excels in visual use of guitar. Like Presley, Hendrix and Townshend, he makes it an integral part of stage act. Classic cuts: 'Born To Run', 'Born In The USA'.

DAVE STEWART One half of Eurythmics (with singer Annie Lennox), Stewart is one of pop's most in-demand producers (Daryl Hall, Dylan, Feargal Sharkey) and forceful live guitar player. Classic cuts: 'Missionary Man', 'When Tomorrow Comes'.

TOMMY TEDESCO Ace West Cost session man who has played with everyone from Frank Sinatra to Frank Zappa, Joan Baez to The Beach Boys. Possibly most recorded guitarist in music history. Classic cuts: 'Then He Kissed Me' (Crystals), 'Good Vibrations' (Beach Boys).

GEORGE THOROGOOD No-nonsense blues rocker whose fiery playing has always been more appreciated live than on record. A noted slide guitarist, fond of jamming with blues and R&B greats such as Albert Collins and Bo Diddley. Classic cuts: 'Willie And The Hand Jive', 'One Bourbon, One Scotch, One Beer'.

Tom Verlaine: a poet's name for a lyrical player.

TOM VERLAINE Founder of important mid-'70s New York band Television, Verlaine has influenced many young guitarists with his fierce and sometimes perverse guitar patterns. Now solo, he may still come to wider recognition. Classic cuts: 'Marquee Moon' (Television), 'A Town Called Walker'.

Led Zep's legendary double act: Plant, Page and double-necked Gibson.

Fast Eddie Van Halen, the man with the dopiest grin in rock.

EDDIE VAN HALEN

MANY REGARD Eddie Van Halen as the greatest rock guitarist playing today. A brilliant player, he combines lightning-fast fingering with a seemingly limitless vocabulary of techniques and effects.

He uses every trick in the book to build excitement – controlled feedback, harmonics, vibrato – but also brings to heavy rock a rare invention and creativity.

Netherlands-born in 1957, Van Halen and his drummer brother Alex eventually moved to California and formed the band (originally named Mammoth) with vocalist David Lee Roth and bass player Mike Anthony. Following a change of name to Van Halen, the outfit signed to Warners and released their first album in 1978.

The record was immediately successful, and Van Halen went from strength to strength gradually adding real humour to their winning blend of energy, machismo and metal mayhem.

After the band found pop chart success with 'Jump' (featuring excellent keyboards by Eddie), Roth quit for a solo career. Many thought Van Halen would founder, but Eddie showed new strength, coming to the front alongside new singer Sammy Hagar. Hits such as 'Why Can't This Be Love' from the excellent '5150' album continued their chart-topping ways.

Eddie's exceptional talent has played a major part in the band's success. Classic cuts: 'Beat It' (Michael Jackson), 'Eruption' (Van Halen).

Steve Vai plays another hot lick.

STEVE VAI A former member of Frank Zappa's band and John Lydon's PiL, Vai made his mark with rock audiences as David Lee Roth's guitar showman – a tough assignment since Roth's previous partner was Eddie Van Halen. Classic cuts: 'Single' (PiL), 'Yankee Rose' (David Lee Roth).

MUDDY WATERS Blues legend who was major influence on '60s rock. Renowned for powerful vocals and incisive single-string bottleneck guitar played with almost frightening

venom. Probably *the* central figure in blues history, he continued making great records till his death aged 68 in 1983 – his last few albums featuring Johnny Winter. Classic cuts: 'I Can't Be Satisfied', 'Long Distance Call'.

CLARENCE WHITE Legendary flatpicker and leader of Kentucky Colonels, widely regarded as best bluegrass group of all time. Went on to join Byrds and help originate country-rock sound. Died in 1972. Classic cuts: 'When You're Smiling' (Kentucky Colonels), 'Eight Miles High' (Byrds, live).

JOHNNY WINTER Texan blues wizard launched to much acclaim in late '60s as albino version of Hendrix, but lost his way in obsession with speed over subtlety. Reurned to blues roots in late '70s with excellent LPs with Muddy Waters. Classic cuts: 'No Time To Live', 'Highway 61 Revisited'.

Muddy Waters, king of Chicago, with Telecaster.

LINK WRAY Pioneer rock player whose reputation is largely based on early '50s million-seller 'Rumble' featuring cavernous guitar sound. Cited as influence by Pete Townshend and Jeff Beck. Classic cut: 'Rumble'.

Frank Zappa finger picks his Les Paul.

FRANK ZAPPA Leader of '60s legends Mother of Invention, and prolific guitarist, composer and producer. Possesses quirky and eclectic guitar style, often plays in odd time signatures. Classic cuts: 'Hot Rats', 'Sheik Yerbouti'.

BUSINESS SECTION

So far, so good. You've read the Instruction Manual, Chord Directory, Buyer's Guide and Who's Who—how to play, what to play, what to buy and who to look out for. You're ready to join the music business. Now how do you get your foot in the door?

That's where our Business Section comes in. In it you'll find a rundown of the various ways you might develop your talent, either as a professional or part-time musician. And to finish the book off, there's a detailed chart of how the music industry works, showing the relationships between all the different people who work in it, and the stages an artist's work goes through on its way to the public. The music business is often referred to as a jungle. We can't tell you how to be king, but we can help you cut your way through to your goal.

CONTENTS

FORMING A BAND

IF YOU'VE followed every stage of this book and put in plenty of practice time, you should now have a good grasp of the basic elements of rock guitar playing. You're ready to take things a stage further – so where do you go from here?

If you decide to put a band together, you'll find there's a lot of practical matters that have to be sorted out. Even on a small scale, running a band is a time-consuming activity – and a great deal of that time is taken up by planning and day-to-day administration.

The first thing to consider is – who's in the band? You're going to end up spending a lot of time together, so compatibility is vitally important. The other members don't have to be your *best* friends, but if you're not all on roughly the same wavelength you'll be in for problems later – either when you start to get successful and there's some money to squabble over, or when you *don't* get successful right away and you start to argue about why.

Again, it makes sense if you're all at roughly the same level of musical ability. Carrying someone who's not really competent slows down rehearsals and recording, puts live performances at risk, and generally ends in tears.

IN REHEARSAL

HAVING SET your line-up, you're going to need somewhere to rehearse – a stumbling-block for many young bands. Ideally of course you need a place where you can leave your gear permanently, that's soundproof and entirely free of charge. The reality usually falls well short of this ideal, but a number of options are available, depending on the kind of area you live in. Church and meeting halls are often available for a reasonable fee, some

"People think of me as a soul fan, but you should have heard my first group—we sounded like Siouxsie And The Banshees. I definitely prefer being in a-group: there's less pressure and you can call on other people's opinions. It can be really boring on your own."　　　　　　　　**ALISON MOYET**

clubs are open during the day for rehearsals, and in many towns there are purpose-built rehearsal rooms – though obviously these charge commercial rates for their accommodation.

If you can get hold of somewhere private but are worried by the noise factor, consider soundproofing the premises yourself. Ideally you need acoustic tiles of the type used in recording studios, but heavy material draped around the walls can make a surprising difference.

Then there's the question of transport. A gigging band needs a truck or van, and this is one area where it's best to spend as much as you can afford. Unreliable transport is really worse than none at all.

Don't forget that you can always hire transport, and in the early days when times are tight this can make a lot of sense.

MONEY MATTERS

WHICH BRINGS us to the question which most often bedevils starting-out bands: money. At the beginning everything – equipment, transport, rehearsal rooms – is going to *cost* you money. You're going to have to make some early decisions on just how you're going to handle these expenses.

Does one member of the band act as treasurer, extracting contributions from the others and handling the bills as they come in? Should you open a bank account in the band's name? Do you all make the same contributions, whether you have day jobs or not?

If you have money coming in from gigs you'll have some floating capital, so proper administration becomes even more vital. How much money goes into each member's pocket, how much into a central band fund? Do you all get equal shares?

The point is, you have to deal with the money angle up front, so that everyone knows exactly what's going on. Make sure that detailed records are kept and you'll reduce the chances of 'misunderstandings' at a later date.

PLAYING IN HARMONY

HOWEVER, RUNNING a band isn't all administration – there's also the question of music! The first thing is to agree amongst yourselves about the type of music you want to play. If three of you are committed punk revivalists and the fourth is a secret admirer of Barbra Streisand, you're not going to get very far.

You're bound to have musical tastes

"My first group was a band in Liverpool called Send No Flowers. I only did two rehearsals and they kicked me out because they said I couldn't sing!"
IAN ASTBURY, THE CULT

that differ to some extent, but as a band you need to be pulling in roughly the same direction. When you've become mega-rich rock stars, *then* you can afford to split up citing musical differences!

ALL YOUR OWN WORK

WHATEVER KIND of music you want to play, at some point you're going to have to think about original material. When you first start playing together you'll probably fall back on the rock standards and twelve-bar blues you all know. This may get you local gigs, but if you've got your eyes set on greater things, sooner or later you're going to have to start writing.

In the next chapter you'll find some detailed advice on how to go about it.

THE FIRST GIG

SO THERE you are. Four or five of you have got together. You've begged, borrowed or even bought most of the equipment you need and you've got somewhere to rehearse. No problems with 'musical direction' – you've already put together an hour's worth of material. How do you get it heard?

Well, don't forget that you've got access to a ready-made public that is disposed to think well of you – a public that consists of your friends and relatives. The chances are that sooner or later your band will be asked to play at a wedding, party or some other private function, and you'll have the perfect opportunity to try out your skills in front of a live audience (assuming you play 'party' music). One booking can lead to another, and if you're lucky you'll soon find you've got some money coming in and the beginnings of a reputation.

THE IMAGE IS THE MESSAGE

LOCAL PARTIES and functions are only the first step on the road to professional employment – nevertheless, you should start as you mean to go on and have a few thoughts about the kind of visual image you want to project.

It doesn't matter that much at this stage, as you'll develop your own visual style as you go along, but it is always worth thinking in terms of impact and originality. What is it that's going to distinguish you from the next band?

WHAT'S IN A NAME?

ANOTHER THING you're going to have to think about at this stage is naming the band – a job which can be quite amazingly time-consuming. You'll probably end up with a shortlist with seventy names on it, and you'll still be convinced that all the best ones have already gone.

Think hard about the kind of impression you want to make – exotic, punky, straightforward – and whatever you choose, try to make it memorable and original. It's generally best to avoid overly offensive names like Garbage Breath or The Haemorrhods – they may seem funny(ish) now, but they're almost certain to become a millstone round your neck at some point in the future.

PRACTICE MAKES PERFECT

YOUR FIRST gig is bound to be a little 'untidy'. The audience might have

"We argue a lot—it's the only way to get something really good. Both of us have to be satisfied with a song. The secret is in editing our own work. If things don't sound good, we don't labour over them, we just reject them. There are plenty of half-finished songs around."

ANNIE LENNOX, EURYTHMICS

enjoyed it, but there *was* that embarrassing moment when half the band thought the number had finished while the other half carried on regardless... You have to admit your performance did leave a little bit to be desired. So what do you do?

You go back to your rehearsal room and work your way through the whole set again. Then you do it again... and again, until you get absolutely everything right, from the introduction of the first number right the way through to the encore.

You should aim at being able to perform your repertoire without thinking – without having to worry about whether you can remember the next chord change or the lyrics to the next verse. Once you've reached this stage you'll be able to concentrate on projecting yourselves, on creating atmosphere, on putting some control and feeling into the music.

Don't waste time when you're rehearsing. Get down to business as soon as possible. How you rehearse depends to a great extent on what kind of band you are. You might have a leader/songwriter who demos his or her song and then tells all the other members of the band

exactly how to play it – or every member of the band might make their own contribution to every arrangement.

However you handle it, try and get every song note-perfect – a good test is whether each member of the band can play his or her part all the way through without accompaniment. Go on until you get it right – but if you really can't seem to get it together, leave it for another day. There's nothing worse than hammering away at a song you're beginning to get heartily sick of.

OFF THE RECORD

ONE FURTHER thought. If you're reading this book, the chances are you're the sort of person who listens to a lot of records. From now on, try and listen analytically. Keep asking yourself questions...

Why is this a hit song? Why is this keyboard solo a classic? Why is this band exciting, that one boring?

In rock, as in all art and entertainment, half the trick is knowing what's good. You can have all the talent in the world, but if you don't know how to edit yourself – how to cut out the overblown, the pretentious and the simply boring – your abilities may well pass unnoticed.

WRITING SONGS

IF YOU want to get ahead in the music business you've got to write your own material. There are artists who make it with other people's songs, but they're few and far between.

The pop industry runs on hit songs, and your writing can influence a manager or record company A&R man just as much as your performing skills.

It's also worth remembering that generally speaking, writers end up richer. Your name in small letters under the title of a song means a whole lot of extra money in royalties. Every time your song is played in an airport lounge, you earn! Every time someone covers your song, you earn! In the case of standards like 'Sunshine Of My Life' and 'Just The Way You Are', cover versions can run into hundreds – and royalty income can run into millions.

GETTING STARTED

SO, HOW do you start? Well, the chances are that you've already fiddled around with a few snatches of lyric and some simple chords – and you've been disappointed because your efforts somehow didn't sound like chartbusters.

Well, don't worry about it – practically everyone who starts writing songs produces a lot of rubbish to begin with. There's only one way to get better – and that's to keep on doing it. There's no substitute for experience, and if you're prepared to be ruthless with yourself and accept constructive criticism from others, the chances are that your writing will gradually improve.

There is no set method of writing songs. For one thing, there is no set goal. Some people just want to write top 50 hits; others have something to say, whether lyrically or musically, and hang the commercial potential.

Even when two writers do share a goal – say, to get a number one single – they very rarely go about it in the same way.

Having said that, if your aim is to get a recording contract, the best thing you can have in your portfolio is a clutch of potential chart songs.

GETTING A HIT

WE CAN'T TELL you how to write a hit song, but we *can* get you in the ballpark.

First, your song has to make musical sense. Think about the relationship between notes and chords you've already learnt – for instance, the way **C**, **Dm**, **Em**, **F**, **G** and **Am** work together in the key of **C**.

If you're a songwriter, music is your

"I keep all the demo tapes of songs I've ever done. I often go back and pick bits out, remodelling them. There are hours and hours of music, some of it really atrocious—trying to construct a song out of different elements and failing miserably—but bits are useful."
HOWARD JONES

language. The better you know it, the more you can do with it. If you want to break the rules, go ahead. But it will help if you know them first – and discordant songs are unlikely to get you signed to CBS.

Secondly, keep it simple. Most hit songs revolve around a limited number of chords, riffs and rhythms. Today's top songwriters such as George Michael and Bruce Springsteen frequently revisit the same musical ground trodden by Smokey Robinson or Bob Dylan in the '60s, and they wouldn't pretend otherwise.

It's even more important for you, as a

new songwriter, to keep your material direct and immediate. You only have a limited time to win over your audience, whether that audience is in a dancehall or behind a record company desk. They need to be able to make sense of it in a hurry.

WORKING METHODS

GOOD SONGS rarely write themselves. Mostly it's hard work. So set aside time for songwriting. If you simply wait for inspiration to strike, you'll end up with a very thin repertoire.

How you actually go about songwriting is of course very largely up to you. Some writers go for a melody and then fit lyrics around it. Some take the reverse approach. Many match snatches of words to melody as they go along, redrafting them into coherent lyrics later. Sometimes a good title can set off a whole song.

Consider right at the start what your strengths and weaknesses are. If you've got a good ear for a melody but fumble over the lyrics, or vice versa, the solution may be to find a partner. After all, some of the greatest rock and pop songs have been written by teams – Lennon/ McCartney, Jagger/Richard, Holland/ Dozier/Holland – the list is endless.

Working in a partnership certainly has advantages. You get built-in criticism, and there's always someone there to help you along when your enthusiasm flags.

SONG STRUCTURE

WITHIN MAINSTREAM pop or rock, songs still tend to follow the traditional song structures: intro/verse/chorus/verse/ chorus/solo/verse/chorus, etc.

If in doubt, use these devices: they give the song pacing, and ensure that it doesn't just drone on and on.

Make sure you know what you want to achieve. The structure can reinforce the mood through repetition, climax, sudden changes of direction. . .

Think about who is to perform it. If you're in a band, some of your songs may not suit the group. Don't let that stop you finishing them: it's all good practice and you may be able to use the song later. But if you're writing with the group in mind, imagine them performing it as you write, and try to build in elements that will flatter their talents.

Above all, give it some shape: a beginning, middle and end if you like.

Once you've got a song on the way, make sure you write down all the elements on paper – chords, melody line, and any ideas you might have for riffs, basslines or solos – using either musical notation or some other system such as our musical grids. There's nothing more frustrating than 'losing' a song.

It's also a good idea to record each song onto tape, even if it's just a portable cassette recorder – for a start, you can hear it more objectively – but don't make this your only record.

One other thing. Once you've got a routine for songwriting. . . break it, at least now and then. Working with the

Lionel Richie (left) onstage with Eric Clapton.
"I'm so wired after a concert that the only way to relax is to write songs. Sometimes I'll write for six hours after a show. On tour I take an eight-track recording machine, two synthesisers and a drum machine to demo my songs. Technology has made it all so simple." **LIONEL RICHIE**

"When I was about 11, I used to muck around on my father's piano. I got a tremendous sense of fulfilment out of it, and it just became an obsession. I used to spend all my time writing songs at the piano, but that's changed now. I've got my own studio, so I can play about with different sounds on the Fairlight or the Emulator. Production has become part of the songwriting. It doesn't matter if people don't fully understand what my songs are about; the most important thing is what they feel. That's what music is really all about: emotion."

KATE BUSH

guitar – or any other instrument – there is a tendency to 'follow your hands'. You ring the changes on the chords you know, and the results can become predictable and repetitive. Don't get yourself in a rut.

SELF-PROTECTION

OK, LET'S say you've done everything right. You've listened to all the top songsmiths and taken in what they're doing, you've formulated your own original style of songwriting, and finally you've come up with a clutch of respectable songs. How do you stop your precious works from being ripped off?

In the first place there's no need to worry unduly. As a general rule, people in the music business don't want to steal your songs. If you have in fact got the ability to write saleable songs, they'd rather sign you to a publishing and/or recording contract so that they make money out of you in the future as well as now.

Having said that, it is true that there are some sleazy types around who are prepared to take your song, change a bit here and a bit there, and claim it as their own. Every year there are court actions involving hits which, it is claimed, have been lifted from other songwriters or old songs. As often as not, the resemblance is judged to be unintentional. There are a limited number of melodies and rhythms in rock, and most of them have been used dozens of times in the past thirty years.

If you happen to create something identical to someone else's work, but completely separately, you hold the copyright to your work. If, however, you copy someone else's work, you're in breach of copyright — even if you copy it unintentionally, for instance by recycling some old song that's lurking at the back of your mind. It's easily done without realising it — but as soon as you do realise it, change the song!

It's even dangerous to 'quote' an old song as a tribute to its author. If you write, "And Bob Dylan said, The answer my friend is blowing in the wind", in theory Dylan could sue you for breach of copyright and a share of your royalties.

As soon as you write something and record it, on paper or on tape, you own the copyright.

The problem is to prove it. One cheap, simple way to do this is to seal it in a package and send it to yourself by registered post. Don't open the package: the postmark proves when it was sealed and posted. In most cases this should be sufficient, but it doesn't guarantee complete legal protection.

Another method is to deposit your tape or manuscript with a bank or solicitor, and get a statement from them saying when it was deposited, and that the person depositing it claimed to be the author.

If you really want to be certain – particularly if you are moving into a position where people in the business are beginning to hear your songs – the best thing to do is consult a lawyer, preferably one with music business experience.

If your songs prove to be commercially viable, the chances are that at some stage you will sign to a publisher. The publisher's job is to try to get your songs used, and to collect royalty payments on your behalf whenever your song is played, recorded or printed.

Once your songs are being performed live, on radio or TV or on record, you will be eligible to join the organisations which exist to collect royalties for composers and songwriters.

In the US these include BMI (Broadcast Music Inc.), ASCAP (American Society of Composers, Authors and Publishers) and the Harry Fox Agency; in Britain the PRS (Performing Right Society) and the MCPS (Mechanical Copyright Protection Society).

Your publisher will be able to advise, bearing in mind that it is in his/her interest to make sure that you receive all the royalties that are due to you.

In the meantime, however. . . just keep on writing. Remember, huge hits have been written in ten minutes – and after all, you've got to have *something* to put on the demo tape. . .

THE DEMO tape is the calling card of the music business. Every morning, all over the world, thousands of cassettes drop onto the doormats of managers, agents, promoters, DJs and record companies. Whether they're good, bad or indifferent, they carry the hopes of countless young people who think they've got what it takes to make a living in music, and maybe become the next big thing.

So what happens to all these musical missives? If you make a demo and send it off to take its chances amongst the armada of tapes floating around, will it even get listened to?

Perhaps surprisingly, yes it probably will. Every band tells stories of demos despatched into the blue never to be heard of again, but in general if you send someone a tape they'll get to hear it – eventually. You may have to wait months to hear from them, you may never hear from them at all – but you can be pretty sure that at some point your tape will have been given a whirl.

It'll get heard because – although the opposite often seems to be the case – the music industry is always desperate for new talent. Very few managers or record companies can afford totally to ignore the tapes that turn up on their doorsteps.

On the other hand, listening to unsolicited tapes is not a priority. Music business professionals are generally going to deal first with acts recommended by people already known to them (one of the reasons why any contact is better than none). Your tape will most likely be heard first by a secretary or junior staff member of the organisation you sent it to. It will only reach the boss by a process of elimination.

Don't forget, if the executive *is* impressed by your tape, he or she probably still has to convene meetings, canvass other people's opinions, and go through the whole corporate decision-making process before getting back to you – so when it comes to submitting demos, patience is a virtue.

WHAT THEY WANT TO HEAR

SO WHAT can you do to make sure that your demo overcomes all the hurdles and makes the best possible impression? What do people in the music business *want* to hear?

As ever, it doesn't do any harm to have some great songs. The ideal demo tape is one which contains one or more obvious major hits, preferably requiring little or no alteration or re-arrangement. If it is of master tape quality, yielding records that can be released without re-recording – so much the better!

Apart from hits, the professionals look for signs of originality – 'newness' if you like – but you don't have to be eccentric or peculiar. At the time of writing, the record business is not going overboard on art-rock, and that situation looks likely to remain the same for some time.

They also want to hear strong, distinctive vocals, at least competent instrumen-

tal skills, and signs' of genuine talent. Don't forget that ultimately they're looking for something they can sell, something that is going to give people so much pleasure that they are actually prepared to pay for it.

Some of the things they don't want to hear are: lengthy instrumental workouts (unless the band in question is working in an essentially non-vocal field like jazz-rock – and then the instrumental skills should be exceptional); cover versions, unless they're done in such a way as to have new and saleable qualities; and solo voice-and-acoustic-guitar performances. The latter were of course staple fare a few years ago, but nowadays the average music business executive tends to reach for the stop button at the first sign of a tinny acoustic chord. .

"We came to London in 1983 and toured all the record companies without success. But we kept making demo tapes, and eventually the manager of the demo studio offered to manage us. The first company he approached signed us up." **MORTEN HARKET, A-HA**

The question is, how can you make your demo stand out from the crowd of hopefuls and also-rans?

PRESENTATION

THE ANSWER can be summed up in one word: presentation. A great many bands let themselves down by a lack of basic professionalism when it comes to demo tapes. Often even the appearance of the demo – scruffy packaging, smudged hand-written titles – is enough to put off potential listeners. When it comes to the music, poor sound quality, badly thought-out arrangements and even fluffed notes often push interesting ideas and genuine talent into the background.

So adopt a professional attitude right from the start. Consider first how much you can afford to spend – bearing in mind that, as in most other fields, you tend to

get what you pay for.

Even if you are operating on a tight budget, you should dismiss the thought of making a demo at home. (Unless you're broke *and* you've got a really brilliant song – most music business professionals pride themselves on their ability to spot an outstanding song however poor the quality of the recording.) Your best bet by far is to book yourself into a professional demo studio.

By doing so you'll not only gain the benefits of professional recording equipment and facilities, you'll also be able to draw on the skill and experience of a professional recording engineer. With a professional behind the mixing desk, you can concentrate on your performance, on making your demo what it should be – a 'demonstration' of your band's ability when playing at the top of its form.

CHOOSING A STUDIO

THE QUESTION then arises – which studio should you pick? The choice is endless, ranging from converted rooms in private houses (these can sometimes be surprisingly good, usually due to the enthusiasm of their owner/operators), through purpose-built professional demo studies all the way up to the major studio complexes where the hits are made.

Costs can also vary enormously, depending on the number of tracks available, the size of the studio, the facilities, the studio's reputation and other factors. But one thing worth bearing in mind is that the hourly rate tends to drop the further you get from the city. Sometimes a lengthy trip can yield surprising dividends in terms of affordable studio time.

The best thing is to ask other musicians. The good (or bad) word about a studio soon gets around, and musicians who have actually used the facilities are the best qualified to judge. A lot of the differences between studios lie in 'feel' or atmosphere – something you have to have experienced to recognize.

If you can't get any word-of-mouth recommendations, you're going to have to do a little research.

Check out the music press by all means – but don't be tempted simply to pick the studio offering the cheapest hourly rate. Call a few studios and compare costs. Ask them how many tracks they offer – studios can be anything from four-track to 48-track – and what facilities. What other bands have worked there?

Once you've hit upon a studio where everything seems right, book your session. But don't relax – your work has only just begun.

PREPARATION

FIRST, DECIDE on the songs you want to record. Go for the ones with the most instant appeal, the ones that really leap out and grab the listener's attention. Whatever kind of music you play, memorable melody lines and catchy 'hook' phrases carry a lot of weight when it comes to demos. Remember, the person who's going to listen to your tape is probably going to do so in a hurry – fast forwarding through your carefully crafted epics, trying to get an instant fix on what it's all about. Make sure your tape is full of solid 'meat', and save the atmosphere-building intros and extended solos for live gigs.

Unless someone already has an interest in your band and has specifically asked for a longer tape, don't plan on demoing more than four or five songs. But once you've decided on them, make sure you *know* them. Rehearse them again and again until you can all play your parts in your sleep – and remember that faults which might go unnoticed live will become glaringly obvious during a recording session.

Having made sure that the band is

"I met Dave Gilmour of Pink Floyd (above) through a friend, and he used his name and money to enable me to make a proper demo tape. I couldn't have done it on my own—I'd go round the record companies, but nobody wanted to know."
KATE BUSH

musically perfect, you should make sure that all your equipment is in equally good shape. Check all your instruments, leads and amps, bearing in mind that any stray buzzes and hums are going to sound horribly worse in the studio.

One other thing – when the day of your session dawns, get there early. The studio will have allowed a period before your session for you to set up your equipment – much better to use that than waste precious recording time.

IN THE STUDIO

HOPEFULLY YOU will have been able to take a look at the set-up before arriving for your session, so you will know roughly what to expect. However, if you've never seen the inside of a studio before, this is what it will look like.

There will be a control room where the

tape machines and ancillary equipment are situated. The room will be dominated by a control 'desk' – size depending on the number of tracks – covered in switches, dials and fader controls. The engineer sits at the desk and looks out through a soundproof window into the studio itself, communicating with those in the studio via a speaker system. (Incidentally, even in the most elaborate studios control room accommodation tends to be cramped – it isn't a good idea to ask friends along to your session.)

The studio itself will be lined with soundproof material and cluttered with mikes, mikestands, headphones and all the other paraphernalia of recording. A portion will probably be screened off to accommodate the drums, to avoid them overpowering other instruments during recording. All except the smallest studios will have a piano. Many will also have synthesisers and drum machines, though you may have to pay extra to use them.

Once you've set up your gear – generally positioned by the engineer or assistant – you'll all be 'miked up', particular concern again being paid to the drum set. Then the engineer will ask you each to play a few runs to get a recording 'level' – and you're ready to go.

Well, some of you are anyway. Recordings are made by building up layers, track by track, and you invariably start by laying down the rhythm track. To keep everything together, the lead vocalist will normally sing a 'guide vocal' along with the rhythm section – this will be scrubbed out later.

Once the rhythm and bass tracks are completed to everyone's satisfaction, the next step might be to record, say, keyboards and guitar. Finally, the finished vocal is added and vocal harmonies, if any, layered on. The vocalists generally have to peform on their own in the studio, with the rhythm track being relayed through headphones – a slightly daunting task if you haven't done it before!

However, recording should be an enjoyable process – provided you know your material and you don't try and do too much in one session. You don't have to get everything right first time. If you're not happy with anything, do it again – and again, if you want. If your vocals were perfect until the last chorus when you forgot the words – no problem. The engineer can 'drop you in' so that the final result will be seamless – a perfect vocal from beginning to end. There's all sorts of studio trickery that can be used to correct imperfections, from strengthening vocals to speeding up the entire finished recording, and the more sophisticated the studio you hire, the more facilities of this type will be available.

Don't forget, the engineer is there to help you. If this is your first demo session, you don't know all the ins and outs of production technique, but you do know what you want the final result to sound

like. However inexperienced, you and your band are paying for the studio and you are the producers – so keep on until you get it the way you want it.

This particularly applies when you have finished laying down tracks and are ready to 'mix' – that is, integrate all the tracks into the final finished product. The 'mix' is one of the most important parts of the whole recording process – to a large extent it determines what your demo is actually going to sound like.

Unfortunately it's also the area at which you, first-time recording artists, are likely to have least experience. There's no easy answer. You have to ask questions, absorb the processes which go into putting together a mix, and be insistent about the result you want.

But remember this is a demo, not an

"The industry is looking for hit singles. I got so many letters saying the tracks on our demo weren't commercial enough and were too long, we should do three-minute singles. We had to build up a live following to get signed."
FISH, MARILLION

album. You needn't bother with some of the enhancing effects which are available at this stage. Managers and A&R men know that anyone can add echo and reverb – they want to hear what you've basically got to offer, unhindered by extraneous technical wizardry.

THE END RESULT

AT THE end of it all you should have a master tape and a number of cassette copies – cassettes rather than reel-to-reel tapes or discs are the accepted medium for demos. You've spent a lot of time and probably quite a lot of money getting to this stage, but you've now got a shop window for your talents, a calling card that can open the door to all sorts of possibilities. With a good demo to your name you're up and running – and ready to stop the rock business in its tracks. . .

IF YOU want to take things a stage further, the next step has got to be performing in public – to an audience of paying customers. But remember, playing in public is a quantum leap away from playing for your friends. The public at large don't care whether you're a nice guy or not, they just want to be entertained.

From your point of view, this means more rehearsal, more individual practice, more day-to-day administration – in fact, a major investment of time and energy. Running a gigging band can take up all your time if you're not careful, so you'd better be sure that it's a commitment you want to make.

You're going to have to be prepared for setbacks too. Until you build a reputation, you're an unknown quantity, which means it's hard to get gigs and even harder to make a success of them when you do get them. Once you're playing for money, at whatever level, you're competing with bands that might have been round for years – and you're going to be judged against them.

DO THE HUSTLE

SO HOW do you set about getting those all-important first gigs, the gigs that will transform your band into a semi-professional if not a professional outfit?

As a means of getting some sort of track record, you might find it worthwhile to play for nothing – or expenses only – to begin with. For example, charities often mount benefit concerts for one good cause or another, and they're generally only too glad to add another band to the bill.

By the same token, local clubs are always promoting talent nights, usually on a slack night of the week. On those nights they will present two or three bands on an expenses-only basis, charging low door prices to attract custom. Again, the benefit is mutual – they cover a slack night and you get to play in public, with the chance, if you impress, of getting a real paid booking at a later date.

THE RIGHT PEOPLE

WHEN IT comes to real, paid bookings, you won't find it easy. Over the last few years the number of small venues – particularly those prepared to take a chance on new talent – has not kept up with the explosion in the number of new bands. Getting a gig has never been easy, but it's more difficult than ever now.

Your biggest problem is simply getting the right people to see or hear you play. Unless you're lucky enough to get spotted at a benefit gig or on a talent night, you're probably going to have to rely on your demo tape – the good old 'calling card' of the music business.

Needless to say, you shouldn't simply send it out to every venue in your area. Club owners, like record companies, get demo tapes arriving by every post, and they have even less time to listen to them.

Instead, do your homework first. Visit all the likely venues in your area. Check out which ones would be right for your kind of music. See if you can find out who does the booking. Make the acquaintance of other musicians, and ask their opinion. Find out which places have a policy of trying out new talent.

Don't send your demo, give it to the booker personally. Make sure it's well packaged and presented, with the name of your band and a number where you can be contacted. Don't bother with photos unless they're of professional standard and they say something about your band – no one's interested in snapshots of you and your drummer in your back yard. Don't include written material about the band, unless you've got a worthwhile story to tell. The fact that you've played a benefit gig and got an encore might be relevant – you bass player's birth sign isn't.

Choose your moment. Don't approach a club owner during a gig, for example. He's going to be far too worried about how *this* evening's going to think about some future occasion involving your band. On the other hand, if you're around after a successful gig, when everyone's celebrating a good night and the club owner's looking forward to a big take, it might be worth approaching him. It's all a question of psychology.

You should let him know if there is any time when he can check you out in person – if you rehearse nearby, for example, or if you have any kind of a performance lined up.

MAKING CONTACTS

BEST OF all, try and find some point of personal contact before you make your approach. Sound out all your acquaintances to see if *any* of them have any connection, however remote, with the people who run venues in your area. Keep your ear to the ground around your local music shop and record store. Always keep in touch with other local musicians. The basic rule is: any contact is better than none.

Having said all that, nothing is going to help you if your band isn't up to scratch. So don't try and get gigs before you're ready. You'll simply make it doubly difficult for yourself when you are ready to take the plunge.

READY FOR ANYTHING

IF YOUR music is good enough, and you're prepared to put in the legwork, sooner or later you'll land a gig. But don't think your troubles have ended, because they've only just begun.

As with any other performance, a good rock show depends largely on preparation. Assuming that you're already well-rehearsed, that means preparation of your equipment.

Make sure it all works. If it doesn't, get it fixed, or hire or buy some more. Always make sure you carry spare leads, strings and so on. You're not going to be able to

Above: Chuck Berry jamming with Dave Edmunds.
"There's something magic about playing live, something you can't describe. Not have played live for a few months, I recently got up onstage with Dave Edmunds and it was great to be in front of an audience again. That used to be normal in the '70s, but it doesn't happen any more. As soon as you step onstage with somebody else, they think you're after their jobs." **GARY MOORE**

"I saw The Who (above) at Live Aid, when Pete Townshend fell over on his back—and Roger Daltrey immediately fell down next to him. That's what being in a band's all about. You can't laugh at a member of your own band, you have to pretend it's part of the show."

PAUL YOUNG

get hold of any on the night of the gig.

MAKING YOURSELF HEARD

THEN THERE'S the question of the PA (public address) system. If you've managed to raise the money to buy your own, then you've no problems – although you should make sure it's powerful enough to fill the venue you've been booked into.

If you haven't got an adequate system, you're going to have to hire one. There are plenty of equipment hire firms where you can rent PA suitable for venues ranging from a small club to a major stadium. Ask other musicians which is the best place to go to, ring round and get quotes, and make sure you know exactly what you are going to get for your money.

Depending on the venue, it is possible that a house PA system will be available to you. Check this out beforehand. Similarly, you may be able to borrow the PA of the headlining group, if there is one. Again, you're going to have to get in touch with the other band and find out beforehand.

Whatever you do, don't just wait until the night and hope for the best.

INSURANCE

SPEAKING OF equipment, you should consider insuring yours. Also, make sure your stuff is clearly identified as yours. Do the same as all working rock groups and stencil your name or logo on your amps and speakers.

ONE TWO THREE TESTING

ON THE day of the gig, your 'be prepared' philosophy should apply even more. Set out early – better to have to kill an hour than arrive late and have to rush setting up your equipment.

Make sure you know what time you're supposed to be playing, and what time your soundcheck is. If you're playing second fiddle to a headlining group, you probably won't be given much time for a soundcheck anyway. For the moment, you represent the downtrodden masses of the music business, and you'll be lucky if you get a few minutes after the main band has been through its entire repertoire including encores.

However long you get for a soundcheck, remember that the idea is to balance your live sound, not rehearse your set. If you have a sound mixer and someone who knows how to operate it, so much the better. If not, you're going to have to get a balance by ear. Either way, it's the last chance you'll get to iron out any unexpected glitches in your sound, so make the best of it.

IF AT FIRST YOU DON'T SUCCEED

AS TO the gig itself. . . well, as ever, how you go down largely depends on how talented you are and how much work you've put into your act. But don't be too disappointed if you don't get three encores. When it comes to playing live, nothing improves a band like playing live – the more gigs you do, the tighter and more professional you'll get. In the early days, you're doing well if you just get asked back.

Trial and error is the name of the game,

but there are nevertheless a few points you should bear in mind when you're playing to a live audience.

RUNNING ORDER

OBVIOUSLY YOU should have a running order, so that you all know what you're going to play next without massive onstage conferences. But don't be afraid to change the order if necessary, depending on how your stuff is going down. If the audience wants to bop, let them bop with some hard, up-tempo numbers – don't slow them down.

Whatever kind of music you play, and whatever order you play it in, try and avoid clichéd announcements on the lines of "are you having a good time?" Unless one of you is a real comic talent, it's best to avoid long announcements of any kind – and in-jokes are definitely out.

As for the music, give your act some sort of shape, pacing it so there is a good balance between fast and slow, loud and soft. Make sure you save a couple of your best numbers for the end, and have a real 'hit-'em-between-the-eyes' number standing by for an encore – just in case!

THE PAYOFF

FINALLY, WHEN the gig's over and the customers have gone home, there comes the moment of reckoning when you actually get a cash sum thrust into your hands, the moment that makes all the sweat and hustle, the cramped van and the even more cramped dressing-room seem worthwhile. You're on your way to becoming professional musicians.

IT SOMETIMES seems as though half the population under thirty is in a band. Yet at the same time, there are fewer opportunities to play live, and even the mighty record business is feeling the pinch.

Despite the record-breaking sales achieved by megastars like Michael Jackson and Bruce Springsteen, sales overall are down.

So currently the supply of bands is somewhat outstripping the demand, and the result is that it's harder than ever to get the break that will turn your outfit from a working semi-pro band into a collection of rock stars.

Having said that, there's always room at the top for someone new, original or just plain lucky. If you've got talent and, even more important, sheer determination, you can still make it in the music business.

A WORD IN YOUR EAR

AS WE discussed previously, contacts are important. Of course if the band's no good, it's not going to help if your uncle is the managing director of a major record company. But if you have got the potential, you need to start off a ripple of word-of-mouth appreciation, a buzz, which is eventually going to reach the ears of the right people in the business.

So whenever you're gigging, try and get people to come and see you – anyone whose opinion is worth something, like local journalists (who sometimes also freelance for national publications), other musicians (particularly those in more established bands) and people on the periphery of the music business proper, like record store and music shop owners. Find out whether record companies have representatives living locally, and ask them along too.

As we've said before, a recommendation, however remote, can make all the difference.

For example, the person who reviews your gig for the local paper might also review records – in which case they're probably on the mailing list of several record companies, and known to their press officers. If you can get that reviewer to submit your demo for you, or even just make a call to the press office before you submit it, you're in with a much better chance.

When you're trying to make these first few contacts, don't forget that the music industry is a small world. Journalists know publicists, managers hang out with record company execs, A&R scouts drink in the same places as agents. So if someone receives your tape and is impressed by it, even if they're not interested in taking matters further themselves, they'll pass it on to someone who might be. So a tape sent to an agent could eventually land you a management contract.

"We don't have a manager, so we discuss all decisions among ourselves. But the more successful we become, the harder it gets—on tour it's a real strain. I wouldn't advise any young group to do it our way. You need a manager if you're looking for a deal."

DAVE GAHAN, DEPECHE MODE

Talking of management, you'll probably find out quite early on that there's no shortage of so-called 'managers' at a minor league level. Typically, these are small businessmen – sometimes on the periphery of the music business – who for one reason or other want to get involved with a band. *You* have to make up your mind whether you want to get involved with *them*.

DON'T GET TIED DOWN

OBVIOUSLY, A LOCALLY based manager can be useful if he (or she) can hustle gigs for you. A manager with funds might be a help in getting equipment, transport and so on. At best, he could help you make those first important contacts.

On the other hand, there's probably not a lot he can do that you can't do yourself, and he is likely to try and tie you down to some sort of contractual agreement. This will probably be bad news if you do start to make some headway in the music business, as record companies generally prefer new bands to come unencumbered by advisers of any kind. They prefer to place new bands with manage-

ment companies of their own choice. Likewise, heavyweight management companies are generally not keen on having to buy out some smalltimer before they can handle you.

On the whole, it's probably better to stay clear of the smalltime local manager. But if you do come across someone who looks as if he can genuinely do something for you, don't sign anything. Keep your relationship on a 'gentlemen's agreement' basis. If he insists on some form of contract, two golden rules apply.

First, you must take the advice of an independent lawyer (something you should do at all important junctures of your career anyway). Secondly, if you must sign, it's the length of the contract that's important. Keep the period down to a year, or two years at most. That way, if the worst comes to the worst, you can always just sit out your contract before making your next move.

JOINING THE MAJOR LEAGUE

WHETHER YOU have a relationship with a local manager or not, when you make your first approaches to the music business you may do well to try management outfits first, rather than record companies.

There are several good reasons for this. In the first place, record companies have a higher profile, and tend to get swamped by hopefuls who have copied down their addresses from record sleeves. What's more, they prefer acts who are immediately recordable. Management companies, on the other hand, work at the coalface of the music business. They are to a greater extent in the business of finding and developing raw talent, and are sometimes prepared to take time and trouble over an act that a record company would regard as simply not ready.

If you're courting, or being courted by, a management company, try and find out as much as possible about them – who their other artists are, the kind of reputation they have, their track record. Music business managers are a notoriously tough breed, and many of them are legendary for their uncompromising business methods. But if you do come up against any types who are reputed to hold those who displease them out of upper storey windows, don't let it necessarily put you off. Such types are often fiercely protective of their artists' interests, and people who receive the window treatment are usually those who owe the act money.

IN THE BUSINESS

WHETHER YOU sign with a management or record company first, the moment you put your signature on the dotted line, you're in. You've joined the music business, become part of the powerful machine that can open the doors to radio, TV, headlining tours and eventual fame and fortune. Your management team and record company will set you up with all the other experts and specialists that a promising young band needs on the road

"We got signed through having a single released on an independent label. It's the fastest way: you can spend years on the concert circuit without getting noticed, and demo tapes can get lost in an office, so indie singles are the best way to attract attention. We did it on a one-off basis, so we wouldn't have to wait for the deal with the indie label to run out."

WAYNE HUSSEY, THE MISSION

"I had to do a lot of different jobs to survive before I got a deal. A&M came to see me performing for six or seven months, but they didn't make a definite offer until the *New York Times* wrote a story about me."

SUZANNE VEGA

moment, you're going to be pretty much treated as a product, to be moulded and manipulated to suit the demands of the current market.

Naturally, it's up to you how much you want to bend with the wind. Some bands will do literally anything for success, others want to do things their way or not at all.

Ideally, the working relationship you establish with your management, record company and other advisers should be one of give and take. Sometimes they're going to be right, sometimes you are. But it's worth remembering that they have one asset that you at this stage don't have: experience. Whatever the music business professionals suggest is probably worth at least some consideration.

HIT POWER

HAVING SAID that, everything changes once you've got a hit record. All of a sudden you can help yourself to albums out of your record company's promotional cupboard, get through to the A&R department within seconds, and order a limo to take you down to rehearsals.

This is what you've been working for, it's when the fun really starts. All the sweaty gigs in backstreet clubs, all the demos sent off in hope, all the carefully laid plans have finally paid off. The rock dream has come true.

IT'S TOUGH AT THE TOP

BELIEVE IT or not, you're still not home and dry, because having done it once, you've got to do it again – after all, you've still got a lot of advance money to pay back! So before all the furore dies down, you've got to come up with another hit.

But if the unthinkable happens, and you find yourself drifting back into the obscurity from which you rose, at least you'll have enjoyed the ride.

to stardom.

Take a look at the chart on the next page and you'll get some idea of how it all works. Naturally this is only intended as a rough guide to the business, as the functions of the various departments and companies often overlap. We've depicted a typical major label, with numerous different departments. Many independent record companies consist of no more than a handful of people, each of whom does whatever has to be done at any given time. But even a small label will have to fulfil all the functions on our diagram.

Any band coming into the business can expect to have dealings with most or all of the different outfits shown on the diagram.

KEEP YOUR EYES OPEN

THE MODERN music business is a complex, sophisticated industry with a huge turnover. It is geared to making money, and as such is full of pitfalls for the unwary and inexperienced. That's why it is so important that you sign nothing without taking legal advice.

Once you're signed to a record company, you should see some fairly immediate improvements to your material standard of living, you'll be playing a better class of gig, staying in a better class of hotel, and using a better class of equipment. Even if you don't see much cash to begin with – and don't forget your expenses will probably be coming out of advance royalties – you're likely to be taken care of on a day to day basis.

As against all this, you're now going to have to consider the opinions and advice of others, from your manager through to the director of your video. For the

"If it was left to record company A&R men, there'd be nothing happening. They believe they predict things, but that's a joke. It's the bands that have the foresight."

PAUL RUTHERFORD, FRANKIE

BUSINESS SECTION

PLAY ROCK GUITAR

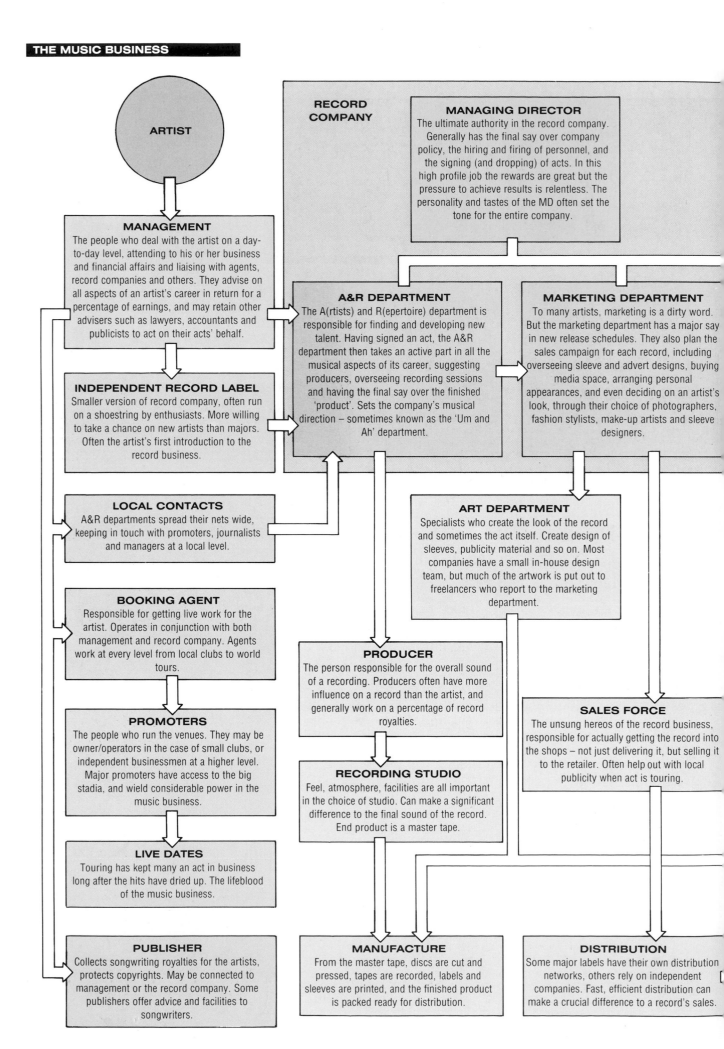

ARTIST

RECORD COMPANY

MANAGING DIRECTOR
The ultimate authority in the record company. Generally has the final say over company policy, the hiring and firing of personnel, and the signing (and dropping) of acts. In this high profile job the rewards are great but the pressure to achieve results is relentless. The personality and tastes of the MD often set the tone for the entire company.

MANAGEMENT
The people who deal with the artist on a day-to-day level, attending to his or her business and financial affairs and liaising with agents, record companies and others. They advise on all aspects of an artist's career in return for a percentage of earnings, and may retain other advisers such as lawyers, accountants and publicists to act on their acts' behalf.

A&R DEPARTMENT
The A(rtists) and R(epertoire) department is responsible for finding and developing new talent. Having signed an act, the A&R department then takes an active part in all the musical aspects of its career, suggesting producers, overseeing recording sessions and having the final say over the finished 'product'. Sets the company's musical direction – sometimes known as the 'Um and Ah' department.

MARKETING DEPARTMENT
To many artists, marketing is a dirty word. But the marketing department has a major say in new release schedules. They also plan the sales campaign for each record, including overseeing sleeve and advert designs, buying media space, arranging personal appearances, and even deciding on an artist's look, through their choice of photographers, fashion stylists, make-up artists and sleeve designers.

INDEPENDENT RECORD LABEL
Smaller version of record company, often run on a shoestring by enthusiasts. More willing to take a chance on new artists than majors. Often the artist's first introduction to the record business.

LOCAL CONTACTS
A&R departments spread their nets wide, keeping in touch with promoters, journalists and managers at a local level.

ART DEPARTMENT
Specialists who create the look of the record and sometimes the act itself. Create design of sleeves, publicity material and so on. Most companies have a small in-house design team, but much of the artwork is put out to freelancers who report to the marketing department.

BOOKING AGENT
Responsible for getting live work for the artist. Operates in conjunction with both management and record company. Agents work at every level from local clubs to world tours.

PRODUCER
The person responsible for the overall sound of a recording. Producers often have more influence on a record than the artist, and generally work on a percentage of record royalties.

PROMOTERS
The people who run the venues. They may be owner/operators in the case of small clubs, or independent businessmen at a higher level. Major promoters have access to the big stadia, and wield considerable power in the music business.

SALES FORCE
The unsung hereos of the record business, responsible for actually getting the record into the shops – not just delivering it, but selling it to the retailer. Often help out with local publicity when act is touring.

RECORDING STUDIO
Feel, atmosphere, facilities are all important in the choice of studio. Can make a significant difference to the final sound of the record. End product is a master tape.

LIVE DATES
Touring has kept many an act in business long after the hits have dried up. The lifeblood of the music business.

PUBLISHER
Collects songwriting royalties for the artists, protects copyrights. May be connected to management or the record company. Some publishers offer advice and facilities to songwriters.

MANUFACTURE
From the master tape, discs are cut and pressed, tapes are recorded, labels and sleeves are printed, and the finished product is packed ready for distribution.

DISTRIBUTION
Some major labels have their own distribution networks, others rely on independent companies. Fast, efficient distribution can make a crucial difference to a record's sales.

LABEL MANAGER

Responsible for co-ordinating the efforts of all the company's different departments. A highly responsible but often thankless position that calls for considerable administrative and management skills. Some companies have a more creative Product Manager in this position to oversee and co-ordinate all marketing; promotion and press activity.

ACCOUNTS DEPARTMENT

Responsible for all the financial aspects of the company, including staff salaries and expenses, payments to suppliers and of course to artists. Generally computerized to deal with complicated royalty payments. In recent years accountants have often risen to the highest positions in the music business, some would say to the detriment of creativity.

INTERNATIONAL DEPARTMENT

Liaises with overseas branches of the company, keeping them informed of new signings and impending releases. The international department swings into top gear when act is touring abroad, making sure that the local office is fully prepared for a promotional and publicity push.

PROMOTION DEPARTMENT

The job of the promotion department is to gain exposure for the company's artists on radio and TV. In special cases independent 'pluggers' are appointed to reinforce the in-house team. This department is often involved with making videos, and producing promotional items such as 12-inch pullout poster gatefold double-pack limited edition picture discs, which help to get a new release moving.

PRESS OFFICE

Press officers are the link between an artist and the press – newspapers, magazines, etc. They set up interviews, press conferences and press receptions, take journalists to see bands on tour or in the studio, write news releases about upcoming tours and records, send out records and concert tickets to reviewers, answer queries from journalists, and so on. Generally, any publicity which is not paid for emanates from the press office.

INDEPENDENT PUBLICIST

Specialist in press relations. Many artists have their own publicists, appointed directly by management. For a big star, the PR may spend most of their time keeping the press away.

PRESS COVERAGE

Essential to keep the artist in the public eye. Can range from profile in national newspaper to gossip in teen magazines. Some artists shun publicity and thus build up mystique.

INDEPENDENT PROMOTION

In special cases, the record company will bring in outside pluggers to gain airplay. They generally work for high fees without guaranteeing results.

RADIO AIRPLAY

Probably the most important element in breaking a record. Record companies compete fiercely with each other for the attention of DJs and radio producers.

VIDEO PRODUCTION

Videos are an integral part of record promotion, and good directors are much sought after. Some bands have been broken almost exclusively through one good video.

TV EXPOSURE

Except for the MTV music channel in the US, rock and pop receive relatively little coverage on TV. Nevertheless, the right TV exposure can break a band almost overnight.

ADVERTISING AGENCY

Plan and execute advertising campaigns for records and artists. Paid advertising is placed with care: ads for rock bands in the music press, for slushy love compilations on TV.

MEDIA SPACE

Media used include the press, posters, radio and TV. Although expensive, TV advertising can be remarkably effective in selling middle-of-the-road artists and compilation albums.

RECORD STORE

The retailer is in the front line of the record business, and can wield considerable influence. Major chain retailers can help to break an artist via point-of-sale displays, in-store record play and personal appearances.

PUBLIC

All figure references which appear in **bold** type relate to captions to illustrations.

ACKNOWLEDGMENTS

THANKS

DEWI EVANS for much good advice and the section on reading music

MARTIN McNEILL for the section on open tunings and bottleneck guitar

PAUL SELWOOD and Level 42's stage crew, for helping to set up the picture on pages 4/5

GRANT-EDWARDS MANAGEMENT for liaising with Stuart Adamson

SASHA STOJANOVIC for interview material

GAVIN WOODS for information on guitars

SONGS

'THE BOYS ARE BACK IN TOWN'
Words and music by Phil Lynott. © Copyright 1976 Pippin The Friendly Ranger Music Co. Ltd., London W1. Reproduced by permission of Chappell Music Ltd. and International Music Publications. Territory: world (excluding USA and Canada). Published in the USA by Chappell & Co. Inc. International copyright secured. All rights reserved. Used by permission.

'PHONE BOOTH'
Words and music by Robert Cray, Dennis Walker, Mike Vannice and Richard Cousins. © Copyright 1985 Calhoun Street Music (administered by Bug Music Group). British publisher Warner Bros. Music Ltd. Reproduced by kind permission.

'THAT'LL BE THE DAY'
Words and music by Norman Petty, Buddy Holly and Jerry Allison. © Copyright 1957 MPL Communications, Inc. and Wren Music Co. © renewed 1985 MPL Communications, Inc. and Wren Music Co. Southern Music Publishing Co. Ltd., 8 Denmark Street, London WC2. By arrangement Melody Lane Publications Inc. Used by kind permission. International copyright secured. All rights reserved.

PHOTOGRAPHS

LONDON FEATURES INTERNATIONAL
All pictures

MIKE PRIOR
All instruction pictures, covers, inside covers and title pages

STEVE RAPPORT
Pages 4/5, shot at Brighton Conference Centre using Level 42's stage set-up

FRONT COVER PICTURES
Richie Sambora Ilpo Musto
BB King Steve Rapport
Eddie Van Halen Ross Marino
Mark Knopfler Ilpo Musto

6 Eric Clapton Frank Griffin
6 Prince Kevin Mazur
6 Ry Cooder Steve Rapport
6 Chuck Berry Sam Emerson
6 The Edge Ilpo Musto
6 Jimi Hendrix Ronnie Sia
6 Gary Moore Ilpo Musto
6 Jimmy Page Michael Putland
6 Carlos Santana Michael Putland
8 Nils Lofgren Phil Loftus
9 Stuart Adamson Andrew Catlin
10 Bruce Springsteen Ron Wolfson
10 Chrissie Hynde Ilpo Musto
10 Pete Townshend Michael Putland
10 Chris Holmes Gene Kirkland
10 Billy Idol Ross Marino
10 Vicki Peterson Frank Griffin
12 Jimmy Page Neal Preston
15 Chuck Berry Ken Regan
16 Albert King Ebet Roberts
20 Elvis Costello Ebet Roberts
21 Buddy Holly LFI
29 Johnny Ramone Gary Merrin
39 Phil Lynott Paul Cox
39 Brian Robertson Gary Merrin
39 Scott Gorham Elaine Bryant
39 Gary Moore Simon Fowler
39 Thorogood/Collins Ken Regan
39 Jeff Beck Michael Putland
45 Robert Cray Ann Summa
46 Hank Marvin Paul Cox

55 Eric Clapton Eugene Adebari
55 ZZ Top Frank Griffin
55 Dave Edmunds Ebet Roberts
57 Jimmy Page Neal Preston
57 BB King Michael Putland
58 George Thorogood Ebet Roberts
58 Rick Nielsen Neal Preston
59 Angus Young Gene Kirkland
60 Robert Cray Geoff Swaine
62 The Beatles LFI
63 Bill Wyman Michael Putland
63 Jaco Pastorius Jonathan Postal
63 Mark King Geoff Swaine
82 Carlos Santana Henry Diltz
82 Angus Young Ebet Roberts
83 Andy Summers Ebet Roberts
83 Stevie Ray Vaughan Jonathan Postal
83 Ace Frehley Ebet Roberts
84 KK Downing Ebet Roberts
84 Rudolf Schenker Gene Kirkland
84 Bo Diddley Neil Jones
84 Frank Zappa Simon Fowler
84 Mike Antony Ross Marino
84 WASP Neil Zlozower
85 Blue Oyster Cult Frank Griffin
85 Rick Nielsen Steve Granitz
85 Nikki Sixx Neil Zlozower
86 Stratocaster Grahame Tucker
86 Susanna Hoffs Frank Griffin
86 Andy Taylor Steve Payne
86 Charlie Sexton Ross Marino
87 Lou Reed Ebet Roberts
87 Les Paul Mike Prior
87 Brian May Ilpo Musto
88 Jimi Hendrix Ken Regan
88 Eddie Van Halen Ebet Roberts
90 Midge Ure Grahame Tucker
93 Ritchie Blackmore Ebet Roberts
93 Paul Weller George Bodnar
95 Jimi Hendrix LFI
98 Stuart Adamson Eugene Adebari
98 Jeff Beck Sam Emerson
98 George Benson LFI
99 Eric Clapton Frank Griffin
99 Carlos Alomar Steve Rapport
99 Bo Diddley Neal Preston
100 Chuck Berry LFI
100 Ritchie Blackmore Ebet Roberts
100 Robert Cray Ann Summa
101 Ry Cooder LFI
101 Duane Eddy LFI

101 Rory Gallagher Paul Cox
102 ZZ Top Frank Griffin
102 Al DiMeola Paul Canty
102 Blue Oyster Cult Gene Kirkland
103 The Edge Gene Kirkland
103 The Edge Sam Emerson
103 Jerry Garcia Barry Wentzell
103 Peter Green LFI
104 Jimi Hendrix Govert De Roos
104 Steve Howe Michael Putland
104 The Smiths Ross Marino
105 Jimi Hendrix LFI
105 Nils Lofgren Jonathan Postal
105 Yngwie Malmsteen Gene Kirkland
105 Queen Steve Rapport
106 John McLaughlin Michael Putland
106 Keith Richards Ebet Roberts
107 BB King Steve Rapport
107 Phil Manzanera Grahame Tucker
107 Wendy Melvoin Ilpo Musto
108 Richie Sambora Ilpo Musto
108 Steve Stevens Neal Campisi
108 Andy Taylor Steve Payne
109 Johnny Ramone Gary Merrin
109 Chic Deborah Feingold
110 Thin Lizzy Gary Merrin
110 Gary Moore Sam Emerson
110 Pete Townshend Paul Cox
111 Angus Young Gene Kirkland
111 Led Zeppelin Neal Preston/Andy Kent
111 Bruce Springsteen Ron Wolfson
111 Tom Verlaine Jill Furmanovsky
112 Eddie Van Halen Ross Marino
112 Muddy Waters Michael Putland
112 Steve Vai Kevin Mazur
112 Frank Zappa Paul Cox
114 The Cult Ilpo Musto
114 Alison Moyet Derek Ridgers
115 Eurythmics Ilpo Musto
116 Howard Jones Phil Loftus
116 Richie/Clapton Nick Elgar
117 Kate Bush Eugene Adebari
118 Morten Harket Eugene Adebari
119 Joey Tempest Eugene Adebari
119 Fish Ilpo Musto
120 Berry/Edmunds Ebet Roberts
121 The Who Frank Griffin
122 Wayne Hussey Ilpo Musto
122 Dave Gahan Steve Rapport
123 Suzanne Vega Geoff Swaine
123 Paul Rutherford Steve Rapport